FEMINIST PERSPECTIVES ON
CONTRACT LAW

FEMINIST PERSPECTIVES ON CONTRACT LAW

Edited by
Linda Mulcahy
and
Sally Wheeler

London • Sydney • Portland, Oregon

First published in Great Britain 2005 by
The GlassHouse Press, The Glass House,
Wharton Street, London WC1X 9PX, United Kingdom
Telephone: + 44 (0)20 7278 8000   Facsimile: + 44 (0)20 7278 8080
Email: info@cavendishpublishing.com
Website: www.cavendishpublishing.com

Published in the United States by Cavendish Publishing
c/o International Specialized Book Services,
5824 NE Hassalo Street, Portland,
Oregon 97213-3644, USA

Published in Australia by The GlassHouse Press,
45 Beach Street, Coogee, NSW 2034, Australia
Telephone: + 61 (2)9664 0909   Facsimile: +61 (2)9664 5420
Email: info@cavendishpublishing.com.au
Website: www.cavendishpublishing.com.au

British Library Cataloguing in Publication Data
Mulcahy, Linda, 1962 –
Feminist perspectives on contract law
1 Contracts – England   2 Contracts – Wales
3 Feminist jurisprudence
I Title   II Wheeler, Sally
346.4'202

Library of Congress Cataloguing in Publication Data
Data available

ISBN 1-85941-742-6
ISBN 987-1-859-41742-3

1 3 5 7 9 10 8 6 4 2

Printed and bound in Great Britain

List of Contributors

Dr Rosemary Auchmuty is a Principal Lecturer at the University of Westminster. Her research interests lie at the intersection of feminist history, law and popular culture.

Professor David Campbell is a Professor of Law at the University of Durham. His research focuses on the law of contract and the interface between law and economics.

Dr Bela Chatterjee is a Lecturer in Law at the University of Lancaster. Her most recent work is on architecture, gender and cyberlaw.

Professor Belinda Fehlberg is a Professor in the School of Law, University of Melbourne. Her research focuses on family law, corporate law and the overlap between the two.

Dr Adam Gearey is a Senior Lecturer in Law at Birkbeck College, University of London. His research focuses on law and literature and the law of restitution.

Professor Peter Goodrich works at Cardozo Law School. He has written extensively in the areas of contract, law and literature and semiotics.

Professor Linda Mulcahy is the Anniversary Professor of Law and Society at Birkbeck College, University of London. Her research focuses on dispute resolution, the regulation of medical work and court architecture.

Bruce Smyth is a Research Fellow in the Family and Marriage Program at the Australian Institute of Family Studies and an accomplished drummer. He has published on a wide range of family law issues.

Professor Sally Wheeler joined the Law School at Queen's University Belfast as Chair of Law, Business and Society. She has published widely in the fields of corporate governance, corporate ethics legal history and contract.

List of Contributors

Contents

List of Cases

Chapter 1

The Limitations of Love and Altruism –
Feminist Perspectives on Contract Law

Linda Mulcahy[1]

Introduction

The law of contract is an area which is ripe for feminist analysis. Of the 'core' common law subjects, it is the one most obviously imbued with values associated with the marginalisation of women and the feminine. The emphasis placed on self-regarding, autonomous and competitive contractors by classical and neo-classical scholars has led to calls that the law of contract is phallocentric and centrally located in a suppression of the feminist voice and feminist values (Pateman, 1988; Sullivan, 2000). Indeed, the identification of a correlation between the characteristics of masculinity and the ethos and philosophy of classical legal doctrine has been central to feminist engagements with the law. Nothing better embodies masculine abstracted relations with each other than the model of the discrete contractual transaction with which the majority of scholarship in the field remains concerned. Those writing in this volume argue that feminist analysis of contract law allows us to identify what dominant discourse has left unsaid about the nature of contractual relationships, and to question the credibility of dominant paradigms.

The task of introducing a feminist perspective on contract law is a difficult one. It has been argued that traditional legal doctrine has, for the last 200 years, systematically neglected alternative ways of thinking (Teubner, 2000). The law's cognition of women has taken place through the eyes of male legislators and male judges.[2] The fact that the majority of writers in the field are male and that authorship of the mainstream texts has tended to pass through a male line is apparent from a review of current publishers' catalogues. When we teach our students about the philosophical underpinnings of contract, we talk of such writers as Smith, Bentham, Atiyah, Fried and Gilmore, and Llewelyn. Later in this volume, Wheeler provides examples of the untold stories of women and contract in her analysis of shopping. She argues that the presence of women in the commercial sphere was significant during the era in which the classical canon was being formed; but the status of married women as agents of their husbands, which the law imposed on them, rendered their role invisible in the cases which came before the courts. Our students are challenged when asked to name leading cases involving women. Even when remembered, those that do exist, including the disappointed newlywed in *Curtis v Chemical Cleaning and Dyeing Co Ltd,*[3] the bargaining sillies in undue influence cases like *Barclays Bank v O'Brien,*[4] the

---

1   School of Law, Birkbeck College, University of London.

2   At the time of going to press, the Lord Chancellor and Secretary of State for Constitutional Affairs, all but one Lords of Appeal in Ordinary, 34 of the 37 Lords Justice of Appeal, all 19 of the Chancery Division judges, 70 out of the 73 Queen's Bench judges and 14 of the 19 Family Division judges are male (Department for Constitutional Affairs, 2003).

3   [1951] 1 KB 805.

4   [1993] 4 All ER 417.

scheming wife in *D and C Builders*,[5] do much more to reinforce prevailing stereotypes of women in the contractual sphere than they do to challenge them.

Introducing an alternative vision of contractual relationships is made even more difficult by the common law's predisposition to look to the past. Critical and socio-legal approaches to the study of law are more popular than ever before, but student textbooks and scholarship in the field continue to focus on analysing legal problems by reference to the test of tradition. The insistence on using precedent means that students are taught to commit to looking to what has gone before in order to determine how to proceed in the future, but this repeated 'performance' of rules lends them an authority and meaning that contributors to this volume contest. The very rules, which rely for their legitimacy on tradition, have helped to structure gendered relations in the law and recreated particular notions of voluntary relations. This can only be a barrier to feminist scholarship, which demands that the gendered structures underpinning modern doctrine are revisited and the notion of voluntary obligation reconfigured.

Feminists have engaged with contract scholarship at several levels. At a general level, feminist work on law has encouraged sensitivity towards the many ways in which legal language and concepts are gendered. It has been argued, for instance, that masculine ways of thinking about relationships determine judicial approaches to problem solving. In particular, it has been claimed that masculine subjects prefer to work with predetermined and logical rules which, although inflexible, produce certainty. This tendency is reflected in classical and formalistic approaches to contracts, which concentrate on certainty, specific events and particular moments in time. Moreover, the emphasis placed by the judiciary on abstract principles and linear reasoning reflects the tendency of the common law to seek universal and guiding principals to frame all decisions. Such generalisations assume universal truths and a neutral or objective way of seeing things, which tend to suppress alternative visions of relationships and the needs of contracting parties. The emphasis of the law of contract on the objectified subject, or reasonable man, is particularly worthy of note in this context. Feminist critiques of law have argued that such rational and objective ordering of apparently gender-neutral persons serves subconsciously to address the essential male only. For many feminists, the root problem with law lies in its pretended impartiality, objectivity and rationality. This has meant that if women are to be reasonable within the legal meaning of the term then they must adopt the male standard of reasonableness (Barnett, 1988).

At a more specific level, a considerable amount of work has focused on contract as an alternative to marriage and the use of contract in intimate relationships more generally. It has been argued, for instance, that contract has the potential to foster a non-exploitative conception of 'private' relationships, although feminists have also argued that using contracts in this sphere could merely entrench existing bargaining inequalities. Recently, there has been some limited discussion of the value of relational contract theory to debate amongst feminists and increasing sympathy towards the view that contractual relationships need to be reconceptualised. This does not so much reflect a movement away from recognition of the oppressive effects of contracts so much as a rediscovery of their potential to privilege notions of

---

5   [1966] 2 QB 617.

connection rather than competition. This has led writers, such as Wightman (2000), to claim that there has been a virtual rehabilitation of contract. This introductory chapter aims to suggest possible ways in which scholars engaged in debate about the future of contract scholarship can be encouraged to be more responsive to feminist perspectives.

The argument that contract law is experiencing a legitimacy crisis has been well plotted by critical legal and socio-legal scholars. The deficit in the explanatory power of neo-classical ideology and doctrine has created a conceptual lacuna, which feminist writers in the field are well placed to inhabit. Despite this, it remains the case that feminist engagement with modern theories of contract remains relatively unexplored.[6] My task then is not merely to undermine the understanding of voluntary obligations, suggested by the classical model, that continue to cast a shadow over developments in the field. That task has been undertaken by many others and is well documented. Instead, I seek to use this critique as a stepping stone to consider how feminist ideas around the notion of an ethic of care can contribute to the ambitious task of persuading lawyers to think differently about why people voluntarily bind themselves to an enforceable agreement with another.

It is important to stress from the beginning that contributors to this volume have many views of feminist approaches to the law of contract.[7] In this chapter, I take as a starting point the view that notions of femininity are best understood as culturally contingent.[8] Viewed in this way, generalisations about 'feminine values', ways of thinking and arguing are seen as socially constructed and transient, rather then genetically anchored. Indeed, it is a sign of a patriarchal society that the values associated with masculine or feminine identities can change, whilst patriarchy does not. So, for instance, Schroeder (1990) has argued that certain ideals, recognised as uniquely feminine by contemporary writers, were seen by European men in the Middle Ages as uniquely masculine. By the same token, it has been argued that the feminist ideals being promoted in this volume were guiding principles in the pre-classical period of contract law; however, whilst it is asserted that patriarchy does not depend for its existence on any one conception of masculinity or femininity, the argument that patriarchal societies, such as our own, privilege male values over female ones, whatever they happen to be, is the foundation upon which the arguments presented here build.

---

6   The interface of lesbian and gay scholarship with relational contract theory is an exception to this. A number of interesting articles have been written about the use of relational contractual sphere in intimate relationships more generally. See, for instance, Wightman (2000); Kingdom (2000); Biggs and MacKenzie (2000).

7   As the name of the series reminds us, a multitude of feminist perspectives exist. Indeed, one of the originators of the series has continued to argue that one of the threats for feminist scholarship is the suggestion that there is a feminist orthodoxy (Bottomley, 2004). I do not take up this particular challenge here, but hope that by making it clear that I am focusing on one strand of feminist scholarship that remains contentious, I am, at the very least, making it clear that feminists disagree about the validity or credibility of notions of an ethic of care.

8   Although generally understood as an essentialist, Gilligan admits of this possibility. Indeed, she has expressed concern that her work has been misunderstood as claiming that women have essential traits.

An ethic of care in contracts?

The gendered way in which contracts are understood has traditionally expressed itself in two main ways in the law of obligations. First, contractual relationships have been understood as being motivated and fuelled by separation, possessive individualism, certainty, security of transaction and standardisation. The classical and neo-classical models of contract, which continue to dominate the formulation of modern law, are associated with these masculine ideals of the discrete arms-length transaction between strangers. Indeed, it is arguable that there is no branch of the law in which the hostile egoism of possessive individualism is more clearly reflected than in the classical model, which takes people away from their pre-existing web of communities and networks. According to this vision, doctrinal analysis of contractual exchange is viewed as a mere expression of economic relationships: a callous cash nexus divorced from intimacy, in which exchanges are the only way in which individuals come to recognise the needs of others.

Numerous examples of this understanding of relationships can be drawn from the field of contract. One of the most obvious is the decision in *Walford v Miles*,[9] in which Lord Ackner famously argued that the concept of a duty to carry on negotiations in good faith is inherently repugnant to the adversarial position of the parties when involved in pre-contractual negotiations. In the alternative, he encouraged each party to pursue their own interests so long as they avoided making misrepresentations. The point is also well illustrated by the way in which doctrines such as intention to create legal relations,[10] and debate around the enforceability of cohabitation contracts exclude certain agreements from the contractual sphere because of their supposed reliance on alternative values. As Fehlberg and Smyth demonstrate later in this volume, consideration of the status of prenuptial agreements has been largely relegated to the sphere of family law, despite the fact that the majority of such contracts involve those concerned to protect proprietorial interests in acquired capital, as well as non-commercial expectations. The issues raised in debate about such agreements suggest that contract lawyers continue to struggle to know how to regulate complex relationships based on a mixture of trust, intimacy and selfishness. Drawing on some of these themes, Auchmuty argues, somewhat ironically, that the law's fear of managing intimacy and abuse of bargaining power in undue influence cases stems from the fact that a defining feature of heterosexuality is a gendered power dynamic which is in turn reinforced by the legal system (see, further, Chapter 3 in this volume).

One of the most important debates to emerge from modern feminism focuses on alternative understandings of what motivates people to form relationships and fulfil their promises to each other. Central to this debate is the idea that feminine subjects have a fundamentally different way of conceiving of, and understanding,

---

9   [1992] 2 AC 128.

10 The overt aim of the doctrine was to ensure that only those who intended to enter into a commercial agreement would be bound by it; but indirectly the doctrine served the purposes of rendering unenforceable agreements made in the 'domestic' sphere between married couples or close relatives. As it is women, rather than men, who have tended to dominate the domestic sphere, such prohibitions have served to leave unheard women's stories of unfulfilled obligations.

relationships than the masculine architects of the classical and neo-classical canon. The argument that a discrete set of ideologies and values exist, which can be labelled feminine, has been the subject of much discussion and has resonance with contemporary discussions about the state of the law of contract.[11] The distinction that Gilligan and others have made between an ethic of justice and an ethic of care accentuates the differences between moral philosophy concerned with the rights of the autonomous, separate, objective self with an orientation towards procedural justice and the responsibilities of the connected, interdependent self with an orientation towards substantive outcomes. Men and women have been shown to adopt both orientations in response to particular needs but it is the former – an ethic of justice – that has been associated with masculinity and the latter 'ethics of care' that has been shown to most dominate the moral reasoning of women.[12] By way of illustration, Baier (1993) has argued that female philosophers have demonstrated a lack of interest in debates about game theory that adopt an individualist and self-interested stance towards problem solving.

The ethic of care represents a distinctive approach to the understanding of relationships and has its own moral vocabulary, moral epistemology and explanatory force. It offers a direct contrast to the classical model in that it stresses the importance of intimacy, community and relational actors embedded in particular contexts. Feminist scholars have argued that the worlds of feminine subjects are worlds in which connection and network rather than bargain give rise to a recognition of responsibility for one another. Applying this reasoning to contracts, the late Mary Jo Frug (1992) characterised as feminine a position that was grounded in a pluralistic, context-sensitive model of contract relationships, which offered a multiplicity of objectives and perspectives. Her work gives us a taste of how feminine theories of contract might impact on contractual doctrines, such as frustration, and provide support for the development of a more sophisticated understanding of such concepts as good faith or unconscionability.

Similarly, in this volume Goodrich returns to his analysis of the marriage contract to remind us that the roots of the postal rule lie in a branch of ecclesiastical law, which recognised difference in the contractual sphere. His argument that it was the marriage contract that emerged as the first type of executory contract also encourages us to temper completely exclusionist readings of the history of gender

---

11 Critics would be right in suggesting that I am sidestepping the essentialist-difference debate. This is because I subscribe to the view put forward by Tronto, that debates about the ethic of care could usefully be centred in a discourse about the ethic's adequacy as a moral theory, rather than located solely in debates around whether there are essential differences between male and female ways of thinking. Some feminists have been wary of equating 'care' with 'the feminine' because of the lack of conclusive evidence and a concern that the identification of difference creates a hierarchy of values where women's ways of reasoning may be seen as inferior to men's. It has been argued, for instance, that women's moral differences may be a function of their subordinate social position. In this way, an ethics of care could be seen as confirming traditional roles and confirming women in their otherness. Writers such as Sevenhuijsen (1998) have argued that this reflects a superficial or inaccurate acquaintance with Gilligan's work, a view with which I concur. Despite this, I remain concerned that I have not fully addressed the concerns raised by Drakopoulou (2000) and that what I am espousing by taking this stance is a humanist, rather than a feminist, argument.

12 Baier (1993) and others remind us of the potency of the argument that women of ethnic identities other than Anglo-Saxon white do not necessarily share these orientations.

and contracts. While ecclesiastical law undoubtedly treated women as being inferior to men, the rule in *Adams v Lindsell* recognised that the consent of women to contracts should at least be true. Through its support for the will theory of contract, it gave legitimacy to the contention that contract law concerned itself with separate individuals who were distinct and differentiated. Goodrich provides a deeper understanding of this well-known case, which brings with it the possibility of modern applications of the rule attending to the plurality of subjects in a way that would be more conducive to feminist readings of law. What his chapter in this volume offers is further hope that unexpected rewards may be reaped through attempts to unravel the complex cultural and philosophical history of a case.

Feminism and relational contract theory

Feminists are not alone in their call for the introduction of new ways of understanding contract. In his grand explanation of the history of contract, written almost three decades ago, Atiyah expressed concern about the lack of a firm ideological foundation for modern contract law and his call has been echoed by modern authors (see, for instance, Adams and Brownsword, 2000; Brownsword, 2000; Campbell, 2000a; Mulcahy and Tillotson, 2004; Wightman, 2000). Writing at the turn of the century, Sheinman (2000) suggested that: '[a]s the century is drawing to a close, it is fair to say that contract law has undergone a theoretical crisis deeper than any other branch of the law.'[13] The quest for a new and more credible philosophical framework for the law of contract becomes even more compelling as contracts as a metaphor and device become the pre-eminent form of social regulation in an age in which many public functions are returning to the private sphere of contract.[14]

Changes to the marketplace and the increasing concentration of economic power have rendered the concept of bargain, on which classical and neo-classical models are based, largely redundant. Globalisation, the retraction of the state from civil society, the growth of long-term supply contracts and franchising are all developments that have led to calls to reconceptualise founding principles of contract. In addition, Bela Bonita Chatterjee has drawn attention to the ways in which the advent of cyberspace has given rise to new challenges and debates for the legal world, which cannot be adequately resolved by reference to traditional doctrine. Adopting a feminist perspective, she has contended that the gendered dimensions of the interface between law and cyberspace need to be interrogated and politicised if regulation of electronic contracts is to gain legitimacy (see, further, Chapter 6 in this volume).

---

13 There are some writers who would contest this claim although some of their arguments, in my view, remain unconvincing. See, for instance, Mitchell (2003), whose criticism of 'socio-legal' approaches to contract is that those approaches have failed to take sufficient account of doctrine. Since the claim of many socio-legal researchers has been that formal law lacks legitimacy because it does not reflect practice, it seems perfectly rational for them to marginalise its significance in such circumstances. Mitchell's claim that there is still life in the classical law is not contested when what she is writing about is the reluctance of the judiciary to move away from the neo-classical concept of discrete exchange.

14 There is something rather ironic about the ease with which politicians have conferred the title of 'contract' on practices which would not be recognised as such by lawyers, whilst the judiciary still struggle with the concept of commercial arrangements between sexual partners.

Dave Campbell has consistently argued that the problems with the classical contract model are no longer a matter of contention. Rather, the problem has been in finding a coherent successor. Neo-classical and welfarist approaches to the subject showed much promise in that they at least conceived of relationships in which individuals sought advantage through the contractual transaction, but were also tied to the success of the mutual venture (Feinman, 1990). Moreover, the welfarist approach takes account of context and has been more sensitive than the classical model to the relative bargaining power of the contracting parties (see, for instance, Macneil, 1990); however, the neo-classical model has favoured a pragmatic approach to the failings of classicalism and lacks a rigorous unifying conceptual structure. It has tended to tinker with the classical model rather than offer an alternative vision which can replace it.[15] For feminists, the greatest disappointment has been that 'masculine' ways of understanding relationships continue to be at the core of judicial reasoning. This means that they are still understood primarily in terms of individual advantage and freedom of contract or as exceptions to this prevailing concept (Belcher, 2000).

An approach which is more sympathetic to the central concerns of feminists has come in the guise of the relational contract 'school', which is increasingly being seen as having the promise to replace classical modes of thinking and revitalise debate about the purpose of law in regulating voluntary relationships.[16] Connections have been made between the two 'movements' (see, for instance, Wightman, 2000: Vincent-Jones, 2000; Belcher, 2000). In the words of Brown (1996):

> What a present, it seems, for feminism: an account of contract law's 'familial' understandings that at the same time can summon the weight of legal realism and critical legal studies, to put 'the feminine' on the side of the nascent counter principles against the dominance of the discrete transaction, and the ideology of freedom and classical individualism. [p 14]

Four main concerns link those interested in the ethics of care and relational contracts. First, it is worthy of note that, in common with many feminists, relationalists have drawn particular attention to the need to address the large gap between theory and practice.[17] Drawing on the work of socio-legal researchers who have studied the everyday world of contracts, the practical outcome has been a call to develop a system that responds to the regulatory needs of those who use it rather than imposing overly abstract concepts upon those who truck and barter on a day to day basis (Collins, 1999; Campbell, 2000b).[18] Such an exercise involves a determination of the modern role of contract in the aftermath of a raft of empirical

---

15 Campbell reminds us that welfarism has also become something of an outdated concept in the successful neo-liberal attack on the welfare state.

16 Relational contract theories have proven to be particularly popular amongst economists and it is in economics journals that much of the modern literature is to be found. See, for instance, Gifford, 1999.

17 Gilligan (1982), for instance, argues that the feminine voice does not ground morality in abstract generalisable principles, but in the daily experiences and moral problems of real people in their everyday lives.

18 Campbell (2000b), for instance, refers to much of what Gunter Teubner (2000) has to say about relational contract theory as woolly rhetoric. Campbell is particularly critical of social theorists who theorise without an adequate appreciation of how contract operates in practice.

studies, which make clear that formal contracts are rarely used or referred to in everyday commercial dealings.[19]

Realist studies of contract in action provide the basis of a second important link between these schools. Such empirical studies have revealed that, contrary to the understanding of relationships that underpin classical model, many of the values labelled feminine have an important role to play in the day to day practice of the commercial sphere. The impact of these findings is that they have the ability to transform the way we think about the common understandings that nurture contractual relationships. They suggest that relational elements in contracts have not just come about as a result in changes in patterns of regulation and governance, but rather that these features are an inevitable attribute of all contracts. Viewed in this way, changes to dominant paradigms are not only justified on the basis that times have changed, but because the classical model was never a true reflection of interactions in the marketplace.[20]

Drawing on his understandings of the day to day formation and performance of contracts, the work of leading relational contract lawyer Ian Macneil brings complexity and a plurality of perspectives to our understanding of contracts.[21] The classical model's preference for certainty has meant that legal doctrine can, at times, be seen as harsh in its formalistic tendencies. By way of contrast, Macneil offers us 'open contracts' in which exact terms and conditions are negotiated as needs arise and reliable information becomes available. His contracts are not set in stone at the 'moment of responsibility', but rather evolve. Thus, we are presented with the idea that contracts are relationships, rather than viewing relationships as contracts. Dealing with such complexity is undoubtedly a challenge. As Macaulay (1977) has surmised:

> If writing about contract were to reflect the empirical operation of the contract system, we might lose the elegance and neatness that once gave us confidence that our doctrine supports and reflects our economic ideals. Instead of a neat system, we would risk being left with an unsatisfying collection of ideas where everything 'depends'. [p 521]

Relational contract theory holds a final promise for feminists. A major concern amongst feminist scholars has been the way in which the classical model rendered certain characteristics of contractual relationships, such as imbalance of power, invisible. The unstated assumption here is that existing patterns of property ownership and rights of liberty are of no significance to classical analysis, which relied on a rather crude and unsophisticated notion of power. Welfarist approaches to contract brought some of this into view, but one of the greatest successes of

---

19 For a general overview, see Macaulay (2003). More specifically, see Johnson *et al*, 2002.

20 Macaulay (1977, p 515) asserts, for instance, that the classical paradigm is an overgeneralisation from a biased sample of litigated cases and that 'economically important contract cases that adjudicate rights are too rare to serve as a solid foundation for the classical model'.

21 In this chapter I refer to the work of relational contract theorists although Macneil's most recent evolution of the theory is known as essential contract theory. I have adopted his earlier label as I am concerned here with the general thrust of his theories rather than the nuances which have led to him distancing himself from other incarnations of his ideas.

relational contract theory is that it renders issues around the creation and restraint of power more visible still.[22]

In common with feminists, Macneil's work on long-term contracts stresses that contracts are embedded in a network of relationships and show a firm commitment to the preservation of ongoing relationships. In the long-term relational contract it is connection, flexibility, trust, co-operation and bilateral settlement of disputes that are privileged as key concepts underpinning the majority of contracts. These values replace the classical canon of separation, isolation and competition. The concern of relational contract theorists has shifted towards the ways in which legal doctrine can recognise and engender trust, and respect the diverse interpretations of legal obligations of the kind that empiricists and feminists have talked about. So, for example, a relational reading of *Marks and Spencer*[23] would have allowed a different reading of relationship as one in which long-term flexible deals could be viewed as more than a series of discrete commercial exchanges. In drawing attention to the possibility of a range of different types of contracts from the one-off discrete to the long-term, Macneil (see, for instance, 1980) offers us an alternative to the conceptual underpinnings of the classical model at the same time as providing feminist scholarship with a space in which feminist ethics can be identified as relevant and, indeed, essential to the real world of contracts.

Context

Not all contracts are long-term, but it has been argued that all have a relational element to them, even if this is no more than adherence to some of the same norms. This is a theme that Macneil has turned to in many of his later writings (see, for instance, 1983). As Macneil's work has developed, so too have the number of norms he considers to be present to some degree in all contracts.[24] Drawing on this work, Collins (1999) has argued that there are three main competing systems of norms that frame each contract. These are the business relation, the economic deal and the agreement enshrined in the formal contract. According to this scheme, a contract which does not necessarily reflect a good economic deal might, for instance, be understood by reference to the long-term goals of the business relationship. Drawing on the insights of systems theory, Collins suggests that these three normative systems are self-referential communication systems, the examination of which promises to reveal what motivates the performance or non-performance of contractual relationships in a way that traditional models have not been able to. His work reminds us that sensitivity to context is a complex task, involving as it does an

---

22   Welfarist approaches to contract law have played an important part in addressing many of the most inequitable repercussions of doctrine founded on classical precepts. As the assumption of equality of bargaining power has been submitted to intense scrutiny, the judiciary has seen fit to provide greater protection for certain categories of people, such as consumers, in order to mitigate the inequalities which have come about as a result of the creation of the welfare state, the growth of large-scale business and globalisation. The success of welfarist approaches has been to encourage adjustments to the classical model so that it better suits the goals of modern policy formation.

23   *Baird Textile Holdings Ltd v Marks and Spencer plc* [2001] EWCA Civ 274.

24   These are role integrity, reciprocity, planning, consent, flexibility, contractual solidarity, procedural justice, creation and restraint of power, propriety of means and harmonisation with the social matrix.

appreciation of not just one, but several contexts or systems, which some have labeled polycontextuality (see, for instance, Teubner, 2000).

Feminist scholars share this interest in context and it is discussion of the circumstances in which events occur, rather than particular fact patterns, has fuelled much feminist debate. Relationalists provide an important link between this feminist moral philosophy and the commercial world by indicating ways in which context could transform judicial reasoning in contract cases. In one of its most radical guises, Macneil's theory does more than suggest that context should be taken into account as an aide to construction of the terms of the contract. Rather, his theory takes context as the *starting* point in understanding the nature of the relationship. That is not to say that normative frameworks are not taken into account in the law of contract at present. Reference to such things as previous course of dealings and common business practice in the case law demonstrates this,[25] but the focus has been on how these understandings supplement the judge's reading of the agreement rather than on Macneil's suggestion that we should start with the context of understandings.

Not only does this reverse the method of analysis traditionally adopted by the judiciary, but it suggests that the values which should inform adjudication should derive from indigenous normative frameworks rather than those of formal law. The significance of this is that it provides opportunities for outsider narratives such as those of feminists and women to be voiced. The importance of drawing on the lived experience of subjects is something that has been much encouraged by feminists who have opined that it is at the interface of theory and praxis that law is most likely to gain legitimacy (see, for instance, Tronto, 1993). It follows from this that the value of taking everyday understandings of what binds the parties to an agreement is important because judicial decisions are likely to become more 'realistic' and gain greater respect within the commercial sphere if informed by prevailing norms. Not only does this approach satisfy the demands of much socio-legal scholarship, but it also accords with the arguments of those who contend that law will only have authority where those bound by it have participated in its formation.

A mush of altruism?

Relational theorists have been criticised on the basis that the values they espouse are naïve and simplistic. The implication is that they would not survive in the cut and thrust of the market place. Criticisms of the credibility of notions of trust, context and co-operation as not being of value in discussions of the nature of contractual relationships are fed by assumptions that the optimum gain for society as a whole is achieved through the pursuit of selfish behaviour on the part of individuals. Similarly, the significance of an ethic of care has been undermined by the tendency to equate it with a specific morality of self-denial and dedication to others in the private sphere. In turn, this makes it of minimal use to those interested

---

25 Clearly, this is not just an issue for those interested in the law of contract. Just as the classical contract model and political theories of the 19th century encouraged us to conceptualise negotiations in terms of the distance between the parties, so too have substantive law, and process in other areas, moved away from respect for the importance of localised understandings and normative frameworks.

in the discrete haggle. The vulnerable and dependent, who have so often become the subjects of women's care in the family and sphere of work, have, in Sevenhuijsen's (1998) view, fuelled the association of women with 'weakness' and 'need' in a way that provides a stark contrast with the autonomous and independent actor of liberal politics and contract theory. Later in this volume, Gearey argues that the neo-classical model of contract continues to struggle with the newfound 'visibility' of women as actors in the commercial arena and to recognise the rights of women against their husbands. His account of the development of restitution suggests that women have yet to be conceptualised as legal subjects in cases involving 'domestic' commercial arrangements if they are to be seen as capable of engaging in bargain and exchange.[26] Instead, the case law suggests the tendency for women to be conceived of as victims, and this in turn has become an inherent part of the granting of legal subjectivity in the field of contract.

The equation of the ethics of care with self-sacrifice reflects a simplistic understanding of relationships in which care is all too readily defined as servitude and subordination. In her discussion of the organising principles of feminist philosophy, Davies (1994) makes clear the ways in which dominant liberal ideologies have impacted on the way lawyers look at relationships. In her words:

> In concentrating on obligations, rather than virtues, modern moral theorists have chosen to look at the cases where more trust is placed in enforcers of obligations than is placed in ordinary moral agents, the bearers of the obligations. In taking, as contractarians do, contractual obligations as the model of obligations, they concentrate on a case where the very minimal trust is put in the obligated person, and considerable punitive power entrusted to the one to whom the obligation is owed. [p 192]

Significantly, Gilligan saw blind self-sacrifice as just one step on the road to moral maturity that was reached when it was recognised that care is related to relationships in which there is reciprocity in the form of a response to what is given.

We don't expect those in intimate relationships to display altruistic and caring tendencies throughout their time together. Why is it then that when looking at the opposite end of the spectrum of relationships, mainstream contract scholars resist the suggestion that contracts can be motivated by something other than a continuous stream of hostile egoism? Why is the expectation of care and support in the future ever-present in divorce settlements, but an anathema to commercial judges in cases where the parties have clearly adjusted their business behaviour in expectation of a long-term relationship and communal goal? As Pohjonen (2000) has surmised, 'in the one, you seek love and personal enjoyment and in the other, profit and material good' (p 51). Both can be seen as self-interested contracts. Both can be seen as relationships based on the common good and give and take.[27]

---

26 A number of academics such as Beatson (1988) have made great claims for restitution as a rival to classical precepts, although not all experts in the field share their assessment of this emerging field. See, in particular, Campbell (1999).

27 Pohjonen (2000) develops this argument in a much more detailed format in his article on this subject and draws out many similarities between the contractual and intimate relationship, such as expectations of loyalty, the increasing recognition of the rights of weaker parties and commitment to long-term goals. However, he also suggests that rather than coming together as concepts they may in fact have passed each other. As legal marriage in Finland has increasingly come to be portrayed as an economic relationship, contract has come to be seen as much more of a human relationship than was previously the case.

Is it possible for feminists to call for a recognition of their alternative understandings of relationships without necessarily glorifying them as sources of moral goodness? The first step to achieving this is surely a recognition that it is natural for human beings to form connections and relationships. Indeed, they develop their moral and rational capacities by interacting with others. Seen in this way, dependency and the giving and receiving of care occurs within complex networks of family, friends and the workplace, and the ability to make and sustain these networks becomes part of the self-identity of all individuals. In other words, dependency and interdependence become aspects of the human condition upon which we all draw on a day to day basis in both the domestic and commercial sphere. Adopting this position as a starting point admits of the possibility that the barriers that have traditionally been erected between the domestic and commercial sphere are not necessary. Instead, branches of law, such as contract, are no longer symbols of altruistic or egotistical tendencies. Instead, it is but one part of the law concerning human co-operation (Pohjonen, 2000).

Macneil (1986, 1990) has specifically discussed these issues in his consideration of household relationships. He acknowledges the differences with discrete commercial exchanges. These include the presence of strong norms of sharing, altruism, 'generalised' reciprocity and the difficulties of identifying calculated, specific and discrete exchanges of things and services; in his view, however, this does not exclude domestic arrangements from theories of exchange or reciprocity. Rather, he embraces them as one type of specialised exchange in which there is intense interdependence and solidarity. Perhaps most importantly, he argues that the selfish individual is not lost in the domestic sphere, for in his view we are all inconsistently selfish and socially committed at the same time. This understanding of relationships has significant repercussions for feminist debate. It allows for the 'private' world of the household to be reunited with the 'public' world of contracts under the auspices of a new ideology of contract that encompasses a wide range of different types of relationships, which display varying degrees of commitment to the self and community. Macneil does much more than find a way to include discussion of domestic relationships within the general law of contract: he argues that they are essential to our appreciation of the notion of exchange. In his words, 'not only is reciprocity essential to the household, the household economy is the very seedbed of human reciprocity, a seedbed stretching back to our evolutionary primate roots' (p 434). According to this argument, the discrete commercial barter displays behaviour that engenders trust in the marketplace just as domestic relationships display some selfish behaviour. At the most simple level, this is because barter is chosen in preference to theft and even the most selfish of exchanges provides information to the market about the value of a good or service, which will be of use in the efficient pricing of services.

In my view, this conceptualisation of relationships undermines the tendency to glorify feminist values whilst nonetheless finding a place for them within debate about the nature of contracts. This introduces a level of complexity in our analysis of contracts that will not be welcomed by all, but which is surely inevitable and necessary in our postmodern state. In support of this view I turn again to Macneil (1983), who has described the position much more eloquently than I am able to:

... we are faced with an illogicality. [Wo]man is both an entirely selfish creature and an entirely social creature, in that [wo]man puts the interests of [her] fellows ahead of [her] own interests at the same time that [she] puts [her] own interests first. Such a creature is schizophrenic, and will, to the extent that it does anything except vibrate in utter frustration, constantly alternate between inconsistent behaviours – selfish one second and self-sacrificing the next. [p 348][28]

A second step is to recognise that an ethic of care or appreciation of the relational self is best conceived of as a reflection of the reality of many commercial relationships rather than as something to which the commercial sector should aspire. If, as many have argued, practitioners see trust and co-operation as having commercial worth, then these norms are only radical if one starts from a misunderstanding of the glue that binds these relationships, as traditional doctrine has. It is in this context that empirical work in the field has proven so valuable to feminists. Take, for example, Macaulay's (1963) finding that people in the business community often prefer to rely 'on a [person's] word in a brief letter, a handshake, or common honesty and decency – even when the transaction involves exposures to series risks' (p 58), or his suggestion that the principles of not 'welshing' on a deal and producing a good product remain the key.

What these studies also reveal is that contractors work hard to satisfy each other and that potential disputes are often suppressed in the interest of keeping a good commercial relationship alive. Macaulay (1963) describes how salesmen take purchasing agents to dinner and buy them Christmas gifts, buyers' engineering staff do favours for long-term partners, executives of firms socialise, serve together on government committees or hold stock in each other's companies. Whilst it might be a mistake to suggest that all contracts worked along these lines, there is now sufficient evidence to suggest that these values are present in stable business networks where the parties have an interest in preserving a good reputation and where they have built up trust and confidence over time. The importance of these fibres of obligation should not be underestimated. In their analysis of relational contracting in countries in the former Soviet bloc, Johnson *et al* (2002) have argued that in jurisdictions lacking workable laws of contract, these relational norms have been used in the place of law to fuel and motivate commercial deals.

Perhaps the most significant aspect of these findings is that the motivation for such behaviour has nothing to do with altruism, as some commentators have disparagingly suggested. These empirical findings should not be taken to suggest that all contractual relationships are 'nice and warm', involving 'communal cooperation and solidarity' (Teubner, 2000, p 400) or 'beautiful nice rainbow people' (Biggs and MacKenzie, 2000). Drawing on this research, Macneil (2000), for one, has argued vehemently that he sees little place for 'unqualifiedly non-reciprocal altruism' (p 213), and this is demonstrated by the emphasis he has placed on conflict within contracts. It would seem then that relational contract theory and the characteristics of working contracts to which it draws attention are about much

---

28 My attention was drawn to this quotation by Macneil (1986), which is in turn reproduced in Campbell's (2001) edited collection of Macneil's work. In that collection, this quotation appears on p 90.

more than encouraging people to be nicer, more open or more generous.[29] Reflecting on the reactions to his theories of contract he has explained:

> A widespread perception has long existed that relational contract theory is an analytical tool biased in favour of state intervention in contractual relations; of co-operation rather than conflict; of communitarian, liberal and/or radical values; of the continuance rather than break up of relations; and many other 'soft and cuddly values' often associated with humanitarianism. [p 208]

There is then, in the relational school, no suggestion that every instance of co-operative contracting reflects a deeply held moral concern for one's fellow contractors. These phenomena can just be easily explained by enlightened self-interest (Brownsword, 2000). Wightman (2000) has also reminded us that:

> Although such terms as trust and co-operation are used here, it is important to see that there is no suggestion that relational contracting is just a mush of altruism, where self-interest has disappeared. The issue is not the existence of self-interest, but the form of its expression. Take, for example, the relationship between a main contractor and various subcontractors on a major construction project such as a large bridge. It will be in the self-interest of all the firms for the project to be completed successfully, but this will not happen if every technical breach is pounced on as an excuse for terminating and claiming damages.

So, for example, if it is not good business sense for one party to take advantage of another's vulnerability, then the classical law's insistence that the seller has no duty to disclose facts in pre-contractual negotiations is undermined. Similarly, the participants in Macaulay's early empirical study are not painted as saints. Despite their commitment to honouring agreements and producing a good product, they were prepared to put pressure on other contractors or terminate contracts where default was a frequent feature. However, it is also the case that there are incentives to co-operate where the costs of finding an alternative trading partner and assessing their credit risk or reliability are prohibitive. Gifford (1999) has argued that there are many economic savings to be made from transactional efficiency in the drafting of relational contracts, which have been under-researched by economists.[30] As a form of governance, relational contracting also has advantages over recourse to the courts. Market participants are more expert than the courts at monitoring the performance of another contractor and can make much more nuanced decisions than the binary decisions taken when recourse is made to the courts.[31] The key point to be made in the context of this discussion is that a range of different models of contractual behaviour exist, which employ relational norms.

At this level of analysis, it is not necessary for feminists to be prescriptive about the values that should govern contracts if the norms identified by relational contract

---

29 Indeed, Macneil criticises Teubner for the 'breathtaking disregard' of everything Macneil has written with which he has distorted his conflict analytical model of contractual relations into the communitarian sense of the word as 'nice and warm'. See Macneil (2000, p 433).

30 She argues that as relational contracts are 'incomplete' in comparison to discrete short-term contracts they require less time to draft and monitor. According to her research, the opportunity cost of writing detailed contracts is neglect of new negotiations and business deals.

31 Macaulay (1963) has argued, for instance, that gossip from long-term partners about other players in the sector provides vital information that can be used to assess risks.

theorists reflect those which feminists have argued should be recognised. Included in this category are those norms such as role integrity, flexibility and broadly defined notions of reciprocity. There is, however, much work to be done by feminists in further investigating the normative frameworks that engender, facilitate and nurture commercial relationships and the ways in which competing systems are accommodated. This is far from an easy task; disciplines such as law and economics are said to be struggling with the concept (Belcher, 2000). It is also in this area, more than any other, that the interests of contemporary writers and feminist scholars in the field are most likely to conflict and the need for a more prescriptive approach to norms can be justified. If, in addition to there being widespread use of relational sanctions outside of the formal legal system, the law of contract were to legitimate such practice and give it priority over judicial reading of contracts, we surely arrive at a system of state sanctioned private governance. The problem for feminists is that reference to localised norms raises the issue of whose norms are to be taken into account and whether the new voices that are to be heard by the judiciary in a relational utopia are those which continue to marginalise feminist perspectives on contract. As Teubner (2000) reminds us:

> ... there are serious limitations to a spontaneous order approach if it is to be used to inform legal decision-makers. Interactional patterns and social customs inform legal arguments only about the results of underlying social conflicts, not about the conflicts themselves. They may be wise or unwise compromise, they may result from balanced negotiations from a unilateral imposition of power, a sophisticated response to conflicting demands or thoughtless compliance with outmoded traditions, rational discourse or blind evolution, but in themselves they do not reveal the collisions between social systems to which the contract is exposed. [p 405]

His argument raises the issue of whether feminist understandings of contract are best served by an 'enlightened' judiciary which imposes a view of the world on the contracting parties, or an enlightened commercial world in which feminist values are used to inform the creation and regulation of obligations. Will this democratisation of contractual values benefit feminist causes or facilitate a moral free-for-all in which dominant discourses continue to dominate? It is to be hoped that barriers to acceptance of feminist approaches to contract are undermined by empirical evidence that the business community already shares an interest in the value of trust and co-operation in contractual performance. Moreover, Teubner suggests that by privileging context and appreciating its significance there is at least a possibility that that difference will be afforded more respect.[32]

Conclusion

Failure to address the ideological and practical issues raised in this introductory chapter will undoubtedly leave the law of contract dangerously outdated and lacking in legitimacy. The importance of returning to first principles is particularly significant when living in an era in which the issue of what constitutes an appropriate balance between the ever-present desire for individual utility and social solidarity is a hotly contested political issue. Within this debate there is much to be

---

32 Teubner (2000) anticipates the 'conflict ridden exposure of contract to a multitude of highly developed social rationalities that collide with each other' (p 339).

gleaned from the examination of existing practice in the marketplace. Empirical research has shown that this provides us with a number of sophisticated, legitimate and workable templates for organising exchange in a way which is much more responsive to the needs of contracting parties. If nothing else, these remain credible because they are grounded in experience and practice. These studies, and their interpretation by relational contract theorists, provide feminists with additional riches because of a shared focus on values associated with feminist ethics. In this context, I would argue that the opportunities for feminist scholars to have influence on emerging theoretical frameworks have never been greater.

This, in turn, provides feminist scholars with a daunting number of challenges. In particular, feminist scholars should be encouraged to pursue the detail of what a feminist reading of a contract would entail. Some targets are undoubtedly easier than others. Feminist writers have already made a considerable contribution to the literature on gendered readings of cases. Commentaries on the undue influence cases provide a particularly good example of this. Moreover, feminist writers have encouraged the breaking down of the falsely constructed barrier between the commercial and domestic sphere enshrined in leading cases on intention to create legal relations. We have also been encouraged to favour a pluralistic, context-sensitive model of contract relationships, which offered a multiplicity of objectives, perspectives and outcomes. What, however, would this mean in practice? Would feminist approaches to formation of contract go beyond Denning's context-sensitive understanding of the business relationships in the Manchester cases?[33] Would it shun the formalist rhetoric of *Williams v Roffey*[34] and abandon the notion of consideration based as it is on the notion of commercial exchange? How might feminists' sympathies towards open-ended notions such as good faith and unconscionability be realised? Perhaps most importantly, do common contract norms become inappropriate because of their gendered assumptions? It is to these details of feminist perspectives that we now turn.

References

Adams, J and Brownsword, R, *Understanding Contract Law*, 3rd edn, 2000, London: Sweet & Maxwell

Atiyah, P, *The Rise and Fall of the Freedom of Contract*, 1979, Oxford: OUP

Baier, A, 'What do women want in moral theory', in Larrabee, MJ (ed), *An Ethic of Care: Feminist and Interdisciplinary Perspectives*, 1993, New York and London: Routledge

Barnett, H, *Introduction to Feminist Jurisprudence*, 1988, London: Cavendish Publishing

Beatson, J and Friedmann, D (eds), *Good Faith and Fault in Contract Law*, 1988, Oxford: OUP

---

33 See *Storer v Manchester City Council* [1994] 1 WLR 1403 and *Gibson v Manchester City Council* [1979] 1 WLR 294. For further discussion of these cases, see Mulcahy and Tillotson (2004).
34 [1991] 1 QB 1.

Belcher, A, 'A feminist perspective on contract theories from law and economics' (2000) 8 *Feminist Legal Studies* 29–46

Biggs, H and MacKenzie, R, 'Gendered readings of obligations: social lore or strict legal forms?' (2000) 8 *Feminist Legal Studies* 1–4

Bottomley, A, 'Shock to thought: an encounter (of a third kind) with legal feminism' (2004) 12(1) *Feminist Legal Studies* 29–65

Brown, B, 'Contracting out/contracting in: some feminist considerations', in *Feminist Perspectives on the Foundational Subjects of Law*, 1996, London: Cavendish Publishing

Brownsword, R, *Contract Law Themes for the Twenty First Century*, 2000, London: Butterworths

Campbell, D, 'Classification and the crisis of the common law' (1999) 26 *Journal of Law and Society* 369

Campbell, D, 'Reflexivity and welfarism in the modern law of contract' (2000a) 20 *Oxford Journal of Legal Studies* 477

Campbell, D, 'The limits of concept formation in legal science' (2000b) 9(3) *Social and Legal Studies* 439–47

Campbell, D, 'Ian Macneil and the relational theory of contract', in Campbell, D (ed), *The Relational Theory of Contract: Selected Works of Ian Macneil*, 2001, London: Sweet & Maxwell

Collins, H, *Regulating Contracts*, 1999, Oxford: OUP

Crawford, A, 'Contractual governance of deviant behaviour' (2003) 30(4) *Journal of Law and Society* 479–505

Cretney, S, 'The little woman and the big bad bank' (1992) 108 *LQR* 534

Davies, M, *Asking the Law Question*, 1994, London: Sweet & Maxwell

Department for Constitutional Affairs (2003), 'The Judiciary', www.dca.gov.uk

Drakopoulou, M, 'The ethic of care, female subjectivity and feminist legal scholarship' (2000) 8 *Feminist Legal Studies* 199–226

Feinman, J, 'The significance of contract theory' (1990) 58 *University of Cincinnati Law Review* 1283

Frug, M, *Postmodern Legal Feminism*, 1992, London: Routledge

Gifford, S, 'Limited attention and the optimal incompleteness of contracts' (1999) 15(2) *Journal of Law and Economic Organization* 468–86

Gilligan, C, *In a Different Voice*, 1982, Cambridge, MA: Harvard UP

Guinier, L, Fine, M and Balin, J, *Becoming Gentlemen*, 1997, Boston, MA: Beacon Press

Johnson, S, McMillan, J and Woodruff, C, 'Courts and relational contracts' (2002) 18(1) *Journal of Law, Economics and Organization* 221–77

Kingdom, E, 'Cohabitation contracts and the democratisation of personal relations' (2000) 8 *Feminist Legal Studies* 5–27

Lange, B, 'The emotional dimension in legal regulation' (2002) 29(1) *Journal of Law and Society* 197–225

Macaulay, S, 'Non-contractual relations in business: a preliminary study' (1963) 28(1) *American Sociological Review* 55–67

Macaulay, S, 'Elegant models, empirical pictures, and the complexities of contract' (1977) 11(3) *Law and Society Review* 507–28

Macaulay, S, 'The real deal and the paper deal: empirical pictures of relationships, complexity and the urge for transparent simple rules', in Campbell, D, Collins, H and Wightman, J (eds), *Implicit Dimensions of Contract: Discrete, Relational and Network Contracts*, 2003, Oxford: Hart Publishing

Macneil, I, *The New Social Contract: An Inquiry into Modern Contractual Relations*, 1980, New Haven, CT: Yale UP

Macneil, I, 'Values in contract: external and internal' (1983) 78 *Northwestern University Law Review* 340–418

Macneil, I, 'Exchange revisited: individual utility and social solidarity' (1986) 96 *Ethics* 567–93

Macneil, I, 'Political exchange as relational contract', in Marin, J (ed), *Generalised Political Exchange: Antagonistic Co-operation and Integrated Policy Circuits*, 1990, Boulder, CO: Westview Press, pp 151–72

Macneil, I, 'Contracting worlds and essential contract theory' (2000) 9(3) *Social and Legal Studies* 431–38

Mitchell, C, 'There's still life in the classical law' (2003) 62(1) *Cambridge Law Journal* 26–29

Mulcahy, L and Tillotson, J, *Contract Law in Perspective*, 4th edn, 2004, London: Cavendish Publishing

Pateman, C, *The Sexual Contract*, 1988, Oxford: Polity

Pohjonen, S, 'Partnership in love and in business' (2000) 8 *Feminist Legal Studies* 47–63

Sally, D, 'Two economic applications of sympathy' (2000) 18(2) *Journal of Law and Economics* 455–87

Sevenhuijsen, S, *Justice, Morality and Politics*, 1998, London: Routledge

Schroeder, JL, 'Feminism historicized: medieval misogynist stereotypes in contemporary feminist jurisprudence' (1990) 75 *Iowa Law Review* 1136

Sheinman, H, 'Contractual liability and voluntary undertakings' (2000) 20 *Oxford Journal of Legal Studies* 205–20

Smith, S, *Contract Theory*, 2003, Oxford: Clarendon

Sullivan, B, '"Its all in the contract": rethinking feminist critiques of contract' (2000) 18 *Law in Context* 112

Teubner, G, 'Contracting worlds: the many autonomies of private law' (2000) 9(3) *Social and Legal Studies* 399–417

Tronto, J, 'Beyond gender difference to a theory of care', in Larrabee, MJ, *An Ethic of Care: Feminist and Interdisciplinary Perspectives*, 1993, London: Routledge

Vincent-Jones, P, 'Contractual governance: institutional and organisational analysis' (2000) 20 *Oxford Journal of Legal Studies* 317

Wightman, J, 'Intimate relationships, relational contract theory and the reach of contract' (2000) 8 *Feminist Legal Studies* 93–131

Wightman, J, 'Beyond custom: contract, contexts and the recognition of implicit understandings', in Campbell, D, Collins, H and Wightman, J (eds), *Implicit Dimensions of Contract: Discrete, Relational and Network Contracts*, 2003, Oxford: Hart Publishing

Chapter 2
Going Shopping
Sally Wheeler[1]

Introduction

This chapter takes shopping as its theme. Shopping as a practice is obviously central to the development and functioning of a capitalist market economy. However, its status within the doctrinal structure of contract law is only as an illustrative mechanism for particular phenomena. In this chapter, I take two case studies that, from different perspectives, consider shopping as a narrative of pleasure. Their aim is to offer readings of shopping that put self-gratification back into it as an activity. The first study examines the reading of shopping that is offered by current contract case law. Onto that examination I then impose an alternative reading that embraces a feminist perspective at the level of doctrinal analysis.

The second case study examines 19th century contracts made for the purchase of women's clothes. The story of shopping begins, for this chapter, in the 18th century. By the end of that century, shops consisted of fixed retail spaces and were beginning, in some locales, to sell the products of empire and industrial revolution.[2] The context of 19th century shopping was that continuing progress in production methods both created and demanded a buoyant consumer market to sustain developments.[3] The beginnings of a transport infrastructure assisted in making this possible.[4] Goods could now be selected in person from the range of fixed shops (Davis, 1966, p 102) rather than from local merchants or travelling salesmen. These developments heralded the arrival of the department store toward the end of the 19th century.

As I explain below, on one level the link between the contract doctrine reading of shopping and the 19th century practice of shopping is found in the symbolism and practical effect of the marriage contract. For the contemporary doctrinal account of shopping, the marriage contract offers the mirror image exchange of promises so worshipped within the formalist accounts of contract formation. In historical terms, the marriage contract for some five centuries denied, in general terms, married women a legal or economic existence.[5] While the specificity of the marriage contract is examined in more detail in Section 2 of this chapter, two preliminary observations are made here. The first is that the marriage contract was used as a form of sexual

---

1   Faculty of Law, Queen's University, Belfast.

2   Walsh (1995). This is not uncontroversial as it departs from the standard retail history account that fixed location shops and the end of the barter economy did not occur until 1850 or so (see Jeffreys, 1954). This is the source text that most subsequent commentary has relied upon. As Walsh points out, however, these assertions reflect the 19th century focus of the primary literature Jeffreys draws upon. For a fully annotated overview of these debates, see Winstanley (1994).

3   For a discussion of the role of consumer demand in this period, see Perkin (1969).

4   In 1830, Britain had under 100 miles of usable railway track; by 1852 this figure had risen to 6,600 miles and by 1901 route mileage was just over 19,000 miles (Freeman, 1999).

5   This statement is obviously subject to some qualifications. Women, married or otherwise, for example, were persons recognised by law for the purposes of criminal law: see the discussion in Naffine (2002) around the idea of abstract personhood within positivist jurisprudence.

identity for women; it delineated those who were sexually available from those who were not. Allied to this is the second point of interest. Prior to the reform of the laws on the disposition of property, both real and personal,[6] by married women, married women operated as the economic agents of their husbands. This created an ideal of married women existing in a genteel state of married bliss with their lives structured around the home and household governance.[7] The home as domain of the married woman was further buoyed up by nascent industrial capitalism which took men away from the home to work. Under a system of accumulation based upon agrarian activity,[8] men had administered their estates largely from the home.[9] The expanding commodity market put pressure on this model of domestic contentment by playing to the economic potential of women as consumers. Recognition of this potential led inextricably on to the debate examined below, concerning the merits, or lack of merits, of consumption and the involvement of married women. Significantly for women, this debate pushed together the narratives of consumption activity and sexual activity: to indulge in the former was also to want to sell the latter.

Contracts made for the purchase of clothes reveal important class and identity dimensions within 19th century society. Manner of dress made important statements about social position and inevitably, given the nature of Victorian society, was also transmogrified into a statement about sexuality and sexual availability. The same clothes that were appropriate on a woman of the upper social echelons were seen as 'showy and dishonest' on a woman from a lower social stratum (Michie, 2002). This form of dress, if worn by a woman from a lower social stratum, was often attributed to the prostitute. Prostitution was frequently seen as the reason why working-class women wore clothes that were considered more appropriate to women of a different social class, and prostitution was also seen as the method by which the purchase of such clothes was financed. At base, clothes had considerable semiotic currency in Victorian analyses of class and sexual morality (Valverde, 1989).

Charles Dickens' *Dombey and Son*, first published in 1848, offers an almost exact fit, in terms of the themes it explores, with this chapter (Moglen, 1992). An early episode in the novel provides the perfect illustration of the semiotic and dramatic

---

6   There is a huge amount of literature on married women, property, reform of the rules on property in this context and the question of property ownership on marital separation. One of the most interesting contributions is that of Mary Poovey. Her account of this is interwoven into her account of the 1857 divorce legislation; it includes discussion of the parliamentary debates on both topics and reveals some of the cultural and stereotypical views of women and some of the contradictions in those conceptions (Poovey, 1988). See also Holcombe (1983, pp 18–36).

7   Many novels, contemporary to both the start of the industrial revolution and the following Victorian years, emphasise the security to be found in this sphere away from the social dirt and economic uncertainties of the market place. See Gallagher (1985).

8   For a discussion of the metaphor of husbanding a wife and husbanding the economic security of the realm which was a theme of mid to late agrarian capitalism, see Braverman (1985, pp 143–47).

9   Agrarian capitalism had its own vocabulary around women and land. Marriage was used as a means to accumulate more land; consequently, an analogy was drawn around the fruits of the land and the fruits of marriage. During enclosure, with its aim of facilitating mass agricultural production, women became 'enclosed' as well within the domestic sphere. See Malcolmson (1994).

importance of clothes and the changing nature of economy and consumption. Florence is rescued by 'Good Mrs Brown' (Dickens, 1985, pp 129–33). The very same then strips Florence of her 'pretty frock' and dresses her in rags. When Florence eventually escapes the clutches of the old hag and makes her way towards the City, hoping to find the premises of Dombey and Son, she encounters indifference and then hostility. Dressed as she is, those working in the City are reluctant to believe that she is lost and give the impression that they know she is there for an altogether more sinister purpose (Marsh, 1991). In essence, her dress codes her now as a potential child prostitute. Before happening upon 'Good Mrs Brown' her 'pretty frock and little bonnet' would have marked her out as the daughter of a successful City dealer. The relevance of this short scene is not clear to the reader until very much later in the novel. Then it appears that the fate wrought on Florence mirrored the fate of Mrs Brown's daughter. Mrs Brown blamed a close associate of Dombey Senior for her daughter's 'fall'.

Exactly what Mr Dombey deals in is never made clear, as his world represents the impenetrable and puzzling world of finance-based capitalism (Clark, 1984). It is this point of uncertainty that opens up the theme of economy and consumption. Solomon Gills, Walter's uncle, makes and sells ships' instruments from their waterside home. His is the world of simple discrete exchange, based on goods paid for and carried away immediately. He struggles to become used to the idea of shoppers rather than customers (Dickens, 1985, p 95). Shoppers browse, looking at this and that. They enter his shop and look at its wares. In pursuit of browsing, they depart, having purchased nothing. Customers, on the other hand, search out a specific item and, having located it, then proceed to buy it. Customers are Uncle Sol's preference but they are a rare breed in the new world. The business world of Dombey and Son is quite beyond Uncle Sol's understanding and experience. He is at a loss as to what Dombey and Son can do in the world of business to generate profit if it is not to stock commodities that are then purchased. The business of Dombey and Son presumably involves the world of paper transactions in futures and stock options (Perera, 1990).

Clothes also played a role in the formulation of some of what we see now as the first functionalist accounts of society. Simmel (1957) and also Veblen (1998), whose position is examined later in this chapter, used fashion and the pursuit of fashion as a key component in explaining social stratification. For my own part, I see fashion as creating an opportunity for Victorian women of the upper and middle classes to create an identity for themselves both by the apparel they purchased and through their participation in the market. The narrative provided by the 19th century cases and their context tells the narrative of women's economic activity, or at least the activity of those women who appeared to be in sufficient funds to purchase new clothes. The theory of female consumption that I set out is a character-action approach (Campbell, 1987) based upon the identity creation opportunities for women offered by the purchase of clothes.

The role of women in the expanding retail sector raised some complex cultural issues in which law, as the expression of the dominant social force, could be harnessed to reinforce one cultural norm over another. Contract law, through the application of doctrinal principles, was being asked to decide between two competing discourses. Capital invested in commercial ventures was more flexible and liquid than that tied to land. It was not so flexible, however, as to prevent network relationships of credit and debt, akin in many ways to the ones recognised in contract scholarship now, from emerging (Wrightson, 2000, pp 292–94). Retailers relied on periodic settlement of debts owed to them to pay wages, secure supplies and generally sustain life. The economic participation of married women in these networks was vital to commercial society but so was the settlement of their debts by their husbands.[10] Conversely, social stability required that women should defer to their husbands' authority in matters of expenditure, even personal rather than household expenditure, as husbands should be the masters in their own homes if the equanimity of family life was not to be disturbed. It is my intention to look at the relationship between women, the market and issues of identity that the experience of shopping for clothes revealed and the response of contract law to these emerging relationships.

Section I

Shopping within contract doctrine

Offer and acceptance

Examining shopping as part of the law of contract requires an engagement with the cases on offer and acceptance because, with the exception of Mrs McNab's wedding dress,[11] this is the primary locus for discussion of retail practice within the canon of contract doctrine. I think here particularly of *Fisher v Bell* and *Pharmaceutical Society of Great Britain v Boots Cash Chemists (Southern) Ltd*.[12] The jurisprudence around offer and acceptance filtered into English contract law during the later part of the 18th century (Atiyah, 1979, pp 44–48; Ibbetson, 1999, pp 222–23) and by the 19th century was established in more or less its present form.[13] These doctrines are of course the clearest possible manifestation of the will theory. Their exact genealogical descent into contract doctrine is a matter of debate. What is indisputable, however, is that, at the time these doctrines established themselves within the will theory paradigm, the exercise of free will as part of the edifice of contract by many women was

---

10 Leach sees these competing discourses as ones which pitted husband against wife in litigation; in fact, the husband was pitted against retailer while the wife and her clothing were discussed as present only in a spiritual sense. See Leach (1984, p 334).

11 Mrs McNab's wedding dress was the damaged item in *Curtis v Chemical Cleaning and Dyeing Co Ltd* [1951] 1 KB 805. This case is normally placed in the common law jurisprudence on exemption and exclusion clauses developed prior to the Unfair Contract Terms Act 1977.

12 [1953] 1 QB 401.

13 See, for example, *Anson's Law of Contract* (1882). The chapter on offer and acceptance contained therein is not dissimilar to the account now provided in texts of this sort in terms of its conceptual language and structures. As Chatterjee's chapter in this volume explains, technological advances have been assimilated into existing doctrinal categories. Novel factual scenarios, such as that in *Harvela Investments Ltd v Royal Trust Co of Canada Ltd* [1985] 2 All ER 966, have been similarly treated.

limited to just one transaction – the marriage contract.[14] This had the effect of removing women's contractual capacity before the law thereafter.[15]

The offer and acceptance cases are the first item on most contract law courses and we are all familiar with the way in which students learn the difference in terms of status, within contract doctrine, of goods on display in a shop window and goods on display in a shop. There follows on from this the manipulation of the fact patterns to enact particular scenarios and test them against the paradigm cases.[16] Collins (1997, p 94) expresses this technique particularly eloquently in the following extract:

> Consider for example the purchase of goods in a self-service store. At what point is an agreement completed by an acceptance? Does the customer accept the offer when he or she places the goods in the wire basket? Or does acceptance take place when the customers present the goods to the assistant at the cash register? Alternatively, we can even argue that the assistant accepts the offer to buy by ringing up the prices of the goods on the cash register. Or is that merely an offer, accepted by the customer by the presentation of the right amount of money?

Doctrine's context

In this approach, shopping as a lived experience is given little recognition. Central to the contest between the two rules is the status of the goods as object of offer and acceptance (Dow, 1991, p 821). Contract law presents shopping as a discrete exchange. Framed into the narrative, because even discrete exchanges exist within a context,[17] are concerns to protect both the retailer from an obligation to supply more goods of a particular type than are physically present in the shop and the shopper from committing themselves to a purchase before they are ready. A desire to complete the contract is indicated by presenting payment and exiting the retail premises. The retail space is preserved as a space for bartering to take place. The demands of freedom of contract are such that both sides to a potential bargain must have access to the process of bargain construction. The complete inappropriateness of this context is recognised by both Treitel (2003) and Beatson (2002) in their respective texts. However, in failing to offer an alternative scheme, both would appear to feel it unnecessary that those initial learned rules should stand in some relevance to the lived world[18] or that shopping as an experience is important

---

14 The extent to which the marriage contract satisfies the principles of market exchange-based contract is open to doubt. Pateman (1988, pp 163–65) points to the asymmetrical relationship between the two forms of contract as regards the negotiation of terms, absence of writing and inequality of bargaining power. See also 'The sexual contract', below in the present chapter.

15 A review of the major debates on this point – in essence the contest between the impact of classic economics, the development of common law jurisprudence and the legacy of civilian jurisprudence, is provided by O'Malley (2000, p 468). Notably, Goodrich stands outside of this debate. While Goodrich acknowledges the role of the civilian tradition, he subordinates it to the input of the law of marriage (Goodrich, 1994, pp 123–24).

16 Arthur Austin (1998) terms this the 'technique of "logic-chopping"'.

17 On the issue of whether discrete exchanges do in fact exist within what surely must be the overwhelmingly correct relational paradigm of contract description, I follow the approach of David Campbell in *The Relational Theory of Ian Macneil* (2001, pp 42ff).

18 Katz (1990, p 218) comments that on one view the rules on offer and acceptance are there to form a co-ordinating function only. The content of the rules does not matter in so much that the system can function provided that there are rules irrespective of what those rules might say. Katz goes on to comment that the offer and acceptance rules have been largely ignored by the law and economics movement. These rules have not thus far been subjected to the scrutiny of other disciplinary approaches either.

enough to be described by rules that actually reflect the reality of that practice. Shops are not a place in which bartering occurs, nor were they in the period in which the offer and acceptance cases were formulated (Adburgham, 1964, p 141). Prices are fixed and the purchaser expects to pay that price.

A possible explanation might be that the analysis they provide is one that foresaw the advent of the self-service supermarket. In other words, the construction of shopping as a battlefield game – in which retailer and shopper try to outwit each other with the advantages and counters that the rules propose each should have – describes an adversarial relationship, which is not only synonymous with contract itself,[19] but all the more adversarial when the parties are strangers to each other and there is an inequality of bargaining power. Even this as an explanation seems somewhat incongruous. The idea of shopkeeper and shopper engaged in adversarial encounter would seem to fit an era in which the shopper was attended to in person by the shopkeeper or one of their assistants. Defoe's (1727) description of the trader engaged in serving customers individually resonates with this. His instruction to the shopkeeper is to have control of his emotions, to exhibit 'no resentment, no passions' while 'he attempts to catch the browsing shopper in her own snare' by offering her an item that is so exquisite she can't resist.[20] Conversely, personal service in the context of shopping at the present time is seen as a novelty for which prior booking is required.

The classic standard problem question, with its references to those sad and lifeless individuals 'A' and 'B', emphasises that what is important is the actuality of the bargain. What must be determined is 'the moment of responsibility'[21] judged objectively.[22] No place is accorded to deliberation, despite the fact that the verb 'to shop' is best explained through the idea of 'choice [and] empowerment, the relation between looking and having' (Friedberg, 1993, p 57).

'Shopping' used as a verb or a descriptive noun does not appear in any of the shopping cases that form part of the doctrinal canon. Instead, the discourse is composed around the idea of 'needs'.[23] In describing goods purchased as satisfying 'needs', the shopping cases seem to be taking on the language of 19th century judgments that concerned themselves with whether categories of persons such as infants and wives, otherwise excluded from contract law as lacking capacity, had contracted for necessaries.

Contract doctrine and the 19th century consumption debate

It was permissible for infants and married women to contract for necessaries; to contract otherwise was not. In the case of married women, a contract for necessaries

---

19 See the judgment of Lord Ackner in *Walford v Miles* [1992] 1 All ER 453 and *contra* Cumberbatch (1992).

20 Defoe (1987, pp 103–05). The choice of gender in the quoted extract follows the original. A more sophisticated reading of Defoe can be found in Kowaleski-Wallace (1997, pp 82–86).

21 'The moment of responsibility' is the terminology used by Collins to describe the focus of the reasoning and inquiry of contract doctrine.

22 Tidwell and Linzer (1991, p 803) themselves criticise a proposition of Richard Epstein (1983, p 1364).

23 *Pharmaceutical Society of Great Britain v Boots Cash Chemists (Southern) Ltd* [1953] 1 QB 401, pp 405–06, *per* Somervell LJ.

was formed with the wife existing within the contract as agent for her husband. As with all agency contracts, consent, express or implied, of the principal was required for the contract to be valid. Thus, the presence of a married woman within the contractual space is entirely internalised, visible not to contract doctrine but only to the other contracting party, and even then visible not as an individual in person but as a spectre of another absent person, her husband. The married woman as a spectral presence appears again in Section 2 of this chapter. The infant, on the other hand, was considered to act as principal in a contract for necessaries. Therefore, the capacity of a married woman to enter into a contract was inferior to that of an infant. In the 6th edition of *Chitty on Contract* (1857, pp 128–270), married women find themselves enclosed within the same chapter space as lunatics, felons and outlaws, amongst others. According to Maine, '[infants] before the years of discretion, [and] the adjudged lunatic ... do not possess the faculty of forming a judgement in their own interests ... they are wanting in the first essential of an engagement by contract' (Maine, 1905, p 141). Married women were at least spared this indignity of designation, but only on the grounds that their interests were subsumed in those of their husbands. The concept of necessaries in relation to married women and contract had existed from the 15th century onwards (Anon, 1738, p 274).

The interplay between the purchasing identities of husband and wife is symbolic of a much larger debate that occupied considerable space within the discourse of political economy from the start of the 18th century onward. This was the debate around the nature of consumption. Was consumption a deviant act[24] pursued by wives who risked bankrupting the state or their husbands with their actions, or was it a practice which, while carrying these dangers, was for the greater glory of their husbands who benefited from the adornment of their wives? That consumption was a feminine activity and that the practice of business was a masculine one was not a significant issue within the contours of this debate. The division of economic activity in this way was taken as a given.[25] As economic life progressed from the household and largely rural agrarian accumulation to capital accumulation based on industrial production, economic discourse reflected this shift as masculine (Wilk, 1996, pp 15–16). There is documentary evidence to support the idea that women, albeit women of a fairly narrow social elite, were significant consumers, particularly so in the context of the type of purchases that this chapter examines, namely clothes.[26] However, the gusto with which later commentators have seized upon the idea of women hungry for consumption does risk overstating the case as a general proposition. There is a growing body of work which places responsibility for consumption, outside of obviously feminine purchases, on men. It is important to see the Industrial Revolution debate around women and consumption as being as much about male desire to retain their role as provision purchasers as about the desire to control female activity (Bohstedt, 1988; Finn, 2000).

24 Porter (1993, p 58) points out the word play on consumption in these debates; consumption means both expenditure and the then fatal disease of tuberculosis.

25 This is not to say that women had never been known to have participated in business. There was, for example, significant female participation in stock dealings in the South Sea Company: see Ingrassia (1995). For a review of contemporary comment on female stock transactions in relation to the South Sea Company, see Banner (1998, pp 69–72).

26 New clothes were not completely beyond the financial reach of working women: see Lemire (1991).

Concern with the consequences of consumption moved from a focus on the finances of the state to those of the family (Brantlinger, 1996, pp 136–50); a spendthrift wife might bankrupt her husband or, at least in the manner of George Eliot's Rosamond, make his life anxious and less comfortable than it might otherwise have been. The boom and bust cycles of the economy in the mid-Victorian period made this fear all the more real (McVeagh, 1981).[27] Mandeville (1705), who was almost alone in his view that consumption of luxuries was a necessary vice within a burgeoning capitalist economy,[28] saw participation in consumption as the activity of a wife.[29] The acquisition of luxuries was, for Mandeville, the reason for male activity in the labour market. He saw men in a Veblen-esque[30] way as spurred on to outdo or outshine their neighbour (Horne, 1978, pp 60–61). Dissenters from Mandeville's model of the virtues and vices contained within capitalist development did not question his view of women's relationship with purchasing. The idea of women as duplicitous and potentially disruptive within society unless controlled, control being something that their new role as consumers threatened to make less possible if not impossible, is one that underscored much discussion in Victorian society. Women occupied the role of object within this paradigm. The marriage contract can be read as supporting object status. Freedom to purchase commodities as consumers disrupted this popular model as women could then enjoy the status of subject (Roberts, 1998). Compartmentalisation of women into the category of object, along with commodities available for sale in the marketplace, created the link between sexual activity and market participation that features so strongly in both the readings of political economy and fiction literature of the period.

Public and private spheres

Subsequent readings of this aspect of Victoriana have linked fears of the disruptive effect of women in the marketplace to ideas of public and private spaces, or spheres of separation (Roberts, 1998).[31] Women as consumers were entering the public sphere or, put another way, the space that hitherto had been the physical and economic zone of male presence only. Women, so the argument goes, had previously been present only in the private sphere of the home. One difficulty with a division such as this is that there are different definitions of private and public (Weintraub, 1997, p 1). In pure spatial terms, we can point to empirically documented examples of the harassment of women when they appear in this male or public space – the assumption being that to appear was making a statement of sexual availability and offering a rejection of ideas of respectability. However, these examples are no different from present day issues around spatial division. It is an uncomfortable fact that the use of space is, and has always been, sexualised (Myslik, 1996, p 159). Space is predominantly male and heterosexual. In narratives that focus

---

27 McVeagh describes bankruptcy 'as an omnipresent calamity in the creative writing of the age' (1981, p 205).

28 See the novels of Frances Burney, in particular *Cecilia* and *Camilla* (1796).

29 Mandeville (1705, line 20), and comments to the 1714 edition in particular: see Harth (1989). See also Mandell (1992).

30 See Cunningham (2000).

31 For an overview of these debates, see Davidoff (2003).

on sexual danger (Walkowitz, 1998), examples of harassment come to the fore. This is not meant as an argument to legitimise or to trivialise the sexualisation of space but rather as an argument to assert that nothing marks out the Victorian period as a more threatening and dangerous time for women using public space than any other period. As the state had yet to recognise a role for itself as the protector of women's and children's rights within the home, private space was not always the safe and comfortable haven some contemporary commentators assumed it was (Isin and Wood, 1999, pp 78–79). The duality of the home as both a location for private acts of violence and a space of safety has continued (Price, 2002).

The empirical evidence of the street experience for Victorian middle-class female shoppers can suggest a much wider enquiry than the use of physical space. This evidence raises questions of the role played by class divisions and issues of participation in civil society. The organisation of space as a political arena moves into the territory of the debate between Jurgen Habermas and Nancy Fraser, both of whom are drawing on accounts of 19th century urban life to support their respective positions.[32] This debate is intellectually challenging and rewarding but moves far beyond the scope of this chapter. The issue of class division can be dealt with more simply. By the 1860s, areas of cities, for example, the West End in London (Rappaport, 2000), were being designated as consumption spaces for retail commodities, and these cities required the presence of female shoppers with disposable incomes. Women who were not visibly, to put it in Veblen's terms, part of the labour force, made railway journeys alone or with female companions (Schivelbusch, 1977) to access these opportunities. This is evidenced not least by the fact that 'appropriate' female toilet facilities were under construction throughout the period (Penner, 2001). A key point is that these public facilities were to be for the use of the female shopping class, not the female working class.[33] The lives of working-class women are used most notably by Amanda Vickery (1993; 1998, pp 3–11) to point out that changes in industrial production and sites of economic activity from the 15th century onward had opened up opportunities for female employment (Earle, 1989). The creation of consumption spaces involved a relocation of feminine economic activity. The streets of most major cities were busy and hectic. Large-scale Victorian construction and engineering projects existed alongside sites of industrial production.[34] Women going shopping would have made their way through busy streets, no doubt passing working-class women (Nava, 1997, p 61). In doing so, the women of the new shopping world rubbed shoulders with sexually available women of a lower socio-economic class. The risk of this casual encounter across class lines lead to fears of harassment and pollution (Pollock, 1988, p 78). The state regulated the sexuality of working-class women (Howell, 2000; Carabine, 2001), assuming that participation in prostitution was as likely as participation in other forms of paid employment (Ryan, 1994, p 51).

Within the realm of the home, the so-called private sphere, entertaining was very important for both acquiring and maintaining social status. Wives and daughters carried out the design and administration of this activity. Once again, this is a class-

---

32 Fraser (1997, pp 69–98). For a more general overview of feminist debate on this point, see Rendall (1999).

33 James Stevenson MD, quoted in Penner (2001).

34 Nead (2000), in particular Part 1.

based activity. Middle-class women welcomed guests to their homes and their homes cannot really be seen as secluded and closed areas. In this chapter, I am careful to use the term 'domestic' as opposed to 'private' in order to avoid a lengthy engagement with a debate that is more subtle and wide-ranging than it first appears.

The contemporary critic who stands apart from the idea of women as subject and object is Marx. For Marx, women equate to goods and he considers both women and goods to be passive objects that can offer no resistance to sale and possession (Bowlby, 1985, pp 22–28). Women can be bought and sold just as commodities can. In his words: '[c]ommodities are things and therefore lack the power to resist man. If they are unwilling, *he* can use force; in other words, he can take possession of them'[35] (emphasis added). To this statement, Marx, in *Capital*, adds a footnote in which he explains that even in 12th century France, an era 'renowned for its piety', wanton women were available for purchase alongside goods such as clothes and shoes.[36] This makes his linkage of women, sexual activity and the market explicit. Its explanatory force is made all the more powerful by the knowledge that Marx would have been aware of the increased volume of market transactions in which women were the purchasers of commodities in the 50 or so years prior to his exposition. The position that Marx takes on the sale and purchase of women is that women are always the objects of exchange – they are neither buyers nor sellers, they are a force, or more properly a power, that can be used by masculinity and belongs to masculinity.[37] This view can be contrasted with the more mainstream view of political economy that saw women as both subjects and objects in contracts for sexual services. This contract was the only one that women moving around freely in urban consumption spaces could be involved in – there was no other rationale that explained their presence in those spaces.[38] Shopping for commodities by women challenges both of these views.

Necessity or luxury?

The idea that goods can be divided into the categories of needs and wants is one that is fundamental to the social sciences and many spin-off disciplines, such as marketing and consumer behaviour (Maslow, 1934), and this basic distinction is at the heart of the functionalist accounts of fashion that were referred to earlier. However, contract doctrine adopted a rather more sophisticated approach to the question of necessaries than pure functionalism would suggest.

Cases such as *Hands v Slaney*[39] and *Peters v Fleming*[40] made it clear that necessaries or needs related to the 'degree and station in life' of the purchaser. Although both these cases concerned infants, this approach transferred directly into the cases on wives' debts. So the question as to whether particular goods were

---

35 The analogy between consumption, or more usually capitalism, and rape and seduction still abound in feminist analyses derived from Marxism: see Gibson-Graham (1996, pp 120–47).

36 Marx, extracted in Simon (1994, p 245).

37 Marx, in Tucker (1978, p 93). See also Helsinger (1991, pp 905–06).

38 For a contemporary example of the expression of such views, see the discussion of the contemporary debates around the establishment of Whiteley's – the Universal Provider, London's first department store, in Rappaport (1996).

39 (1800) 8 TR 578.

40 (1840) 6 M & W 314.

necessaries or not (Leiss, 1976) depended not only on forming a judgment as to the class of the purchaser (meaning the husband, of course) and from that constructing a distinction between his needs and wants (Wharton, 1853, p 369), but also on the movement of goods themselves between categories (Mintz, 1986; Taylor, 1999, pp 40–43).

In relation to the first point, the husband as defendant was placed in the position of arguing that his station in life was not sufficient to support his wife's taste in clothes. In *Atkins v Curwood*,[41] we learn that a barrister who was both 'in considerable standing at the bar' and 'in the station of a gentleman'[42] may nevertheless not be in a financial position to support the purchase of a boa,[43] a figured lilac satin dress, a black velvet skirt and black blonde[44] sleeves and five or so French cambric handkerchiefs.[45] An argument that such items are luxuries and not necessaries is the converse of Veblen's idea of conspicuous consumption. Veblen's proposition, dealt with in more detail in Section 2 below, was that men adorned their wives as indicators of their own socio-economic status. Husbands can avoid liability by successfully claiming that their socio-economic status does not support their wives' desire for fashionable clothes.

In relation to the second point, the developing industrial production systems rendered goods to the market place both in greater numbers and ever more cheaply (Abelson, 1989, p 35), thus extending the availability and affordability of goods down through the hierarchy of Victorian society.[46] In terms of women's clothes, these production developments can be seen in the advances in the mechanisation of calico printing and the invention of the sewing machine. The introduction of, first, engraved copper plates and, then, steam powering of the same considerably speeded up the printing process for cloth.[47] Sewing machines were widely used by 1864. Although they could not be used for the construction of entire garments, in the context of women's dresses they enabled seam decorations and other individualisations to be added very cheaply (Forty, 1986). The increasing availability of goods, the expansion of shopping spaces and the development of transport meant that wants were often converted to needs through the mediums of envious looking and extensive advertising.[48] Marcuse (1964, p 24), in an essentially

---

41 7 Car & P 756.

42 *Per* Lord Abinger CB.

43 Traditionally, this was a roll of fur worn around the neck. See the comments of Veblen (1894, p 69) on the use of the 'pelt of the arctic fur seal' in preference to fabric. Veblen was more concerned with what he considered to be wasteful expenditure than the fate of the seal: see 'Veblen on marriage, conspicuous consumption and comfort', below in this chapter.

44 Despite the spelling of 'blonde' (one would have expected the spelling 'blond'), this I assume is a reference to blond lace. This was a fine mesh lace with patterns worked in silk. It could be natural or black in colour.

45 A very fine, thin linen.

46 See the contemporary intervention of Harriet Martineau, who makes exactly this point and attributes it to the beneficial effects of industrialisation (Freedgood, 1995).

47 Prior to the introduction of steam rollers, six pieces of cloth could be printed per day per table. With steam rollers, 500 pieces a day could be printed. Annual production rose from 1m pieces to 16m pieces between 1796 and 1840. See Turnbull (1951).

48 There is some debate about the extent to which contemporary fashion journals saw themselves appealing to women directly or, conversely, engaging in a Veblen-esque way with the idea that women dressed for men (see Breward, 1994, pp 80–81). In relation to household furnishings, there was a strong bias towards the home as a female concern (see Cunningham, 2000).

Marxist account of consumption, shared surprisingly by Galbraith (1977), specifies 'false needs' as a method of social control in a society which permits free acquisition. For him, consumption is not a gendered activity, but is itself a manipulative force. The rehabilitation of shopping as a site of pleasure occurs later through the disciplinary focus provided by cultural studies (Nava, 1992, pp 185ff).

A broader frame for doctrine?

The shopping interaction is characterised by the certainty and absoluteness that the classical model of contract is predicated upon. It could be asserted that what contract doctrine is doing here is reflecting the idea of 'doing the shopping' as a routine activity in which, for example, the food products required for the forthcoming week are assembled. However, as both Bowlby and Miller make clear from different perspectives, shopping even for mundane and frequently purchased items is never a routine practice. For Bowlby, the way in which self-service stores are arranged and rearranged marks the fine line between shopping as a diversion and shopping as a chore. Lists are no longer part of the food shopping trip, she argues, because the customer knows that everything required and more will be passed on a journey around the store (Bowlby, 1997, pp 102–04).

Contract doctrine frames out of its narrative any place for pleasure, enjoyment and love. There is no space for reverence at the beauty or simplicity of a product, or delight at locating a much sought-after or longed-for object and certainly no role for Miller's concerns in exploring the human relationships that are contained within the act of purchasing – love, for example, for those whom goods are purchased for (Miller, 1998, pp 23–36). A purchase is presented as an atomistic and abstract moment divorced from any other moment. The exclusion of the idea of gift, through purchasing activity for example, is clear from the recent Law Commission discussions of privity of contract. The recipient of a purchased gift acquires contractual rights of redress in relation to the seller of the gift only through the activities of the original contracting parties and not as a result of their status as donee.[49]

The values transmitted by contract doctrine through its construction of the shopping scene are ones of individualisation, autonomy and conflict. Excluded are ideas of co-operation, care and relationship. One way of analysing this picture is to tie it into the so-called feminist characteristics debate which centres around the work of Carol Gilligan (1982). There are two difficulties with this approach. The first is that Gilligan herself disavows any gender connection for her work.[50] The second difficulty is that, even if we ignore Gilligan's assertions to the contrary and take her work as the foundation of the idea that masculine and feminine value and ethics are different, her work has been used almost without critique within feminist jurisprudence (Sherry, 1986). This has resulted in the creation of stereotypical characters embodying the masculine and the feminine. Ascribed to the feminine are exactly the sort of mothering and nurturing qualities that have been used in the past as a partial rationale for the subjugation of women. In the 19th century, it was this

---

49 Law Commission (1996, paras 7.41–42 and 7.54–56) and Contracts (Rights of Third Parties) Act 1999, s 1.

50 Gilligan (1993, p 209; 1987, p 20).

view of women that ensured their exclusion from the Lockian idea of the proprietary self; the division between, on the one hand, self as labour-provider and recipient of surplus value and, on the other hand, self as exploited by the endeavours of others and the cycles of the economy.[51] Similar problems with essentialist applications of Gilligan's work have occurred in the fields of feminist philosophy and feminist ethics. Those debates are amply covered elsewhere[52] and are touched upon in Linda Mulcahy's first chapter in this volume.

In my view, a less controversial approach is to take the cultural stereotypes of masculine and feminine interests which patriarchal society has constructed[53] and see where, if anywhere, these characteristics are positioned by contract doctrine.[54] This would involve seeing women socialised as non-aggressive caregivers and as individuals who create and maintain relationships (Anderson, 1990, p 1807). Women care more about gifts than striking self-seeking bargains. Men are constructed as inflexible, confident, self-seeking individuals interested in outcome.[55] The late Mary Jo Frug, who was at best ambivalent towards the ways in which feminist jurisprudence had adopted particular readings of Gilligan's work, used this approach with considerable success in her reading of two competing analyses of the impossibility doctrine or, in UK terms, the frustration doctrine. Frug saw as masculine a position which stressed the plausibility of only one outcome in a model of contract that was predicated on discrete and abstract relationships, offering a literal interpretation of the relevant contract texts. She characterised as feminine a position that was grounded in a 'pluralistic, context-sensitive model of contract relationships' (Frug, 1992, p 116). This model offered a multiplicity of objectives and was centred on good faith, forbearance and sharing. Frug linked this feminist analysis to the work of Ian Macneil. The debate about whether Ian Macneil found feminism or whether it found him (Brown, 1996, pp 11ff) is taken up in this volume by David Campbell, in Chapter 9.

Section 2

Victorian shopping activities

The marriage contract

Contract doctrine, in its outcome-centred account of shopping, dismisses the possibility of shopping as a practice in its own right. Shopping owes its presence within the doctrinal structure to its usefulness in providing an illustration of the mirror-image requirement of contract formation. Two final ironies emerge from this

---

51 Locke (1970); for an explanation of property in the moral person and property in the body, see Dickinson (1997, pp 64–91).

52 See Wheeler (2002, p 154) and Traina (1999, pp 141–42).

53 The social artifice that is gender distinction has been commented on from Mill (1869) to Butler (1990). See also Butler (1993).

54 A not dissimilar approach is taken in Belcher (2001, pp 36–37).

55 From the celebrations of positive masculinity that have followed world events post 11 September 2001 we could add bravery, mental and physical strength and leadership: see Allen (2002).

observation. First, that the case that forms the lynchpin of the doctrinal account should centre on something as phallic and violent as a flick knife. The sharp, quick and thrusting nature of the flick knife is the complete antithesis of the thoughtful nature of shopping identified above. Secondly, that the mirror-image idea of contract formation, of which the 'shop' cases form a part, should itself mirror exactly the words and symbolism of the contract which is the ultimate symbol of female non-existence within legal accounts – the exchange of vows in the marriage contract.

Blackstone provides the most celebrated legal definition of marriage in his *Commentaries on the Laws of England*:[56]

> By marriage, the husband and wife are one person in law: that is, the very being or legal existence of the women is suspended during the marriage, or at least incorporated and consolidated into that of the husband: under whose wing, protection and *cover* she performs everything; and is therefore called in our law-french a *feme-covert*.

A number of comments flow from this definition. *Covert* and its extended noun *coverture*, when taken with the idea of a woman 'incorporated and consolidated' into another human form, pushes us to consider the married woman of Blackstone's era as one contained within the home of the husband for *breeding purposes*[57] and to *augment* his financial position. The wife is 'covered'[58] by her husband in the same way that a mare at stud would be by a chosen stallion (Dorré, 2002); at the same time, she is assimilated into the flesh of her husband through 'incorporation'. The married woman is 'covered', as in hidden from view, by her incorporation into the body of her husband. He stands as a protective shield between her and the world outside their union. The husband's death removed this shield and at that point the wife, now widow or relict, occupied an existence of her own before the law.

Aside from the legal qualities of marriage explained by Blackstone, the marriage ceremony itself, which forms the outward expression of the theocracy of marriage, can also be subjected to a feminist critique. Although the Reformation removed, for members of the Anglican community at least, the status of sacrament from the religious aspect of marriage and the Elizabethan reforms of the Prayer Book introduced reforms to the service itself, as a religious institution the marriage ceremony still retained its basic character. The central focus of the marriage service is on the giving of the woman from one man, the father or other prominent male family member, to another man, the husband-to-be. Property settled on the woman then passed from her birth lineage family to that of her husband's family. One reading of this is that it is the zenith of female disempowerment. A woman is being passed with her property from one man to another as the object of an exchange. She

---

56 1765–69, Vol 1, Chap 15, p 430.

57 In a debate in 1868 on reform of the property-holding capacity of married women, the Earl of Shaftesbury commented: 'Would she [ie, the wife] hold [property] with all the usual rights, privileges, and profits? For instance, could she quarrel with her husband and eject him, or refuse him admission to her house; and, while keeping him out of it, might she admit everyone else?' Shaftesbury's point here is that access to the home for only the husband equates to his sexual rights over his wife; if she the wife is allowed sole control of the home she can invite in whomsoever she wishes and, of course, enjoy sexual relations with them. See Harman (1988, p 355), from which both the Shaftesbury quote and the following point are taken.

58 The 10th suggested use of the word 'cover' as a verb in the *Oxford English Dictionary* is as a way of describing the sexual union between mare and stallion.

is also the subject of the exchange in the sense that she gives her consent, but this consent is, at best, one given to a standard form contract (Goodrich, 1996, p 25) that facilitates her passage from one private sphere to another. In any event, the exchange of promises involved in the marriage service is subordinate in importance to the event of the 'giving of the bride'. The formulaic content of the marriage promises and the prescribed responses to them fit neatly the mirror-image requirement of the rules on offer and acceptance. However, in both legal and theocratic terms it is not the case that they encompass the passage of spinster and bachelor to wife and husband. The promises are evidence only of the presence of a greater force. The priestly injunction 'those whom God hath joined together' makes this clear. The reading of marriage that I have given here of course ignores the theological nicety that the bride is being given to God through the intermediacy of the conducting priest who then tacitly facilitates her moving swiftly on from God to her earthly husband.[59]

The analogy between marriage as a contractual arrangement and contract in the private law sense of exchange was commented on by Defoe.[60] Defoe advised the same checks of spousal suitability as would be applied to potential business partners, and saw the marriage contract as being fulfilled according to mercantile ethics of fairness and reciprocity. His values did not extend to giving women a choice of spouse as their reasoning powers were too weak. The civil registration legislation of 1837 brought these debates to the fore once more. It is the civil contractarian aspect of marriage that forms the background for the 20th century critique of Carol Pateman (1988).

The sexual contract

Pateman's work on the political character of the social contract is the obvious starting point for all feminist critiques of contract (Sullivan, 2000). Pateman's critique, of course, exists at a level above the private ordering arrangements that feature in this volume.[61] She is concerned with the social contract that underpins the relationship between citizens and the state. The existence of this relationship allows individuals to make the private legal arrangements that feature in this volume, secure in the knowledge that they can, if they deem it necessary, resort to civil law to enforce these arrangements. The intersection between the social contract and the legal idea of contract occurs in the marriage contract. Pateman presents a damning comparison between the rules that are offered by the state for private exchanges and those that are offered in the context of marriage (1988, pp 57–62). Marriage, for Pateman, is about a woman surrendering her autonomy to a man who himself then goes on to participate in social contract arrangements. These social contract arrangements can occur only after a prior sexual contract has been concluded in which wives are subordinated to their husbands. This offers a construction of society through three cumulative levels: the initial sexual contract, which creates the subjugation of women in marriage; the cultural phenomenon of the family; and an

---

59 For a more detailed overview of the liturgical elements of the service and the differences between Catholic and Common Prayer Book versions, see Cressy (1997, pp 336–49).

60 Defoe (1727). See also Latta (2002).

61 For a more detailed account of how Pateman's work fits into feminist legal theory, see Buker (1999, pp 35–39).

assembly brought about by the activities of the male members of these family units. These facilitate the growth of civil society, governed by patriarchal authority. The creation of civil society allows a regime of law, sufficient to secure private exchange relationships, to evolve.

Central to Pateman's critique is the point that women are not the equals of men in a society that embraces this contractual structure. Their participation in civil society is secured only through marriage. The idea of a social contract based on liberal contractarianism has not freed women from patriarchal structures. Pateman's goal is the casting aside of contract as the basis of social relations (1988, p 220), and as such it lies beyond the horizons of this chapter. However, concerns that Pateman raises in her discussion of contract do resonate with themes that were contemporary to the 19th century. The issue of equality and the contractual nature, or not, of marriage was an important feature of those 19th century debates that existed outside the religious dimension. For Mill, the absence of equality between the parties made a contractual analogy for marriage unacceptable (Mill, 2001).

Mill's position on capitalism was that it was a civilising force, one that would end the feudal nature of society, such that arrangements like marriage would become co-operative arrangements akin to business partnerships.[62] Mill and those associated with him,[63] such as Harriet Taylor,[64] stood apart from their contemporaries on this point. Most business practices were constructed as embodying concepts far from equality. Commercial relationships were seen as rude, uncivilised and cut-throat. In contrast, the home, the domestic sphere, was revered as a space of respite from the commercial world. A commercial analogy for the relationship that underscored domestic existence was most unwelcome (Searle, 1998, p 152). Contract was seen, as one would expect within the liberal paradigm, as empowering and as the conveyer of rights.[65]

Veblen on marriage, conspicuous consumption and comfort

Veblen provided the earliest theoretical account of consumption and it remains a critique of influence in the area of fashion, if not consumption in general (see, for example, Tilman, 1992; and Simich and Tilman, 1984). It is an account contemporary with the debates of political economy outlined here and also addresses itself, *inter alia*, to the issue of women's dress. Veblen's account of dress is concerned with married women in particular rather than women in general. He places his comments within an anthropological framework which sees women as the captured trophies of successful male warriors (1894, p 23). He then places a more modern reading on this idea, which translates servitude through capture or acquisition into marriage. On marriage, a woman becomes part of her husband's social and

---

62 Marriage as a commercial partnership would, of course, have been soluble at will. The infelicities associated with divorce, and particularly divorce by the female partner, saw Mill distance himself from this proposition and take the position that obligations owed to third parties, in other words the children of any union, would prevent divorce at will. For the consequences of divorce or desertion for the female partner, see Turano (1998).

63 For an account of the possible influences on Mill and his view of women, see Jose (2000).

64 For example, Bessie Raynor Parkes (1865, p 149).

65 It is, of course, this view of contract that saw it used as a descriptor for relationships between the service providers and service users in sectors, such as public service, where contract as a legal relationship is certainly not present: see Harden (1992).

economic unit. In a sophisticated society, a married woman has moved on from being a mere chattel, but her continuing status as property is reflected in her consumption activities. These activities are entirely vicarious, done to evidence the strength of the economic unit to which the woman belongs. Conspicuous and unproductive consumption or, to put it another away, the market-based acquisition of luxury goods draws attention, according to Veblen, to the 'pecuniary strength' of the social unit. The key to displaying pecuniary strength is to engage in a display of waste. Unproductive in this sense is used to denote the purchase of items that do not of themselves increase wealth or offer material comfort.[66] Expenditure on dress falls into this category but expenditure on clothing does not. For Veblen, clothing and dress are almost incompatible. In a manner reminiscent of the legal language that surrounded women's consumption activities, Veblen saw clothes as necessaries but dress as a luxury. Changes in clothing fashion were driven entirely by the need to provide an opportunity for conspicuous waste.

The main targets of Veblen's criticisms in relation to female comfort were the corset and the crinoline (1998, p 181). The former he presumably saw as restricting breathing and the latter as restricting movement. These garments would, in Veblen's scheme, only have been worn by women with access to considerable financial support. Veblen was not alone in his criticism of 19th century female fashion. His objections on health and practicality grounds are both separately endorsed by other contemporary commentators and echoed by subsequent 20th century scholars (Negrin, 1999). Adolf Loos[67] launched a stinging critique of female fashion, considering it to be both impractical and an indulgence that could be afforded only by the wealthy. In an extension to Veblen's views, Loos considered that women, as economically subservient to men, required ornate fashion to attract future male support. In an argument reminiscent of the public/private spheres debate, Loos contended that men could create an identity for themselves through their public activities whereas women had to fashion their identity through the clothes they wore. Below, I offer a more positive reading of the link between dress and identity. Another source of functionalist critique came from the members of the Rational Dress Society.[68] The Society drew on a broad base of support from both within and without its membership ranks.[69] Ostensibly, its argument was that 19th century fashion compromised health and hygiene for women (Montague, 1994). The society suggested that women should wear loose flowing clothes, possibly even pantaloons. However, not the least of their aims was to equip women better for the world of work and politics.[70] The inheritors of the 'dress and fashion as oppression'

---

66 Veblen's precise position on 'comfort' is not clear. In *The Theory of the Leisure Class* (1899) his position seems to be that comfort might be achieved by dint of 'fortuitous circumstances' (p 82). However, earlier, in 'The economic theory of woman's dress' (1894) (from where the page references cited here are taken), he appears to say (pp 73–75) that women can never achieve comfort when they buy fashionable clothes.

67 Loos (1982). See the support offered for this view by Summers (2001).

68 This was formed in 1881 by a Lady Harberton. One of its main demands was that women should not have to wear more than seven pounds of underwear.

69 Within this alliance there were a number of distinct and contradictory positions: see Newton (1974).

70 This is made clear from the Society's statement of purpose which was in part to promote the wearing by women of some form of bifurcated garment for business purposes.

movement, such as Orbach (1978), have moved the argument on to the oppression of women present in the body-shaping industries of diet, exercise and plastic surgery.

There is another narrative of dress which asserts that Victorian fashion devolved to women exactly what the functionalist critiques of fashion claimed it did not, namely comfort. If we take two of the items of clothing that the functionalist critique took particular exception to, the crinoline and the corset, the picture is very different. The crinoline, far from constraining women's movement, was viewed as a device that would enhance it. The wire frame allowed the heavy underskirts that had previously been employed to be abandoned. The skirt swung from the waist on the frame leaving the body unencumbered from the waist down. This was ideal for activities as diverse as dancing and household management. Expansions in the technology of travel broadened the horizons of activity for many women and a folding crinoline appeared in 1866 to facilitate these new activities. The crinoline was accommodated in travel by the adoption of new kind of carriage called the Victoria. This had a cut away seat to house full skirts (Laver, 1934). The corset has become something of a *cause célèbre* within Victorian studies (Craik, 1993). Some, supporting the functionalist critiques, see it as the classic symbol of female oppression. For others it has a much more significant role in subsequent accounts than it in fact played in the fashion of the period.[71] The corset has become a key element in analyses of Victorian positions on female sexuality. There are suggestions that the much maligned, tightly laced corset was worn by very few women and that stories of organ damage and dislodged bones were based on a small number of workhouse corpses (Hollander, 1994, p 198). Supporters of the corset suggest that it gave women a sense of completeness, a sense of protection and highlighted their femininity.[72]

Clothes and identity

If we go further than these foundational garments and examine outer clothes, then stripped of functionalist assumptions, fashion becomes an opportunity for Victorian women to construct and assert their identity. Women can create a personal narrative based upon the symbiotic relationship between clothes and the body. The body is a surface to be worked upon and sculpted in the way women choose for themselves and not for anyone else's pleasure (Wilson, 1987). Ready-made clothes for women did not appear until the end of the 1880s. Before that, design, fabric and colour were a matter of individual choice. Fabrics were based upon seasonal colours but this was not a handicap to constructing a colourful outfit. Winter ranges, for example, included 'brown, navy blue, olive-green, myrtle green and the numerous shades of red'. New fabrics emerged from the northern mill towns throughout this period. It was no longer the case that warmth could only be achieved through the layering of cotton fabric. Light tweeds, cashmeres, *paillasson* and *bouclette tibet* were all possible fabrics that could be employed to give garments that touch of individuality (Taylor, 1999, pp 6ff), along with colour choice and design choice.

---

71 See, for example, the debate between Helene Roberts and David Kunzle (Roberts, 1977; Kunzle, 1977).

72 The principal pro-corseter currently is Valerie Steel (2001).

Several of the paintings of Alfred Stevens, the Belgian artist, illustrate the idea of dress as narrative and personality. In *The Lady in Pink*, the subject wears the fashion popular in that year, 1866. The clothes themselves are presented in great detail. The skirt is ruffed and layered, the sleeves are doubled and there are decorated clasps of silver in evidence. However, the setting accorded to the subject invites us to view her not as an object dressed to be seen but as an individual woman occupied with her own private thoughts (Hollander, 2002, p 165). She is pictured studying intensely a doll or figurine of possibly Japanese or Chinese origin.[73] She is comfortable in the clothes she wears; they are part of her, not an adornment that stands separately from her contemplative state. In *The Blue Dress*, also known as *The Duchess*, the scene presented is a similar one. The subject is fashionably attired in a flowing dress of deep blue, and has her face turned into shadow away from the light. She is meditating on an opened letter, which rests in her lap, and on a portrait in the distance. Perhaps the portrait is of the letter writer; perhaps the letter contains news of the figure in the portrait. We do not know. What we do know is that her dress blends into her thoughts. She is not conscious of her exquisite clothes, as they are part of her. We view her not as a very well-dressed female subject, but as a woman contemplating the import of letter-borne news.[74]

Dress becomes liberation rather than oppression. This theme of liberation is reflected also in the shopping experience; the selection of materials, and the design and the eventual finishing decoration of clothes are narcissistic acts. As she chooses fabrics and gives directions to the draper or dressmaker, the married woman does so as her own person. The choices she makes are part of her uniqueness as an individual. Clothes are worn as a statement of inner feelings. The ball gown or the morning dress, as well as having a social context as a piece of clothing, is also given a meaning by its wearer. Present in the process of shopping for the Victorian married woman are the same emotions that we have already taken contract doctrine to task for ignoring: desire, care and love. The retailer, as draper or tailor perhaps, who attends her assists in the project of identity creation as the female shopper is viewed as she is – a woman choosing clothes. To draw on a vocabulary from later cases surrounding issues of identity, the retailer intends to contract with the person standing in front of him.[75] The wider world of consumption opened up by travel opportunities resulted in the replacement of the community nexus, enjoyed, for example, by Lydgate in George Eliot's *Middlemarch*, with a cash nexus not bounded by geography. Consequently, in all likelihood, the retailer would know no more about his customer than her taste in fabrics and dress design. He could not therefore enter a contract possessed of any intention other than to form an exchange relationship with the woman standing in front of him.

---

73 Stevens was one of the first painters of this era to become interested in Asian, particularly Japanese, art. The screen on the left hand side of the subject in *The Lady in Blue* is of Japanese design.

74 For an examination of several of Stevens' works featuring women, see www.clarkart.edu/museum_programs/exhibitions/interventions, where there is a commentary by Griselda Pollock on the Interventions Exhibition of October 2000.

75 *Phillips v Brooks Ltd* [1919] 2 KB 243; *Ingram v Little* [1961] 1 QB 31; *Lewis v Averay* [1972] 1 QB 198.

Contract's response

Who is the female customer the retailer sees? Assuming the customer is a married female with no separate property of her own, as was the norm, then vision and identity are set on a collision course. Vision gives the purchasing customer an identity as an individual sentient being. This identity was unlikely to exist. The legal status given to the marriage contract rendered the female party to it invisible in both a metaphysical and legal sense. She could exist as herself in a spectral form only. Hers was a liminal[76] presence 'betwixt and between'[77] two fixed states. In the liminal period of existence, 'the subject ... is ... structurally, if not physically "invisible"' (Turner, 1967, p 95). In the first state, the married woman as customer was operating within the parameters of the economic existence set for her by her husband, thus she was the representation of her husband. In the second state, she was operating outside of these parameters. In this instance, she was a representation of herself but her personhood was incomplete. In the language employed by the cases on identity mistake, she lacked the attribute of creditworthiness.[78] Marriage had removed her property rights and so left her as a being without the capacity to make a contractual arrangement although the vision of her before the draper might well have been that of a competent and autonomous individual.

These issues fell to be examined by the House of Lords in *Debenham v Mellon*.[79] To the already complex metaphysical questions of presence, partial presence, vision and identity involved in this scenario, contract doctrine felt compelled to add another layer. This concerned the issue of the ostensible or apparent authority that accompanied the agency relationship between husband and wife. The idea that the purchasing relationship within the Victorian household was one of agency is not a new one. It is an obvious consequence of the marriage contract. As with any agency contract, there must be a delegation of authority and, if there can be a delegation of authority, there can also be a revocation of authority. Delegation of authority was not, in contrast to the agency relationship itself, something that occurred simply as a result of marriage. The presence of delegated authority was instead a question of fact that required an inquiry into the nature of the cohabitation between husband and wife and the establishment they shared. Close upon the need for this inquiry followed the need for one surrounding revocation of delegated authority. Revocation could take place, it seemed, secretly at home in the world of domestic bliss. If authority to pledge a husband's credit had been revoked in this way or had never been given (perhaps authority was vested in a bailiff or salaried household manager rather than in the wife), then there was an absence of authority in the agency relationship or, more importantly for a tradesperson or retailer, the absence of a person with creditworthiness within the contractual matrix.

---

76 Liminal is used here as part of the lineage of the term established by Arnold Van Gennep and Victor Turner. In this sense, it belongs to the literature on rites of passage where these are not just culturally constructed life crises but also the stages that accompany the change from one state to another: see Turner (1967, pp 93–111).

77 'Liminal entities ... are betwixt and between the positions assigned and arrayed by law, custom, convention ...' (Turner, 1969, p 95).

78 *King's Norton Metal Co Ltd v Edridge Merrett & Co* (1897) 14 TLR 98. It is clear from the judgment in this case that creditworthiness is part of a greater personhood and not the sole determinant of it.

79 (1880) 6 App Cas 24.

This allocation of contractual responsibility was invisible to the capitalist economic system that existed outside the marital home. It became visible only if a married woman undertook shopping activities wearing a label announcing her status, as regards both her marital position and her financial allowance, or if a retailer was so presumptuous as to address these questions and demand supporting evidence. The question of giving notice to capitalist society that a wife could no longer pledge her husband's credit arose only if the husband had previously indicated that such transactions would be sanctioned, by settling the account perhaps. In short, a prior trading relationship had to be severed by the husband's explanation and a new trading relationship could only be commenced by label-wearing or rather indelicate inquiries. The effect of this was to subordinate the market-based contract for dresses to the writ of the marriage contract. Retailers could have been forgiven for thinking that sales to married women were fraught with difficulties.[80]

The items of clothing for which credit had been wrongly pledged in the *Debenham v Mellon* case are never described. We may deduce from an aside of Lord Blackburn's that the clothing was millinery wear, but we have no more details. The objects that Mrs Mellon desired are framed out of the legal account of her dealings with William and Frank Debenham, drapers of London. These mystery items are referred to throughout the case as necessaries, so we know that Mrs Mellon was not seeking to purchase for herself dresses and other items of apparel that were beyond her husband's financial means or inappropriate to his socio-economic status. However, Alfred Mellon apparently gave his spouse Mrs Mellon a dress allowance. This was large enough to cover the purchases in question but Mrs Mellon had already spent this allowance on other things in the way a child might spend their pocket money in haste and without any thought as to the funding of future desires. It is the presence of this apparently ample and generous allowance that excludes consideration of the doctrine of necessaries. In fact, both the Court of Appeal and the House of Lords were at pains to stress that the doctrine had no impact on this case. This point did not prevent the Court of Appeal, in the person of Lord Justice Bramwell, and the House of Lords, in the person of Lord Blackburn, suggesting that the category of necessaries could be subdivided into items of need and items that were not needed. According to Bramwell LJ, the articles Mrs Mellon purchased were necessaries but not necessaries '… in the sense that she stood in need of them'. The pledging of her husband's credit in relation to items such as those that might be found on a butcher's bill, for example, might well have produced a different answer. According to Lord Blackburn, some items, like household expenditure, may always be procured on the husband's credit, but whether millinery items came within this head was a matter of serious doubt for him.

Delegation of authority and revocation of authority are questions that arise only in relation to items that are non-needed necessaries – a hitherto unknown category of commodity. These sentiments support Veblen's division between clothes and dress – a wife needs to be clothed but not dressed – but their end point is very different. A husband will have more concern for what is on his dinner table than

---

80 See the references to contemporary journals, such as the *Warehouseman and Drapers Trade Journal* and the *Drapery Record*, cited by Rappaport (2000, Chapter 2, notes).

what is on his wife's back seems to be the effect of these statements. The marriage contract once again triumphs over the market relationship.

There appears to be an assumption, certainly on the part of the Court of Appeal through Lord Justice Bramwell, that the consequence of deciding otherwise on the delegation and revocation of authority would be that retailers 'eager for profit' would take advantage of 'foolish' women and thereby do a 'serious injury' to husbands. Women, it seems from this, could only be the unwitting instruments of plots to ruin their husbands. However, the facts of Debenham suggest that women could be part of a very different strategy, one where they colluded with their husbands to defraud retailers. Lord Selborne, the Lord Chancellor, referred in his judgment to an incident some years before in Westward-Ho in Devonshire where 'there were some people who did give credit to the husband, the wife then acting as his agent'. The husband then revoked the wife's agency. The Mellons were resident in Bradford-on-Avon in Wiltshire when the debts being considered by the House of Lords were incurred. It is possible to read into this story of mobility and previous experience in the credit economy that Mr and Mrs Mellon were repeat-players in the structuring of debt. It is possible that they had obtained commodities through playing with the labels of authority and delegated authority at the expense of unknowing retailers.

Conclusion

This has been a story of visibility and invisibility of women and values that might be described as feminine. Contract doctrine has moved from ignoring the female presence to refusing to clothe acts with their appropriate context. The final foray into the world of shopping belongs to Mrs Mellon. We do not know what she bought. We do not know what her first name was. After this litigation she fades even further away from us. She does not appear on the 1881 census. Alfred Mellon does. He has moved again and appears as the general manager of the Grand Hotel in Bristol. The census return tells us that he was married but Mrs Mellon, despite an exhaustive search under numerous spellings and variations of her name, has simply vanished into thin air. Of course, contract doctrine would have us believe she was never there at all.

References

Abelson, E, *When Ladies Go A-Thieving*, 1989, Oxford: OUP

Adburgham, A, *Shops and Shopping 1800–1914*, 1964, London: Allen and Unwin

Allen, C, 'Return of the guy' (2002) *Women's Quarterly* (internet version)

Anderson, E, 'Women and contracts: no new deal' (1990) 88 *Mich LR* 1792

Anon, *Baron and Femme: A Treatise of Law and Equity Concerning Husbands and Wives*, 1738, London

Anson's Law of Contract, 2nd edn, 1882, Oxford: OUP

Ardzrooni, L (ed), *Essays in Our Changing Order*, 1934, New York: Kelley

Atiyah, P, *The Rise and Fall of Freedom of Contract*, 1979, Oxford: OUP

Austin, A, *The Empire Strikes Back*, 1998, New York: New York UP

Banner, S, *Anglo-American Securities Regulation*, 1998, Cambridge: CUP

Beatson, J, *Anson's Law of Contract*, 2002, Oxford: OUP

Belcher, A, 'A feminist perspective on contract theories from law and economics' (2001) 8 *Fem Legal Studies* 29

Blackstone, *Commentaries on the Laws of England*, 1765–69 (reprinted 1979), Chicago: Chicago UP

Bohstedt, J, 'Gender, household and community politics: women in English riots 1790–1810' (1988) LXX *Past and Present* 97

Bowlby, R, *Just Looking*, 1985, Cambridge: CUP

Bowlby, R, 'Supermarket futures', in Falk, P and Campbell, C (eds), *The Shopping Experience*, 1997, London: Sage

Brantlinger, P, *Fictions of State*, 1996, Ithica, NY: Cornell UP

Braverman, R, 'Capital relations and the way of the world' (1985) 52 *ELH* 133

Breward, C, 'Feminity and consumption: the problem of the late nineteenth century fashion journal' (1994) 7 *Journal of Design History* 71

Brown, B, 'Contracting out/contracting in: some feminist considerations', in Bottomley, A (ed), *Feminist Perspectives in the Foundational Subjects of Law*, 1996, London: Cavendish Publishing

Buker, E, *Talking Feminist Politics*, 1999, Lanham, MD: Rowman & Littlefield

Burney, F, *Camilla, or A Picture of Youth*, 1972 edn, Oxford: OUP

Burney, F, *Cecilia, or Memoirs of an Heiress*, 1986 edn, London: Virago

Butler, J, *Gender Trouble: Feminism and the Subversional Identity*, 1990, New York and London: Routledge

Butler, J, *Bodies That Matter: On the Discursive Limits of 'Sex'*, 1883, New York and London: Routledge

Campbell, C, *The Romantic Ethic and the Spirit of Modern Consumerism*, 1987, Oxford: Basil Blackwell

Campbell, D, *The Relational Theory of Ian Macneil*, 2001, London: Sweet & Maxwell

Carabine, J, 'Constituting sexuality through social policy: the case of lone motherhood 1834 and today' (2001) 10 *Social and Legal Studies* 291

Chitty on Contract, 6th edn, 1857, London: H Sweet

Clark, R, 'Riddling the family firm: the sexual economy in *Dombey and Son*' (1984) 51 *ELH* 69

Collins, H, *The Law of Contract*, 3rd edn, 1997, London: Butterworths

Craik, J, *The Face of Fashion*, 1993, London: Routledge

Cressy, D, *Birth, Marriage and Death*, 1997, Oxford: OUP

Cunningham, C, 'Hints on household taste and the art of decoration: authors, their audiences, and gender in interior design', in Bellamy, J, Laurence, A and Perry, G (eds), *Women, Scholarship and Criticism*, 2000, Manchester: Manchester UP, p 159

Cumberbatch, J, 'In freedom's cause: the contract to negotiate' (1992) 12 *OJLS* 568

Davidoff, L, 'Gender and the "Great Divide"' (2003) 15 *J of Women's Hist* 11

Davis, D, *Fairs, Shops and Supermarkets*, 1966, Toronto: University of Toronto Press

Defoe, D, *Conjugal Lewdness or Matrimonial Whoredom; A Treatise Concerning the Use and Abuse of the Marriage Bed*, 1967 (first published 1727), London: Scholars Facsimiles

Defoe, D, *The Complete English Tradesman*, Vol 1, 1987 (first published 1726–27), London: Alan Sutton

Dickens, C, *Dombey and Son*, 1985 (first published 1848), London: Penguin Classic Edition

Dickinson, D, *Property, Women and Politics*, 1997, Cambridge: Polity

Dorré, GM, '"Horses and corsets": *Black Beauty*, dress reform and the fashioning of the Victorian woman' (2002) 30 *Vic Lit and Culture* 157

Dow, D, 'Law school feminist chic and respect for persons: comments on contract theory and feminism in the flesh colored Band Aid' (1991) 28 *Hous LR* 819

Earle, P, 'The female labour market in the late seventeenth and eighteenth centuries' (1989) 42 *Econ Hist Rev* 328

Epstein, R, 'A common law for labour relations: a critique of the New Deal labor legislation' (1983) 92 *Yale LJ* 1357

Finn, M, 'Men's things: masculine possession in the consumer revolution' (2000) 25 *Social History* 133

Forty, A, *Objects of Desire*, 1986, London: Thames & Hudson

Fraser, N, *Justice Interruptus*, 1997, London: Routledge

Freedgood, E, 'Banishing panic: Harriet Martineau and the popularization of political economy' (1995) 38 *Vic Studies* 33

Freeman, M, *Railways and the Victorian Imagination*, 1999, New Haven, CT: Yale UP

Friedberg, A, *Window Shopping: Cinema and the Postmodern*, 1993, Berkeley, CA: University of California Press

Frug, MJ, *Postmodern Legal Feminism*, 1992, New York: Routledge

Galbraith, JK, *The Age of Uncertainty*, 1977, London: Deutsch

Gallagher, C, *The Industrial Reformation of English Fiction 1832–1867*, 1985, Chicago: Chicago UP

Gibson-Graham, JK, *The End of Capitalism (As We Knew It)*, 1996, Oxford: Blackwell

Gilligan, C, *In a Different Voice*, 1982, Cambridge, MA: Harvard UP

Gilligan, C, 'Moral orientation and moral development', in Kittay, E and Meyers, D (eds), *Women and Moral Theory*, 1987, Lanham, MD: Rowman & Littlefield

Gilligan, C, 'A reply to my critics', in Larrabee, M (ed), *An Ethic of Care*, 1993, London: Routledge

Goodrich, P, *'Jani anglorum'*, in Douzinas, C, Goodrich, P and Hachamovitch, Y (eds), *Politics, Postmodernity and Critical Legal Studies*, 1994, London: Routledge

Goodrich, P, 'Gender and contracts', in Bottomley, A (ed), *Feminist Perspectives on the Foundation Subjects of Law*, 1996, London: Cavendish Publishing

Grant Campbell, D, 'Fashionable suicide: conspicuous consumption and the collapse of credit in Frances Burney's *Cecilia*' (1990) 2 *Studies in Eighteenth Century Culture* 131

Griswold, C, *Adam Smith and the Virtues of the Enlightenment*, 1999, Cambridge: CUP

Harden, I, *The Contracting State*, 1992, Oxford: OUP

Harman, B, 'In promiscuous company: female public appearance in Elizabeth Gaskell's *North and South*' (1988) 31 *Vic Studies* 352

Harth, P (ed), Mandeville, B, *Grumbling Hive or Knaves Turn'd Honest*, 1989 (1714 edn), London: Penguin

Helsinger, K, 'Consumer power and the utopia of desire: Christina Rossetti's "Goblin Market"' (1991) 58 *ELH* 903

Holcombe, L, *Wives and Property*, 1983, Toronto: University of Toronto Press

Hollander, A, *Sex and Suits*, 1994, London: Claridge Press

Hollander, A, *Fabric of Vision*, 2002, London: National Gallery

Horne, T, *The Social Thought of Bernard Mandeville*, 1978, Basingstoke: Macmillan

Howell, P, 'A private Contagious Diseases Act: prostitution and public space in Victorian Cambridge' (2000) 26 *Journal of Historical Geography* 376

Ibbetson, D, *A Historical Introduction to the Law of Obligation*, 1999, Oxford: OUP

Ingrassia, C, 'The pleasure of business and the business of pleasure: gender credit and the South Sea Bubble' (1995) 24 *Studies in Eighteenth Century Culture* 191

Isin, E and Wood, P, *Citizenship and Identity*, 1999, London: Sage

Jeffreys, J, *Retail Trading in Britain 1850–1950*, 1954, Cambridge: CUP

Jose, J, 'Contesting patrilineal descent in political theory: James Mill and nineteenth-century feminism' (2000) 15 *Hypatia* 151

Katz, A, 'The strategic structure of offer and acceptance: game theory and the law of contract formation' (1990) 89 *Mich L Rev* 215

Kowaleski-Wallace, E, *Consuming Subjects*, 1997, New York: Columbia UP

Kunzle, D, 'Dress reform as antifeminism: a response to Helene E Roberts "The exquisite slave: the role of clothes in the making of the Victorian woman"' (1977) 2 *Signs* 570

Latta, K, 'The mistress of the marriage market; gender and economic ideology in Defoe's *Review*' (2002) 69 *ELH* 359

Laver, J, *Fashion and Fashion Plates 1800–1900*, 1934, London: Penguin

Law Commission, *Contracts for the Benefit of Third Parties*, 1996, London: Law Commission

Leach, W, 'Transformation in a culture of consumption: women and department stores, 1890–1925' (1984) 71 *J of Am Hist* 319

Leiss, W, *The Limits to Satisfaction: An Essay on the Problem of Needs and Commodities*, 1976, Toronto: University of Toronto Press

Lemire, B, *Fashion's Favourite: The Cotton Trade and the Consumer in Britain, 1660–1800*, 1991, Oxford: OUP

Locke, J, *Two Treatises of Government*, 1970, Cambridge: CUP

Loos, A, 'Ladies' fashion', in *Spoken into the Void: Collected Essays 1897–1900*, 1982, Cambridge, MA: MIT Press

Maine, H, *Ancient Law*, 1905, London: Routledge and Sons

Malcolmson, C, 'The garden enclosed/the women enclosed: Marvell and the Cavalier poets', in Burt, R and Archer, J (eds), *Enclosure Acts*, 1994, Ithica, NY: Cornell UP

Mandell, L, 'Bawds and merchants: engendering capitalist desires' (1992) 59 *ELH* 107

Mandeville, B, 'The grumbling hive or knaves turn'd honest', in *The Fable of the Bees*, 1705, London: Penguin

Marcuse, H, *One Dimensional Man*, 1964, Boston, MA: Beacon Press

Marsh, J, 'Good Mrs Brown's connections: sexuality and story-telling in dealings with the firm of *Dombey and Son*' (1991) 58 *ELH* 405

Marx, K, 'Economic and philosophical manuscripts', in Tucker, R (ed), *The Marx-Engels Reader*, 1978, New York: Norton

Marx, K, *Capital*, Vol 1, extracted in Simon, L (ed), *Marx: Selected Writings*, 1994, Indiana: Hackett

Maslow, A, *Motivation and Personality*, 1934, New York: Harper and Row

McVeagh, J, *Tradeful Merchants*, 1981, London: RKP

Mendes da Costa, D, 'Criminal law', in Graveson, R and Crane, F (eds), *A Century of Family Law 1857–1957*, 1990, London: Sweet & Maxwell

Michie, E, 'Dressing up: Hardy's *Tess of the D'Urbervilles* and Oliphant's *Phoebe Junior*' (2002) 30 *Vic Lit and Culture* 305

Mill, JS, *Subjugation of Women*, 1869 (2001 edn), Alexander, E (ed), London: Transaction

Miller, D, *A Theory of Shopping*, 1998, Cambridge: Polity

Mintz, S, *Sweetness and Power: The Place of Sugar in Modern History*, 1986, New York: Penguin Books

Moglen, H, 'Theorizing fiction/fictionalizing theory: the case of *Dombey and Son*' (1992) 35 *Vic Studies* 159

Montague, K, 'The aesthetics of hygiene: aesthetic dress, modernity and the body as sign' (1994) 7 *J of Design History* 91

Myslik, W, 'Renegotiating the social/sexual identities of places', in Duncan, N (ed), *Body Space*, 1996, London: Routledge

Naffine, N, 'In praise of legal feminism' (2002) 22 *Legal Studies* 71

Nava, M, *Changing Cultures*, 1992, London: Sage

Nava, M, 'Modernity's disavowal: women, the city and the department store', in Falk, P and Campbell, C (eds), *The Shopping Experience*, 1997, London: Sage

Nead, L, *Victorian Babylon*, 2000, New Haven, CT: Yale UP

Negrin, L, 'The self as image' (1999) 16 *Theory, Culture and Society* 99

Newton, S, *Health Art and Reason*, 1974, London: John Murray

O'Malley, P, 'Uncertain subjects: risks, liberalism and contract' (2000) 29 *Econ and Soc* 460

Orbach, S, *Fat is a Feminist Issue*, 1978, London: Arrow

Pateman, C, *The Sexual Contract*, 1988, Oxford: Polity

Penner, B, 'A world of unmentionable suffering' (2001) 14 *Journal of Design History* 35

Perera, S, 'Wholesale, retail and exportation: empire and the family business in *Dombey and Son*' (1990) 33 *Vic Studies* 603

Perkin, H, *Origins of Modern English Society*, 1969, London: Routledge

Pollock, G, *Vision and Difference*, 1988, London: Routledge

Poovey, M, *Uneven Developments*, 1988, Chicago: Chicago UP

Porter, R, 'Consumption: disease of the consumer society', in Brewer, C and Porter, R (eds), *Consumption and the World of Goods*, 1993, London: Routledge

Price, J, 'The apotheosis of home and the maintenance of spaces of violence' (2002) 17 *Hypatia* 39

Rappaport, E, '"The halls of temptation": gender, politics and the construction of the department store in late Victorian London' (1996) 35 *J of British Studies* 58

Rappaport, E, *Shopping for Pleasure*, 2000, Princeton, NJ: Princeton UP

Raynor Parkes, B, *Essays on Woman's Work*, 1865, London: Alexander Strahon

Rendall, J, 'Women and the public sphere', in Davidoff, L *et al* (eds), *Gender and History*, 1999, Oxford: Basil Blackwell

Roberts, H, 'The exquisite slave: the role of clothes in the making of the Victorian woman' (1977) 2 *Signs* 554

Roberts, M, 'Gender, consumption and commodity culture' (1998) 103 *Am Hist Rev* 819

Ryan, J, 'Women, modernity and the city' (1994) 11 *Theory, Culture and Society* 35

Schivelbusch, W, *The Railway Journey: Trains and Travel in the Nineteenth Century*, 1977, Berkeley: University of California Press

Searle, G, *Morality and the Market in Victorian Britain*, 1998, Oxford: Clarendon Press

Sherry, S, 'Civic virtue and the feminist voice in constitutional adjudication' (1986) 72 *Va Law Review* 543

Simich, J and Tilman, R, 'On the use and abuse of Thorstein Veblen in modern American sociology' (1984) 43 *Am J of Econ and Soc* 103

Simmel, G, 'Fashion' (1957) (1904) 62 *Am J of Soc* 541

Simon, L (ed), *Marx: Selected Writings*, 1994, Indiana: Hackett

Steel, V, *The Corset: A Cultural History*, 2001, New Haven, CT: Yale UP

Sullivan, B, '"It's all in the contract": rethinking feminist critiques of contract' (2000) 18 *Law in Context* 112

Summers, L, *Bound to Please: A History of the Victorian Corset*, 2001, Oxford: Berg

Taylor, L, 'Wool cloth and gender: the use of woolen cloth in women's dress in Britain 1865–85', in de la Haye, A and Wilson, E (eds), *Defining Dress*, 1999, Manchester: Manchester UP

Tidwell, P and Linzer, P, 'The flesh-colored Band Aid: contracts, feminism, dialogue and norms' (1991) 28 *Hous L Rev* 791

Tilman, R, *Thorstein Veblen and His Critics 1891–1963*, 1992, Princeton, NJ: Princeton UP

Traina, C, *Feminist Ethics and Natural Law*, 1999, Washington, DC: Georgetown UP

Treitel, G, *The Law of Contract*, 11th edn, London: Sweet & Maxwell

Tucker, R (ed), *The Marx-Engels Reader*, 1978, New York: Norton

Turano, M, 'Jane Austen, Charlotte Brontë and marital property law' (1998) 21 *Harvard Women's LJ* 179

Turnbull, G, *A History of the Calico Printing Industry of Great Britain*, 1951, Altringham

Turner, V, *The Forest of Symbols*, 1967, Ithica, NY: Cornell UP

Turner, V, *The Ritual Process*, 1969, New York: Aldine de Gruyter

Valverde, M, 'The love of finery: fashion and the fallen woman in nineteenth century social discourse' (1989) 32 *Vic Studies* 169

Veblen, T, 'The economic theory of woman's dress' (1894) XLVI *Popular Science Monthly* 198 (reprinted in Ardzrooni, L (ed), *Essays in Our Changing Order*, 1934, New York: Kelley)

Veblen, T, *The Theory of the Leisure Class*, 1998 [1899], London: Prometheus Books

Vickery, A, 'Golden age to separate spheres? A review of the categories and chronology of English women's history' (1993) 36 *Hist J* 383

Vickery, A, *The Gentleman's Daughter*, 1998, New Haven, CT: Yale UP

Walkowitz, J, 'Going public: shopping, street harassment and streetwalking in late Victorian London' (1998) 62 *Representations* 1

Walsh, C, 'Shop design and the display of goods in eighteenth-century London' (1995) 8 *J of Design History* 157

Weintraub, J, 'The theory and politics of the public/private distinction', in Weintraub, J and Kumar, K (eds), *Public and Private in Thought and Practice: Perspectives on a Grand Dichotomy*, 1997, Chicago: Chicago UP

Wharton, JJS, *An Exposition of the Laws Relating to the Women of England: Showing Their Rights, Remedies and Responsibilities in Every Position of Life*, 1853, London

Wheeler, S, *Corporations and the Third Way*, 2002, Oxford: Hart Publishing

Wilk, R, *Economies and Cultures*, 1996, Boulder, CO: Westview

Wilson, E, *Adorned in Dreams: Fashion and Modernity*, 1987, London: Virago

Winstanley, M, 'Concentration and competition in the retail sector 1800–1900', in Kirby, M and Rose, M (eds), *Business Enterprise in Modern Britain*, 1994, London: Routledge

Wrightson, K, *Earthly Necessities*, 2000, New Haven, CT: Yale UP

Chapter 3
The Rhetoric of Equality and the Problem of Heterosexuality

Rosemary Auchmuty[1]

> It is important that a wife (or anyone in a like position) should not charge her interest in the matrimonial home to secure the borrowing of her husband (or anyone in a like position) without fully understanding the nature and effect of the proposed transaction and that the decision is hers, to agree or not to agree.[2]

With this seemingly uncontroversial declaration, a restatement of the undue influence principle as it applies to mortgages of the family home, Lord Bingham opened the 90-page House of Lords decision in *Royal Bank of Scotland v Etridge (No 2)*. His words were greeted with general approval: 'Lord Bingham ... put the matter succinctly and his words bear repetition and need no elaboration', wrote Martin Dixon.[3] However, Dixon to the contrary, Lord Bingham's statement was not without ambiguity. In speaking of 'a wife (or anyone in a like position)' and 'a husband (or anyone in a like position)', he left unclear the precise target of the rule. In fact, the great majority of cases concern actual wives alleging undue influence against actual husbands, including all eight appeals in *Etridge (No 2)*. The ambiguity lies in the words 'or anyone in a like position'. For whom, actually, is in 'a like position' to a wife or to a husband?

Aim of this chapter

The aim of this chapter is to examine the statements made by the House of Lords in *Barclays Bank v O'Brien*[4] and *Etridge (No 2)* concerning the application of the undue influence rule to married and unmarried, heterosexual and homosexual couples alike. Statements which have been welcomed as modern and inclusive are, I would argue, problematic and misleading, deflecting attention away from the real issue at stake. These statements do not go to the heart of the doctrine – *Etridge (No 2)* has now extended the rule to encompass *all* non-commercial relationships – but they are important as an indication of contemporary judicial and social analysis of the factors which give rise to the exercise of undue influence within relationships.

Specifically, this chapter focuses on the House of Lords' formulation of undue influence as a consequence of intimacy between the parties. I argue that the case law reveals that undue influence is the consequence not of the dangers of intimacy *per se*, but of the dangers of heterosexual intimacy, or simply of heterosexuality itself. The fact that we have yet to see an undue influence case between lesbian or gay partners is not, to my mind, surprising. That is not to say that we never will see one; heterosexuals do not have a monopoly on bad behaviour, and all relationships

---

1   School of Law, University of Westminster.
2   *Royal Bank of Scotland v Etridge (No 2) and Other Appeals* [2001] 4 All ER 449, p 456.
3   Dixon (2002, p 59).
4   [1993] 4 All ER 417.

exhibit some of the inequalities of bargaining power that facilitate the exercise of pressure by one individual on another. However, one factor is absent from lesbian and gay relationships which makes the exercise of undue influence much easier between a man and a woman than between two people of the same sex. That factor is the gendered power dynamic which feminist theorists have identified as the defining feature of heterosexuality.

'Heterosexuality is institutionalised as a particular form of practice and relationships of family structure and identity', writes Diane Richardson in *Theorising Heterosexuality*,[5] but it is not simply one form among many. It is, on the one hand, a form which is privileged above all others, and, on the other, one which 'depends for its meaning on gender divisions' (unlike gay and lesbian relationships).[6] Crucially, as Stevi Jackson explains: '[a]s it is institutionalised within society and culture, heterosexuality is founded upon gender hierarchy: men's appropriation of women's bodies and labour underpins the marriage contract.'[7] It is certainly true that marriage has traditionally displayed the features of heterosexuality at their most glaring. One of the insights of Second Wave feminism was that women's problems with gendered power differences did not disappear either with the introduction of more egalitarian marriage laws or with experiments in cohabitation outside legal marriage. The problems were embedded in society's construction of heterosexuality itself. This chapter will therefore set the House of Lords' statements in *O'Brien* and *Etridge (No 2)* in the context of feminist theories on heterosexuality and will then examine the stories of the women involved in the eight appeals to the House of Lords in *Etridge (No 2)* in the light of those theories.

Undue influence and mortgages

The equitable doctrine of undue influence applies in situations where one party procures the execution of a document or the entry into an obligation by another party, through the exercise of influence or dominance by the one party over the other. Equity regards such behaviour as a species of constructive fraud since the influence of the more powerful party causes the victim to bind herself not through free will but through impaired judgment or a psychological inability to resist. The doctrine has a place in property law and in contract law and, in situations concerning mortgage agreements, in both simultaneously. A finding of undue influence allows a court to undo the transaction between influencer and influenced, but the situation is more complicated when a third party – such as a mortgagee – is involved. In the past 20 years, the House of Lords has laid down no fewer than three sets of rules to determine in which circumstances a mortgagee will be bound by a transaction obtained through undue influence. The current rule is that a mortgagee will be put on notice of undue influence in any transaction where the relationship between surety and debtor is a non-commercial one.[8] Recognition of this non-commercial relationship will oblige the mortgagee to take certain clearly

---

5 Richardson, D (1996, p 2).
6 *Ibid.*
7 Jackson (1996, p 30).
8 *Royal Bank of Scotland v Etridge (No 2)* [2001] 4 All ER 449, p 466.

defined steps to avoid being fixed with notice; steps designed to ensure that the surety really knows what she is doing and understands the risk she is running in signing the agreement – namely, that she may lose her home.

Since these undue influence cases, linked to mortgage transactions, have been so much in the news over the last decade or so, it is easy to forget that they are a relatively recent phenomenon. The extension of homeownership beyond the very wealthy, which began in the 1920s and 1930s, increased inexorably in the post-war years under the impetus of consistent government support for the mortgage industry. Co-ownership between married couples, however, first recognised after the Second World War, only became common in the 1970s, and usual in the 1980s, following the landmark case of *Williams & Glyn's Bank v Boland*.[9] Mortgage disputes were not, therefore, the focus of early undue influence cases (those of the 19th century and first three-quarters of the 20th), which tended to be concerned with other types of contracts and settlements. The 1970s saw the doctrine applied to mortgages in two famous cases, both associated with Lord Denning MR, in which sons influenced elderly parents to mortgage their homes.[10] *National Westminster Bank v Morgan*[11] was the first case to recognise the undue influence of a husband on a wife in respect of their shared matrimonial home. Of that case it can truly be said that it opened the floodgates.

The *O'Brien* rules

The guidelines laid down by the House of Lords in *Morgan* were very soon recognised as insufficient to deal with problems of undue influence. This, coupled with widespread dissatisfaction with the Court of Appeal's judgment in *Barclays Bank v O'Brien*,[12] prompted the second intervention by the House of Lords and a new set of guidelines from Lord Browne-Wilkinson, the latter of which was widely considered to be a model of its kind.

It was Lord Browne-Wilkinson who extended the undue influence guidelines in *O'Brien* to encompass situations where homes were shared by unmarried couples:

> The 'tenderness' shown by the law to married women is not based on the marriage ceremony but reflects the underlying risk of one cohabitee exploiting the emotional involvement and trust of the other. Now that unmarried cohabitation, whether heterosexual or homosexual, is widespread in our society, the law should recognise this.[13]

To extend the focus of the jurisdiction beyond husband and wife to encompass unmarried couples appeared, on the face of it, to make perfect sense in a society where marriage was decreasing in importance and more and more people were cohabiting. Nevertheless, it was a curious move. Neither *O'Brien* nor *Pitt*,[14] which

---

9 [1981] AC 487.
10 *Lloyd's Bank v Bundy* [1975] 1 QB 327 and *Avon Finance v Bridger* [1985] 2 All ER 281 – a case from 1979, but reported much later, presumably when its significance became clear.
11 [1985] 1 AC 686.
12 [1992] 4 All ER 983.
13 *Barclays Bank plc v O'Brien and Another* [1993] 4 All ER 417, p 431.
14 *CIBC Mortgages plc v Pitt and Another* [1993] 4 All ER 433.

was heard at the same time, concerned unmarried cohabitees. Moreover, although the higher courts had considered a number of co-ownership disputes concerning unmarried heterosexual couples,[15] there had not been a single reported undue influence claim by a heterosexual cohabitee, let alone a homosexual one.[16] All the reported cases on mortgages on shared homes, up to this point, had concerned wives alleging undue influence against their husbands.[17]

This means that Lord Browne-Wilkinson's statement that 'the "tenderness" shown by the law to married women is not based on the marriage ceremony' was disingenuous, to say the least. It was factually misleading because, as we have seen, the case law was so overwhelmingly about married women's disputes with their husbands that it could fairly be described as a jurisdiction defined by marriage. More to the point, the statement was historically inaccurate because the 'tenderness' of the law (or, more properly, equity) towards married women was indeed based on the marriage ceremony or, more precisely, on married women's legal and material disabilities under coverture.

While the inclusion of heterosexual cohabitees within the rule can be understood in the light of the courts' experience with co-ownership disputes, the position of homosexual couples is more difficult to explain. At the time it was widely welcomed: Anna Lawson, for instance, wrote that Lord Browne-Wilkinson's words demonstrated an 'encouraging' willingness on the part of senior judges to consider social change.[18] It seems to me that the reference to homosexuals can only be seen as a response to the gay rights activism which had gathered force in the campaign against s 28 of the Local Government Act 1988. One of the ironic results of the dominance of the discourse of inclusion within the gay and lesbian legal lobby at that time (and still today) is that lesbians and gay men sometimes find themselves included in unsought and, in truth, unsuitable discourses.

As we know now, the *O'Brien* guidelines failed to stem the flow of undue influence mortgage claims. The rest of the 1990s saw intense Court of Appeal activity in the area, the great majority of cases concerning, as before, allegations by wives of undue influence perpetuated on them by their husbands or ex-husbands. Once again, however, although there was one reported case of a husband

---

15 Eg, *Eves v Eves* [1975] 1 WLR 1338; *Burns v Burns* [1984] Ch 317; *Grant v Edwards* [1986] Ch 638.

16 Pawlowski and Brown (2002, p 57) draw our attention to one unreported case concerning heterosexual cohabitees: *Rhoden v Joseph* (1990).

17 See, eg, *Kings North Trust v Bell and Others* [1986] 1 WLR 119; *Midland Bank v Shephard* [1988] 3 All ER 17; *Midland Bank v Perry and Another* (1987) 56 P & CR 202; *Bank of Baroda v Shah and Another* [1988] 3 All ER 24; *Bank of Credit and Commerce International SA v Aboody and Another* [1990] 1 QB 923; *Barclays Bank plc v Kennedy and Kennedy* (1988) 58 P & CR 221; *Barclays Bank v Khaira* [1993] 1 FLR 343. Pawlowski and Brown (2002, p 53) note one unreported case where a husband alleged undue influence by his wife: *Simpson* (1992) (unreported).

18 Lawson (1995, p 289). See also Dixon (1994, p 23).

successfully proving undue influence against his wife,[19] there were no cases involving heterosexual or homosexual cohabitees.

The *Etridge* rules

Etridge (No 2) was also a case about married couples – eight of them – and in their deliberations on the rule, all five Law Lords used the word 'husband' when describing the archetypal undue influencer and the word 'wife' when describing the typical victim. In the leading judgment of Lord Nicholls, for example, paras 27–46 dealt with 'a wife's guarantee of her husband's bank overdraft, together with a charge on her share of the matrimonial home'.[20] However, when it came to framing the principle, 'husband' and 'wife' were rejected in favour of more general terms. One supposes that this was done for three reasons: first, because the House of Lords was concerned to reiterate its repudiation of the notion that there should be any special protection for wives;[21] secondly, because the House of Lords was conscious that a handful of cases existed where the undue influence was not by a husband on a wife, and they wanted to find an expression which encompassed those situations; and, thirdly, for policy reasons – to demonstrate their recognition of the place of unmarried cohabitation in the modern world. Finding an expression to fit all the possible relationships of influencer and influenced proved difficult. Lord Bingham's words were, as we have seen, both ambiguous and too limited. They did not seem to cover homosexual couples (unless they could be seen as in a like position to 'husband' and 'wife' – not the usual approach of the courts in other areas of law), and they assumed cohabitation (since Lord Bingham spoke of 'her share in the matrimonial home'). Lord Nicholls, however, insisted that '[c]ohabitation is not essential'[22] and was careful to repeat Lord Browne-Wilkinson's inclusion of homosexual couples.[23]

Lord Nicholls's initial choice of the defining feature was that the relationships were 'sexual'. *Barclays Bank v O'Brien*, he explained, was a case '… concerned with

---

19 *Barclays Bank v Rivett* [1999] 1 FLR 730. Fehlberg (1997) also interviewed two husbands who had brought cases against their wives. For cases between *O'Brien* and *Etridge (No 2)* involving husbands and wives, see, eg, *Allied Irish Bank plc v Byrne* [1995] 2 FLR 325; *Banco Exterior Internacional v Mann and Others* [1995] 1 All ER 936; *Castle Phillips Finance v Piddington* (1995) 70 P & CR 592; *Bank of Baroda v Rayarel and Others* [1995] 2 FLR 376; *Halifax Mortgage Services Ltd (formerly BNP Mortgages Ltd) v Stepsky and Another* [1995] 4 All ER 656; *Halifax Building Society v Brown and Another* [1996] 1 FLR 103; *Britannia Building Society v Pugh* [1997] 2 FLR 7; *Barclays Bank plc v Thomson* [1997] 4 All ER 816; the eight appeals in *Royal Bank of Scotland plc v Etridge (No 2) and Other Appeals* [1998] 4 All ER 705, not all of which were appealed to the House of Lords; *Barclays Bank plc v Boulter and Another* [1998] 2 All ER 1002; *Barclays Bank plc v Caplan* [1998] 1 FLR 532; *Cooke v National Westminster Bank* [1998] 2 FLR 783; *Turner v Barclays Bank plc* [1998] 1 FLR 276; *Davies v Norwich Union Life Insurance Society* (1999) 78 P & CR 119; *Abbey National v Tufts* [1999] 2 FLR 399; *Scottish Equitable Life plc v Virdee* [1999] 1 FLR 863; *Bank of Cyprus (London) Ltd v Markou and Another* [1999] 2 All ER 707; *Alliance and Leicester plc v Slayford and Another* (2000) 150 NLJ 1590; *Leggatt and Another v National Westminster Bank plc* [2001] FLR 563; *National Westminster Bank plc v Breeds* (2001) 151 NLJ 170.

20 *Royal Bank of Scotland v Etridge (No 2)* [2001] 4 All ER 449; *Barclays Bank plc v O'Brien and Another* [1992] 4 All ER 983 (CA), p 462.

21 See *Barclays Bank plc v O'Brien and Another* [1992] 4 All ER 983 (CA), pp 1008–09.

22 *Royal Bank of Scotland v Etridge (No 2)* [2001] 4 All ER 449, p 466, citing *Massey v Midland Bank plc* [1995] 1 All ER 929 as authority for the point.

23 *Royal Bank of Scotland v Etridge (No 2)* [2001] 4 All ER 449, p 466.

formulating a fair and practical solution to problems occurring when a creditor obtains a security from a guarantor whose sexual relationship with the debtor gives rise to a heightened risk of undue influence'.[24] This might seem to be a fair summary of Lord Browne-Wilkinson's explanation of the rule, except that *O'Brien* was not really seen as a case about sexual relationships at the time. It was seen as a case about husbands and wives.

No doubt Lord Nicholls chose the expression 'sexual relationship' as an inclusive label covering all relevant categories of parties within the rule: husband and wife, unmarried heterosexual couples, gay and lesbian couples; but as a description of what is really at stake in the undue influence case law it is inaccurate and misleading. First, as a label, 'sexual relationship' is at once too broad and too narrow to contain the institution of marriage. It is too broad because a married couple's relationship may not, in fact, be sexual: many husbands and wives who have slept apart for years would be (ruefully or indignantly) surprised to have their relationship described as a sexual one. As for those husbands and wives who do maintain physical relations, they would surely be taken aback to have their marriage reduced to mere sex. Most spouses feel that their marriage is a much bigger thing than simply one of a range of ways of relating sexually, and they are right. Marriage is an institution of dwindling but still significant legal, social and religious status. In this sense, then, 'sexual relationship' is too narrow a description.

Secondly, one of the effects of de-privileging marriage in this way is to render invisible its oppressive features, in particular the very feature identified by 19th century feminists as working to women's disadvantage: its facilitation of male power over women legally, socially, economically, physically and psychologically. Thus, a statement which seems inclusive and egalitarian is actually depoliticising.

Thirdly, as Lord Nicholls himself admitted, not all undue influence cases are about people in sexual relationships. In *Credit Lyonnais Bank Nederland NV v Burch*,[25] a young woman was subjected to undue influence by her male employer. In *Banco Exterior Internacional SA v Thomas*,[26] a middle-aged widow guaranteed the borrowings of a younger male 'friend'. In *Steeples v Lea*,[27] an older woman mortgaged her home at the behest of her male boss. None of these relationships were sexual. Perhaps it is not surprising, then, that Lord Nicholls abandoned 'sexual' and slipped quickly to 'non-commercial'. 'As noted earlier, the reality of life is that relationships in which undue influence can be exercised are infinitely various', he declared. 'They cannot be exhaustively defined. ... Human affairs do not lend themselves to categorisations of this sort.'[28]

'Non-commercial' certainly covers all the situations in the case law – and a great many more besides. However, in choosing such a bland, cover-all description Lord Nicholls lost sight of (or deflected attention away from) the important features which most of the cases have in common: the fact that the vast majority of undue influencers are men, that the victims are almost always women or elderly people,

---

24 *Ibid*, p 474.
25 [1997] 1 All ER 144.
26 [1997] 1 All ER 46.
27 [1998] 1 FLR 138.
28 *Royal Bank of Scotland v Etridge (No 2)* [2001] 4 All ER 449, p 475.

and that the sexual relationships between the parties, where they exist, are heterosexual ones. It is not intimacy *per se* which provides a site for the abuse of power which underpins undue influence. It is intimacy in the context of a relationship of unequal power, or sometimes something less than intimacy in the context of a relationship of unequal power. The problem that lies at the heart of undue influence is the problem of male power, not simply the fact that men continue to have greater power than women but that men continue to have power over women, and the place where the exercise of that power is most commonly and obviously facilitated is within the heterosexual relationship.

Theorising heterosexuality

Heterosexuality is not much talked about. The reason, of course, is because it is not perceived to be a problem: it is the norm, the acceptable, the rewarded form of sexuality. It is the default position in discussions of sexuality, just as whiteness is the default position in discussions of race, and does not therefore need to be named.[29]

That heterosexuality has long been organised in the service of social goals is well known to anyone who has studied the history of marriage in the Western world. To the feminists of the First Wave, marriage as it was constructed in 19th century Britain and America was an institution that controlled women through the denial of legal and economic rights to wives under the common law rules of coverture. Ironically, however, it was two happily married women – Barbara Bodichon, who led the movement for reform of the married women's property law, and Josephine Butler, who campaigned against the exploitation of prostitutes in Victorian Britain – who made the bold connection between sexuality and legal and economic rights, pointing out that there was little difference between the situations of the virtuous wife and the prostitute: both sold their bodies for a subsistence.[30]

This theme was taken up by Cicely Hamilton in *Marriage as a Trade*, published in 1909. Hamilton argued that 'marriage for woman has always been not only a trade, but a trade that is practically compulsory'.[31] Girls were rigorously trained to get a husband and, as this was a universal goal, the effect was to inculcate into women the kinds of traits and behaviours best suited to the conditions of patriarchal marriage. Hamilton contended, therefore, that 'woman, as we know her, is largely the product of the conditions imposed on her by her staple industry'.[32] Central to this construction of woman was women's desire to put other people's happiness before their own.

And it is well to note that the 'making of others happy' is not put before the girls as an ideal, but as a duty and means of livelihood. They are to be self-sacrificing as a matter of business – a commercial necessity. It is because man realises that self-

---

29 Indeed, heterosexuality was not named as such until about 100 years ago when the word was coined in response to the naming of homosexuality. See Wittig (1992, p 41).

30 Bodichon (1857); Butler (1869); see also Matthews (1983, p 102) and Uglow (1983, p 156). On 19th century feminist theorising around marriage, see Spender (1982); Maynard (1998); Shanley (1989); Caine (1997).

31 Hamilton (1909, p 28).

32 *Ibid*, p 17.

sacrifice in woman is not a matter of free-will, but of necessity, that he gives her so little thanks for it.[33]

Hamilton may have been writing almost a century ago, but these words could serve as a description of the situations in which so many victims of undue influence in recent case law find themselves. The last sentence seems particularly resonant given the way the courts take for granted the idea that women will naturally want what their husbands want.

After the domestic backlash of the interwar years and the 1950s, marriage came under fire again with the coming of the Second Wave of feminism. Enormously influential in the United States was Jessie Bernard's *The Future of Marriage*, which demonstrated that marriage was good for men but bad for women according to a range of measures, including physical, mental and economic well-being.[34] In Britain, books with titles like *Wedlocked Women*[35] reflected the feminist perception that, while most of the worst legal disabilities of marriage had now gone, it remained an institution that constrained women economically and psychologically. Socialist feminists drew attention to the profound social and economic disadvantages for women, with concomitant *advantages* for men, which followed from married women's assumed and imposed responsibility for housework and childcare.[36]

When sexuality first entered the Second Wave agenda, it was as a consequence of calls by gay-rights activists and lesbian feminists for an end to the heterosexual monopoly of feminist concerns and for a recognition of other sexual preferences and choices. With the rise of radical feminism, however, this plea for inclusion was transformed into a vigorous critique of heterosexuality itself, which paralleled the earlier critiques of marriage in linking sexuality, law, and the material oppression of women. Adrienne Rich's influential article 'Compulsory heterosexuality and lesbian existence' (1980) was written, as she explained afterwards, not only to point out the extent of the silencing of lesbian experience in history and daily life, but also '… to encourage heterosexual feminists to examine heterosexuality as a political institution which disempowers women – and to change it'.[37] In an uncanny echo of Cicely Hamilton, she demonstrated that heterosexuality was as 'compulsory' as marriage had been 70 years before. The difference was that economic motives alone could not explain why most women were heterosexual:

> If women are the earliest sources of emotional caring and physical nurture for both female and male children, it would seem logical, from a feminist perspective at least, to pose the following questions: whether the search for love and tenderness in both sexes does not originally lead toward women; *why in fact women would ever redirect that search*; why species survival, the means of impregnation, and emotional/erotic relationships should ever have become so rigidly identified with each other; and why such violent strictures should be found necessary to enforce women's total emotional, erotic loyalty and subservience to men.[38]

---

33 *Ibid*, p 42.
34 Bernard (1972).
35 Comer (1974).
36 The literature is huge, but see, eg, Oakley (1974); Malos (1980); Barrett and McIntosh (1982).
37 Rich (1980, p 23).
38 *Ibid*, p 35.

In outlining the 'violent strictures' employed to achieve this subservience, Rich demolishes any idea that heterosexuality is innate, natural, or even a choice. She demonstrates again and again the connections between law, economics and sexuality: as in the example borrowed from Catharine MacKinnon's (1983) work on sexual harassment of women in low-paid, low-status jobs such as secretaries or waitresses where heterosexual attractiveness as a 'requirement' of the job and sexual harassment as an associated hazard connect women's sexuality inexorably to their livelihood – and help to keep women under men's control. I suggest that this model can be applied to the situations of the defendants in *Burch* and *Steeples v Lea*,[39] both junior employees of powerful men for whom the women agreed to mortgage their homes – their only asset. Though Miss Burch was young and Mrs Lea middle-aged, both acted in ways which (though almost incomprehensible to the judges – see Nourse LJ's comments in *Burch* at p 150j) are explicable in terms of the heterosexual imperative for women to please men, even to the point of self-sacrifice.

Rich's central argument is that heterosexuality will always be, at least, potentially oppressive for women as long as they have no choice to be anything other than heterosexual and, given the extent of the silencing and stigmatisation of the alternatives, women really do not have a choice. Does that then mean that all heterosexual relationships should be condemned? No, says Rich, but they must be examined. The spotlight must move from the 'problem' of lesbianism to the 'problem' of heterosexuality:

> Within the institution exist, of course, qualitative differences of experience; but the absence of choice remains the great unacknowledged reality, and in the absence of choice, women will remain dependent upon the chance or luck of particular relationships and will have no collective power to determine the meaning and place of sexuality in their lives.[40]

For Rich, then, the inability to choose any alternative way to live or love limits women's ability to resist heterosexual oppression or even to envisage any different form of social organisation.

What Rich's paper is chiefly remembered for is her suggestion that all women exist along a 'lesbian continuum':

> I mean the term *lesbian continuum* to include a range – through each woman's life and throughout history – of woman-identified experience, not simply the fact that a woman has had or consciously desired genital sexual experience with another woman. If we expand it to include many more forms of primary intensity between and among women, including the sharing of a rich inner life, the bonding against male tyranny, the giving and receiving of practical and political support, ... we begin to grasp breadths of female history and psychology which have lain out of reach as a consequence of limited, mostly clinical, definitions of *lesbianism*.[41]

The idea that *all* women could be considered to be (in some respect) lesbian proved unsurprisingly controversial among many self-defined lesbians, who objected to the idea that a woman could be called lesbian without genital contact or at least desire for a woman, and many self-defined heterosexuals, who rejected a label associated

---

39 *Credit Lyonnais Bank Nederland NV v Burch* [1995] 1 All ER 144; *Steeples v Lea* [1998] 1 FLR 138.
40 Rich (1980, p 67).
41 *Ibid*, pp 51–52.

with deviance, but it succeeded in making those heterosexual women who had never questioned their sexual 'orientation' realise what it was like to be compulsorily (as it were) positioned within a sexuality that did not match their experience or self-perception. More significantly, by expanding the definition of lesbianism, Rich's paper spurred heterosexual women to new explorations of the definition of heterosexuality, taking forward (though on their own terms) the lesbian feminist critiques.

The gendered power dynamic

The shift towards a wider understanding of heterosexuality was initiated by radical feminists focusing their attention on sexual practice in the early years of the Second Wave. In attempting to understand what motivated men's 'deviant' sexual acts against women (such as rape, prostitution and pornography), in considering wherein lay the difference between these and 'normal' heterosexual acts (if indeed there was any difference), and in insisting that no area of human experience, *not even sexual desire*, was exempt from the necessity of deconstruction, these radical feminists came face to face with the stark realisation that heterosexuality, as constructed in Western culture, was premised upon the principle of male dominance and female submission. From there it was but a short step to the recognition that heterosexual relations were 'neither natural nor inevitable but resulted from a hierarchical ordering of gender'.[42]

This analysis was not and is not shared by all feminists. One cannot really be surprised that disagreements over matters of sexual practice proved to be among the most bitter and fundamental in the women's movement. Followers of Freud, who believed that sexuality has a biological basis, reacted angrily to the radical feminist call to examine and if necessary change our sexual behaviours, and labelled the social constructionists prudes, deluded idealogues, and even sex police.[43] Those who accepted the idea that sexuality did play a part in the oppression of all women and not simply those women who were victims of recognised sexual exploitation, fell into two broad camps. One camp argued that precisely *because* heterosexual relations were socially constructed in the hands of those individuals with knowledge and the will to do so, they could be reworked and made egalitarian. For others, however, this understanding of heterosexuality was too narrow. Of course, heterosexual women could negotiate (up to a point) the forms that their sexual life took and even (again, up to a point) the wider issues within their individual relationships. However, these feminists argued, what you do in bed is linked to how you organise other roles and responsibilities in your relationship and this, in turn, depends not simply on the personalities and wishes of the parties concerned, but on the norms of the society in which you live. Most concretely (and here the argument goes back to the understandings of the First Wave feminists), it is linked to money.

---

42 Jackson (1996, p 25).
43 For the debates, see Cartledge and Ryan (1983); Snitow, Stansell and Thompson (1984); Douglas (1990); Walby (1990).

So, for example, *she* may agree to have sex with him when he wants it and she is not keen, in return for *his* promise to mind the kids on Saturday afternoon so that she can go out. In the absence of this bargain, the assumption would have been that *she* would stay home with the kids; this assumption would be made, first, because she is a woman and childcare is a woman's responsibility, and, secondly, because she is in a weaker bargaining position in the relationships since *he* is the breadwinner and the whole family depends on his income – thus, what *he* says goes.

These interchanges went on in households throughout the Western world in the 1970s and 1980s and, for all I know, they go on still; but what is significant about them is that, although they appear to be personally negotiated exchanges between two free individuals in the privacy of their relationship the discussions are mediated through social norms which limit the ability of the woman to negotiate and make the outcome almost a foregone conclusion and the same across the whole range of couples. In addition, although the initial point of discussion is the sexual act, it is inextricably linked to money: not simply the way that the couple organises its household economy, but the way that heterosexuality (certainly in the 1970s and 1980s, and to a large degree still today) organises material power.

The question that then arises is whether this accepted paradigm of male dominance/female submission in modern constructions of heterosexuality, from the fairy tale to the Mills & Boon novel, from the sex advice manual to the rape trial and the undue influence case, merely reflects patriarchal power in society, or whether it preceded it. For Andrea Dworkin, the very act of heterosexual intercourse is central to women's oppression: 'The right of men to women's bodies for the purpose of intercourse remains the heart, soul, and balls of male supremacy.'[44] It follows that refusing heterosexual intercourse becomes an act of resistance to male power, an idea that was developed by revolutionary feminists in Britain who contended, quite logically, that the one way to bring about a feminist revolution would be for all women to become lesbians.[45]

Catharine MacKinnon, adopting Dworkin's analysis, named sexuality as the root cause of gender oppression:

> Women and men are divided by gender, made into the sexes as we know them, by the social requirements of heterosexuality, which institutionalizes male sexual dominance and female sexual submission. If this is true, sexuality is the linchpin of gender inequality.[46]

The idea that sexuality is the *cause* of women's oppression has, however, been rejected by other feminists. Stevi Jackson argues robustly against the 'over-privileging of sexuality' in these (and other) feminist analyses (and in Western culture generally). Her explanation of heterosexuality encompasses both 'specifically sexual desires and practices' and also 'divisions of labour, power and resources' between the sexes.[47] Christine Delphy prioritises men's exploitation of

---

44 Dworkin (1983, p 83).
45 Leeds Revolutionary Feminist Group (1981).
46 MacKinnon (1982, p 533).
47 Jackson (1999, p 4).

women's labour in the home over sexual practice as the basis of women's oppression in heterosexuality.[48] For this reason, Delphy and Jackson (and others who incorporate in their analysis economic understandings originally explored by Marxist feminists) call themselves materialist feminists.

Both radical and materialist feminist theories depend on the recognition that the significance we attach to categories of gender is political in nature; that is, we would not consider gender difference worthy of notice unless the categories of 'man' and 'woman' were highly important in our society – as, of course, they are. A parallel with race can be drawn: it can only matter whether a person is 'white' or 'not white' if whiteness and non-whiteness carry certain rewards or penalties – as, of course, they do. (We do not distinguish, for example, between people with blue eyes and those with green eyes, since neither reward nor penalty accompanies this particular difference *per se*.)

If we accept the premise that the significance attached to the categories of gender is political rather than natural, then we have to consider *why* those categories of 'man' and 'woman' have come to have the importance they have. Jackson explains:

> For Marxists, classes only exist in relation to one another: there can be no bourgeoisie without the proletariat and vice versa. Similarly 'men' and 'women' exist as socially significant categories because of the exploitative relationship which both binds them together and sets them apart from each other. Conceptually there could be no 'women' without the opposing category 'men', and vice versa.[49]

She goes on:

> The consequences of this are indeed radical. The political goal envisaged is not the raising of women's status, nor equality between women and men, but the abolition of sex differences themselves. In a non-patriarchal society there would be no social distinctions between men and women, or between heterosexuality and homosexuality ... [50]

Clearly, Jackson, who is herself heterosexual, does not imagine we are anywhere near reaching this goal. However, in *O'Brien* and *Etridge (No 2)* the House of Lords pronounced on the equality of all intimate relationships as if society had already reached this happy situation.

Partly in reaction to what were perceived as essentialist tendencies in radical feminism, queer and postmodern analyses have posited different approaches to heterosexuality. Postmodernists view the social categories of gender as (merely) discursive constructs, subject to an ongoing process of contestation and renegotiation. In rejecting grand theories, they repudiate the notion that these constructs might be rooted in a hierarchical material structure.[51] Queer theorists recognise the oppressiveness of the normative rules of sex and sexuality, but argue that these rules can be confounded and destabilised by subversive performance. There is no place in this agenda for a broader definition of sexuality based on a

---

48 Delphy (1984). See also Delphy and Leonard (1992).
49 Jackson (1995, p 13).
50 *Ibid*, p 14.
51 Nicholson (1990).

gendered power dynamic.[52] Personally, I find it hard to see how anything can change unless heterosexual sex is seen as inextricably linked to heterosexual power in other areas of social life, especially the economic: as Jackson puts it, 'the experience and practice of heterosexuality is not just about what does or does not happen between the sheets, but about who cleans the bathroom or who performs emotional labour on whom'.[53] In the context of undue influence, neither postmodernism nor queer theory can adequately explain the combination of factors which propel women into undue influence situations. An analysis of women's oppression must take account of both symbolic and material conditions.

Feminists are motivated by a concern to explain and improve the lives of real women – to link theory to practice. Stevi Jackson declares:

> I doubt that it is possible to produce *a* theory of gendered and sexual subjectivity, but we can begin to try to conceptualize it in ways which do make sense in terms of everyday sexual desires and practices. This demands that we cease to theorize at an entirely abstract level and pay attention to what is known about material, embodied men and women going about the business of living their sexualities.[54]

This understanding – based on the Second Wave principles that the personal is political and that feminist theory should emerge from, rather than be imposed upon, women's experience – motivated the editors of the journal *Feminism and Psychology* to solicit, in 1992, contributions from heterosexual feminists working in the academic field for a special issue devoted to heterosexuality. Their brief was to write about how their sexuality influenced their feminism and their work. The results were fascinating. Alison Young, then a law lecturer at Lancaster, wrote of her unease at being asked to defend her heterosexuality, until that moment unquestioned and unquestionable in an academic context:

> To be invited to write *in the name of heterosexuality* by another is to experience the force of being positioned as Other. ... No longer the subject of the text, I experience objectification and remember as illusory my previous sense of autonomy and self-control.[55]

But the flip side of breaking the silence about the non-problematic nature of heterosexuality was that it allowed women to name the very real problems they experienced within heterosexuality. As Nira Yuval-Davis pointed out: 'Lesbians might be oppressed in the public domain, but heterosexual women – according to all feminist analyses and especially radical feminist separatist ones – enter unequal partnerships in which sexist norms and power relations prevail.'[56]

Several contributors agreed with her but denied that heterosexual relationships were *inevitably* oppressive for women. Carol Nagy Jacklin, an American psychology professor, claimed that she knew of many equitable heterosexual relationships

---

52 Butler (1994).

53 Jackson (1995, p 21).

54 Jackson (1999, p 26).

55 Wilkinson and Kitzinger (1993, p 37). The journal was republished in an expanded version as *Heterosexuality: A Feminism and Psychology Reader*, and it is from this volume that my references are taken.

56 *Ibid*, p 52.

(including her own) as well as inequitable lesbian relationships *but that the asymmetry of power is more common in heterosexual relationships.*[57]

Two features consistently emerged from such analysis. One was that the influence of heterosexuality, for these women, extended far beyond the limits of sexual desire. The other was that gender difference was not merely an incidental feature of heterosexuality, but raised questions of power. In effect, a relationship of different genders in a patriarchal society *means* a relationship of unequal power, even of power by one partner over the other.

In heterosexuality, then, we have the essential prerequisites for the exercise of undue influence by men over women. With this in mind, I turn now to the reported stories of the real people involved in the eight cases on appeal in *Etridge (No 2)* in the House of Lords.

First, the discourse

Reading one undue influence case after another reminds me of the consciousness-raising groups which were a feature of the early years of the Second Wave of feminism. Women would sit around in a circle and share their personal experiences of the topic of the day. Each would tell her story while the others listened. 'My husband said this ...', 'My husband did that ...', 'My boyfriend always ...', 'My boyfriend never ...'. As each woman had her turn, light began to dawn. Every story seemed to be a variation on the same theme, and we realised that, if this were true, then perhaps the problems of which we all complained were structural, not merely personal.

So it is with the case reports on undue influence: so many women in 'relationships of trust and confidence' with their husbands; so many betrayals by those husbands; so many promises, so many lies! So much bitterness and disillusionment. Reading the quite extensive body of undue influence case law from the past 20 years can give rise to a profound sense of unease about the relationships of men and women in the late 20th and early 21st centuries.

We are fortunate in England that the facts of cases are both considered and reported in great detail. It is possible through the words of the judgments to form a picture of the parties and grasp the essential issues as seen through the eyes of the judges. This is not, of course, the same thing as seeing the parties and the issues as the women alleging undue influence would have seen them, but imagining wherein lie the differences can be instructive in itself. Consider, for example, the main thrust of the undue influence rules. In the context of mortgage contracts, the rules exist to provide protection for lenders against being fixed with constructive notice of undue influence or misrepresentation by the mortgagor against his surety. They do not exist to protect the surety. As a result, judgments focus on whether or not the lender has taken adequate steps to avoid being fixed with notice. They do not dwell on whether or not undue influence has actually taken place, since a mere presumption will suffice to put the bank or building society on notice. That means that most of the judgment will be taken up with the wife's position vis à vis the bank and/or the

---

57 *Ibid*, pp 34–35.

solicitor, not her position vis à vis her husband. In addition, since most reported cases are appeal cases, the issue of undue influence has often been decided in the lower court and is, therefore, able to be glossed over in the appeal court. So what actually happened between husband and wife is of much less concern in the case reports than whether the bank or building society will be affected by it.

Already, therefore, the case report will differ in significant ways from the woman's own understanding of the events. For her, the real issue is her husband's behaviour: his lies, his false assurances, the emotional pressure, the breach of trust in the non-legal sense. The courts, however, focus on the bank's liability because they are less interested in the marriage than in the mortgage. For them, the questions to be adjudicated are, in the words of Lord Scott in *Etridge (No 2)*, 'contractual questions, not questions relating to competing property interests'.[58] This is, of course, the bank's point of view. Its sole concern is to get its money back. From the woman's point of view, however, the question is one of competing property interests: whether she keeps her home or the bank gets it.

That the courts have long been aware that the undue influence jurisdiction has its roots in inequalities of bargaining power, which are structural rather than purely individual, is evident from the many lengthy discussions in the case law about equity's 'special tenderness' towards married women.[59] In the cases of undue influence, the English courts (unlike their Australian counterparts)[60] always rejected the idea of an automatic presumption of undue influence between husband and wife but nevertheless purported to cast a fastidious eye on voluntary transactions by a woman for the benefit of her husband. Why is it called a 'special tenderness' for women, as if women were the difficulty? A 'special suspicion' of men would more accurately describe the problem to be addressed. 'If language constructs as well as expresses the social world, these words support heterosexual values', writes Catharine MacKinnon.[61] In any event, the case law makes it plain that the 'tenderness' is a great deal more limited and selective than the existence of a general rule would suggest. In fact, women rarely benefit from any 'special tenderness'; there are almost always stronger claims to the court's sympathy – for example, in the undue influence cases, the banks. Unguarded judicial comments make it clear that the courts do not expect very high standards from husbands. In *O'Brien*, Lord Browne-Wilkinson spoke of the possibility of '*a substantial risk* that the husband has not accurately stated to the wife the nature of the liability' (emphasis added).[62] Likewise, in *Etridge (No 2)* in the Court of Appeal, Stuart-Smith LJ admitted that 'where a woman is asked to stand surety or provide collateral security for her husband's indebtedness, there is *an ever-present danger* that he may have misrepresented the position to her' (emphasis added).[63] If these 'substantial risks' and 'ever-present dangers' are *normal*, why should equity *ever* come to women's assistance?

---

58 *Royal Bank of Scotland v Etridge (No 2)* [2001] 4 All ER 449, p 498.
59 *Barclays Bank plc v O'Brien and Another* [1992] 4 All ER 983, pp 998–1009.
60 See Stone (1999).
61 MacKinnon (1982, p 517 (fn 2)).
62 *Barclays Bank v O'Brien* [1993] 4 All ER 417, p 429.
63 *Royal Bank of Scotland plc v Etridge (No 2) and Other Appeals* [1998] 4 All ER 705, p 715.

For a judge, the process of listening to half a dozen cases with similar facts must make men's bad behaviour seem normal indeed! This problem of desensitivity is exacerbated when, as in *Etridge (No 2)* in both the Court of Appeal and the House of Lords, eight separate appeals were heard together (though they were not all the *same* eight). There is always the tendency to measure all cases against the facts of the worst, in comparison with which the rest do not seem so bad. Of the eight women in the *Etridge* appeals in the House of Lords, Mrs Bennett seems to have suffered the greatest ill-treatment by her husband: the trial judge described 'moral blackmail amounting to coercion and victimization'.[64] Mrs Coleman, however, fared worst at the hands of the professionals – the bank and the solicitors – and, perhaps for that reason, attracted most sympathy from the court. Reluctantly dismissing her appeal, Lord Hobhouse said: 'This is not because of any inherent lack of merit in her case; she has been appallingly badly served.' He went on:

> Her account (which the judge accepted) gives a pertinent reminder of the gap between theory and reality and illustrates the type of charade which, as Sir Peter Millett has observed, lenders will know may occur and should not be tolerated or sanctioned by equity.[65]

The paradox is that because equity's interventions are never based solely on the extent of the injustice suffered by a defendant, Mrs Coleman lost her case while Mrs Bennett and several of the other women won theirs.

Compared with Mrs Bennett and Mrs Coleman, the remaining six wives in *Etridge* had little enough to complain of. Mrs Moore, it is true, was importuned by her husband to sign a blank mortgage application form and did so, after he had misrepresented the amount of the loan to her; he then filled in the remaining parts of the form fraudulently.[66] To add to her grievances, she received no legal advice, but then neither did Mrs Etridge or Mrs Wallace. Clearly, this was par for the course in undue influence cases. A judicial tendency to excuse facts which are less than extreme is particularly marked in the judgment of Lord Scott. Of the bank's failure to note the risk of undue influence between husband and wife in *Harris*, for example, he commented: 'the extent of the risk was not ... very great. There were no special features to put the bank on enquiry.'[67] Therein lies the problem for women: the impossibility of demonstrating 'special features' that would mark the proceedings out from ordinary marital interactions.

Now, the lives

Late 20th century marital relationships of middle-aged people were characterised by a range of gendered role assumptions. It would be normal for *him* to be the (main) breadwinner. It would be normal for her to earn (much) less than he does. If he were a businessman, he would take charge of the family finances. She would do the physical and emotional caring work for the home, children and husband.

---

64 *Royal Bank of Scotland v Etridge (No 2)* [2001] 4 All ER 449, p 530.
65 *Ibid*, p 494. The reference to Millett LJ was to an article in which, writing ex-judicially, he voiced 'serious misgivings' about banking practice and equity's reluctance to assist surety victims of undue influence.
66 *Royal Bank of Scotland v Etridge (No 2)* [2001] 4 All ER 449, p 493.
67 *Ibid*, p 518.

Modern notions of 'equality' would ensure that she would co-own the house with her husband or, as in the case of Mrs Etridge, be sole proprietor for tax reasons. But his economic power within the relationship would give him the right to tell her what to do in financial matters. Her deference would be inevitable, even without the reinforcement of her ignorance and lack of experience of the business world. Within such a paradigm it becomes very difficult to say when a normal relationship of male economic dominance and female economic subordination slips into an abnormal one of undue influence.

Lord Scott demonstrates this dilemma in his assessment of the case of Mr and Mrs Harris:

> The relationship of trust or confidence was certainly present. Mr Harris conducted the businesses from which the family income was derived. It was he who negotiated the financial arrangements with Barclays Bank. He did not explain the arrangements to his wife. He simply asked her to sign the legal documentation. His statement, express or implied, that he would be able to trade his way out of his financial difficulties may have been an expression of over optimism but cannot be, and has not been, suggested to be a misrepresentation. There was no allegation of any bullying of Mrs Harris or of any pressure on her to sign that could be characterised as excessive. She signed, without knowing what she was signing, because she trusted him.[68]

Lord Scott did not believe that undue influence was present in this transaction, nor did the judges in the three lower courts who heard the case before it came to the House of Lords.

In the Court of Appeal, Mrs Harris was represented as someone who, because she was a director and shareholder in two companies, would obviously benefit from the loans to her husband's businesses secured on the matrimonial home. In fact, as the House of Lords' judgment made clear, she played no part in the running of the businesses and was described in the company documents as a 'housewife'. It seems that the courts want to have it both ways: Mrs Harris's reliance on her husband's financial expertise situates her as a 'normal' wife, ignorant of business matters, but their refusal to accept any manifest disadvantage in the arrangement with the bank allows them to conceptualise her simultaneously as a businesswoman acting with a shrewd eye to profit.

This construction could hardly be placed on Mrs Coleman who, as a Hasidic Jew, had been raised '… to expect and to accept a position of subservience and obedience to her husband'.[69] However, once again Lord Scott rejected the idea that the granting of a large legal charge over her home, for the benefit of her husband's business interests, was manifestly disadvantageous to her:

> The legal charge, supporting her husband's business ventures on which he engaged in order to support his family, was no more disadvantageous to her than any transaction in which a wife offers to become surety in order to support her husband's commercial activities. The presumption arose, in my opinion, out of their relationship, in which Mrs Coleman was not merely disinclined to second-guess her husband on matters of business, but appears to have regarded herself as obliged not to do so.[70]

---

68 *Ibid*, p 517.
69 *Ibid*, p 524.
70 *Ibid*, p 526.

The curious verb 'to second-guess' in the last sentence may perhaps be taken to be a euphemism for 'to disagree with', but how do the courts treat wives who argue with their husbands over these financial dealings? One might assume they would consider a good wife to be one who did not interfere in matters she did not understand, but Lord Scott's words almost suggest that a wife who put up a struggle might win more respect in the courts.

Not so – not if she eventually backed down. Evidence of disagreement avails a wife little in these cases. Mrs Gill, for example, described the 'heated altercation between herself and her husband'[71] when he asked her to sign a mortgage of the family home. In the end, however, pressured to act quickly, and under the impression (shared by the solicitor who advised her) that the charge was for a loan of £36,000, whereas in fact it was for one of £100,000, she felt she 'had no alternative but to sign'.[72] The words make it clear that her bargaining position was weak. She told the court:

> I did sign the documents put in front of me, but with time for more reflection, and in less urgent circumstances, with proper advice to think about it, and time to consult a solicitor of my own, I would never have done so.[73]

Indulging in a little second-guessing of their own, the court decided that nevertheless Mrs Gill would have supported the larger charge if she had known of it, and was therefore not the victim of any undue influence.[74]

Similar reasoning was used in the case of Mrs Etridge who, like Mrs Gill, lost her appeal. The court accepted that no explanation of the effect of the charge (in this case, an unlimited one) had been given to her, but decided that she would have signed the documents even if she had had proper advice.[75] Once again, the court found no undue influence because there was no manifest disadvantage to her in the transaction. In his judgment, Lord Scott sought to clarify the meaning of 'manifest disadvantage':

> It is not a divining rod by means of which the presence of undue influence in the procuring of a transaction can be identified. It is merely a description of a transaction which cannot be explained by reference to *the ordinary motives by which people are accustomed to act* [emphasis added].[76]

This reference to normative values begs the question of how we expect people to behave within a marriage. What the *law* expects is made clear in Lord Scott's account of the relationship of Mr and Mrs Etridge:

> Their relationship was, as one would expect of a married couple living together with the family income being provided by the husband's business activities and with financial decisions affecting the family being taken by the husband, a relationship of trust and confidence by her in him. But there was no evidence of abuse by Mr Etridge of that relationship, or of any bullying of Mrs Etridge in order to persuade her to support his

---

71 *Ibid*, p 522.
72 *Ibid*.
73 *Ibid*, p 524.
74 *Ibid*, p 494.
75 *Ibid*, p 512.
76 *Ibid*, p 513.

decisions. Both the transactions under attack had been entered into in part in order to provide finance for the purchase of the Old Rectory and in part to obtain financial support for Mr Etridge in his business enterprises. Both had elements disadvantageous to her and elements that were to her advantage.[77]

The mortgage certainly enabled Mrs Etridge to acquire half-a-million-pounds-worth of home (and this was in 1988) which, of course, by losing this case she then surrendered to the bank. The fact that she was 'quite unaware' that the house was mortgaged at all, still less that her husband's business liabilities were secured against it, would seem disproportionately disadvantageous. Her ignorance of her husband's real intentions would make any bullying by him unnecessary, for if she did not realise there was any risk (and no one told her), then she would have no reason to resist the transaction. However, although there was no way she could have made an informed assessment of whether it was in her best interests or not, Mrs Etridge was still held responsible for her legal actions. This kind of sleight of hand enables the courts on the one hand to approve married women's legal and financial dependence on men and on the other to punish them for it by treating them as free legal agents who must take the consequences of the legal and financial decisions they make.[78]

My conclusion is that undue influence is difficult for a woman to prove against her husband because undue influence is hardly distinguishable from normal gendered behaviour within marriage. For men to take the lead in financial matters is normal; for women to go along with their husband's wishes is normal; a little exaggeration, a certain amount of pressure (but not too much – certainly no bullying), the odd lie or omission – these are all within the parameters of normal behaviour in a marriage. What, then, lies outside it?

When the courts try to draw the line between normal economic interactions between husband and wife and those, such as undue influence, which go beyond the bounds of normality, they come up against the same sorts of difficulties they face in trying to decide what is acceptable sexual behaviour between men and women and what is not. As Catharine MacKinnon explains:

> The point of defining rape as 'violence not sex' or 'violence against women' has been to separate sexuality from gender in order to affirm sex (heterosexuality) while rejecting violence (rape). The problem remains what it has always been: *telling the difference*. [emphasis added][79]

Just as the law of rape turns on the woman's consent to sex, so the law of undue influence turns on whether the woman's consent to the transaction was freely obtained. Of the rape situation, MacKinnon asks: 'What is reasonable for a man to believe concerning a woman's desire for sex, when heterosexuality is compulsory?'[80] One could equally ask, in the context of undue influence: what is reasonable for a man to believe concerning a woman's desire to mortgage her home,

---

77 *Ibid*, p 514.
78 This point has been made by a number of other feminist legal scholars – eg, Richardson, M (1996); Fehlberg (1997); Kaye (1997); Belcher (2000).
79 MacKinnon (1983, p 646).
80 *Ibid*, p 654.

when men's economic dominance and women's economic subordination are compulsory within heterosexual relationships?

Conclusions

When the House of Lords chose to extend the undue influence rule in *O'Brien* beyond married couples to encompass other relationships of intimacy, including homosexual ones, the implied message was that we are all in the same boat when it comes to vulnerability to undue influence within our relationships. Yet the judgment made it clear that Lord Browne-Wilkinson was not unaware of the material and psychological reasons why married women in particular might find themselves under pressure from their husbands, and why they might succumb to that pressure:

> ... although the concept of the ignorant wife leaving all financial decisions to the husband is outmoded, the practice does not yet coincide with the ideal. ... In a substantial proportion of marriages it is still the husband who has the business experience and the wife is willing to follow his advice without bringing a truly independent mind and will to bear on financial decisions. The number of recent cases in their field shows that in practice many wives are still subjected to, and yield to, undue influence by their husbands.[81]

What Lord Browne-Wilkinson left unsaid was that the economic and psychological subordination of married women to their husband's will is a normal and, it could be said, inevitable feature of the heterosexual relationship. His common sense view of sexuality as 'intimacy' did not allow him to see heterosexuality as a political institution which extends beyond intimacy and determines not simply to whom you are attracted and with whom you sleep but also how your household is organised and how society is organised – 'a gendered hierarchy involving not just sexual desire but also the appropriation of women's bodies and labour', as Stevi Jackson puts it.[82]

My aim in this chapter was to examine the rhetorical shift in the undue influence case law from a jurisdiction designed to protect wives from husbands to one based on an idea of ungendered intimacy, a shift which looks, on the face of it, both progressive and sensible, but which obscures what I see as a highly significant change in emphasis. The undue influence doctrine evolved over the centuries to protect those in a weaker bargaining position from those in a stronger one. It is not accidental that it has been invoked most frequently by wives against husbands, not simply in the bad old days of coverture when married women's legal disabilities were substantive, but also in the supposedly egalitarian last 20 years. It is a doctrine which recognised and aimed to redress actual differences of power between the sexes: specifically, men's power over women. So Lord Bingham actually had it right when, in the passage quoted at the beginning of this chapter, he spoke of the rule as being relevant to 'a wife (or anyone in a like position)' in relation to transactions proposed by 'her husband (or anyone in a like position)'.[83]

---

81 *Barclays Bank plc v O'Brien* [1993] 4 All ER 417, p 422.
82 Jackson (1996, p 29).
83 *Royal Bank of Scotland v Etridge (No 2)* [2001] 4 All ER 449, p 456.

I am not suggesting that undue influence is only a problem for women in heterosexual relationships, that men can never experience it (the case law refutes this idea), or, indeed, that we will never see an undue influence case involving a gay or lesbian couple. Clearly, other dynamics of power are present within relationships besides the gendered one, and power is always open to abuse, but I believe that restating the undue influence rule in its new inclusive form masks the gendered power dynamic that accounts for most undue influence and makes it harder for women to prove that their losses are not of their own making but the result of structural forces ensuring men's economic dominance and women's economic subordination. The rhetoric of equality encourages the courts to hold women responsible for decisions made under pressures the judges do not recognise as problematic because they are normal manifestations of the heterosexual relationship. The result is that large numbers of women experience some form of undue influence, which may or may not be accepted as such by the courts, but which more often than not results in the loss of their home, their capital and their marriage. The result of *that* is women's continuing economic subordination.

What is the way forward? The narrow view would be to insist that the courts recognise the part played by gender in the existence and facilitation of undue influence within heterosexual relationships, and that they problematise 'normal' gendered behaviour in the way men obtain consent from women to financial transactions (as other courts must problematise 'normal' gendered behaviour in the way men obtain consent from women to sexual transactions). I am not advocating the introduction of a special rule for women but, rather, an acknowledgment that the 'normal' expectations of gendered roles and conduct within heterosexual relationships are neither inevitable nor natural but socially constructed, structurally inequitable, and potentially oppressive for women. Lesbian and gay relationships may (paradoxically in view of the courts' generous extension to them of equity's protection from undue influence) offer models of more egalitarian decision-making because they are free of the gendered power differential that puts women at risk in heterosexual relationships.[84]

A stronger measure would be a ban or limitation placed on the availability of the family home as security for business debts. This would represent a prioritisation of what is important to most women – their home and family – over the masculine concern for business profits, but nothing in the judgments to date gives any indication that this view would ever be countenanced by the courts, and governments have always been reluctant to interfere with the power of the finance industry.

In the final analysis, however, a bold feminist would not be content to look to either the courts or Parliament to act in defence of women. Her goal would be nothing less than the empowerment of women to carry out acts of resistance to the institution of heterosexuality. 'Women are not passive victims of patriarchy', Sylvia Walby reminds us;[85] Monique Wittig insists that 'breaking off the heterosexual contract is a necessity for those who do not consent to it'.[86] Only when we

---

84 See Cain (1991); Boyd (1999); Diduck (2001).
85 Walby (1990, p 125).
86 Wittig (1992, p 45).

dismantle the institution of heterosexuality (in Wittig's sense of a 'regime which rests on the submission and appropriation of women')[87] will the categories of gender cease to have political significance. Only then will the 'equality' of the sexes match the rhetorical promise of the law.

References

Barrett, M and McIntosh, M, *The Anti-Social Family*, 1982, London: Verso

Belcher, A, 'A feminist perspective on contract theories from law and economics' (2000) 8 *Feminist Legal Studies* 29

Bernard, J, *The Future of Marriage*, 1972, New York: World Publishing Co

Bodichon, BLS, *Women and Work*, 1857, London: Bosworth and Harrison

Boyd, SB, 'Family, law and sexuality: feminist engagements' (1999) 8 *Social and Legal Studies* 369

Butler, J (ed), *Women's Work and Women's Culture*, 1869, London: Macmillan

Butler, J, 'Against proper objects' (1994) 6 *Differences* 1

Cain, PA, 'Feminist jurisprudence: grounding the theories', in Bartlett, KT and Kennedy, R (eds), *Feminist Legal Theory: Readings in Law and Gender*, 1991, Boulder, CO: Westview

Caine, B, *English Feminism 1780–1980*, 1997, Oxford: OUP

Cartledge, S and Ryan, J (eds), *Sex and Love: New Thoughts on Old Contradictions*, 1983, London: The Women's Press

Comer, L, *Wedlocked Women*, 1974, Leeds: Feminist Books

Delphy, C, *Close to Home: A Material Analysis of Women's Oppression*, 1984, London: Hutchinson

Delphy, C and Leonard, D, *Family Exploitations: A New Analysis of Marriage in Contemporary Western Societies*, 1992, Cambridge: Polity

Diduck, A, 'A family by any other name ... or Starbucks™ comes to England' (2001) 28 *Journal of Law and Society* 290

Dixon, M, 'The special tenderness of equity: undue influence and the family home' (1994) 53 *Cambridge Law Journal* 21

Dixon, M, 'The limits of undue influence explained (again)' (2002) 35 *Student Law Review* 59

Douglas, CA, *Love and Politics: Radical Feminist and Lesbian Theories*, 1990, San Francisco: Ism Press

Dworkin, A, *Right-Wing Women: The Politics of Domesticated Females*, 1983, London: The Women's Press

---

87 *Ibid*, p xiv.

Fehlberg, B, *Sexually Transmitted Debt: Surety Experience and English Law*, 1997, Oxford: Clarendon Press

Hamilton, C, *Marriage as a Trade*, 1909, London: Chapman and Hall

Jackson, S, 'Gender and heterosexuality: a materialist feminist analysis', in Maynard, M and Purvis, J (eds), *(Hetero)Sexual Politics*, 1995, London: Taylor & Francis

Jackson, S, 'Heterosexuality and feminist theory', in Richardson, D (ed), *Theorising Heterosexuality*, 1996, Oxford: OUP

Jackson, S, *Heterosexuality in Question*, 1999, London: Sage

Kaye, M, 'Equity's treatment of sexually transmitted debt' (1997) V *Feminist Legal Studies* 35

Lawson, A, '*O'Brien* and its legacy: principle, equity and certainty?' (1995) 54 *Cambridge Law Journal* 280

Leeds Revolutionary Feminist Group, 'Political lesbianism: the case against heterosexuality', in *Love Your Enemy? The Debate Between Heterosexual Feminism and Political Lesbianism*, 1981, London: Onlywomen Press

MacKinnon, CA, 'Feminism, Marxism, method, and the state: an agenda for theory' (1982) 7 *Signs: Journal of Women in Culture and Society* 515

MacKinnon, CA, 'Feminism, Marxism, method, and the state: toward feminist jurisprudence' (1983) 8 *Signs: Journal of Women in Culture and Society* 635

Malos, E (ed), *The Politics of Housework*, 1980, London: Allison and Busby

Matthews, J, 'Barbara Bodichon: integrity in diversity', in Spender, D (ed), *Feminist Theorists: Three Centuries of Women's Intellectual Traditions*, 1983, London: The Women's Press

Maynard, M, 'Privilege and patriarchy: feminist thought in the nineteenth century', in Millett, PJ, 'Equity's place in the law of commerce' (1998) 114 *Law Quarterly Review* 214

Nicholson, L (ed), *Feminism/Postmodernism*, 1990, New York and London: Routledge

Oakley, A, *The Sociology of Housework*, 1974, London: Martin Robertson

Pawlowski, M and Brown, J, *Undue Influence and the Family Home*, 2002, London: Cavendish Publishing

Rich, A, 'Compulsory heterosexuality and lesbian existence' (1980), in *Blood, Bread and Poetry: Selected Prose 1970–1985*, 1986, London: Virago

Richardson, D (ed), *Theorising Heterosexuality*, 1996, Buckingham: OUP

Richardson, M, 'Protecting women who provide security for a husband's, partner's or child's debts: the value and limits of an economic perspective' (1996) 16 *Legal Studies* 368

Shanley, ML, *Feminism, Marriage, and the Law in Victorian England, 1850–1895*, 1989, Princeton, NJ: Princeton UP

Snitow, A, Stansell, C and Thompson, S (eds), *Desire: The Politics of Sexuality*, 1984, London: Virago

Spender, D, *Women of Ideas (and What Men Have Done to Them)*, 1982, London: Ark

Stone, E, 'Infants, lunatics and married women: equitable protection in *Garcia v National Australia Bank*' (1999) 61 *Modern Law Review* 604

Uglow, J, 'Josephine Butler: from sympathy to theory', in Spender, D (ed), *Feminist Theorists: Three Centuries of Women's Intellectual Traditions*, 1983, London: The Women's Press, pp 146–64

Walby, S, *Theorizing Patriarchy*, 1990, Oxford: Basil Blackwell

Wilkinson, S and Kitzinger, C (eds), *Heterosexuality: A Feminism and Psychology Reader*, 1993, London: Sage

Wittig, M, *The Straight Mind and Other Essays*, 1992, Hemel Hempstead: Harvester Wheatsheaf

Chapter 4
The Posthumous Life of the Postal Rule: Requiem and Revival of *Adams v Lindsell*

Peter Goodrich[1]

The significance of a case is often less a matter of what it determined than of what subsequent courts took it to mean. The case of *Adams v Lindsell* is a remarkable illustration of such a maxim.[2] The decision concerned a misdirected letter of offer. The judgment is a brief paragraph in length and it determines that the offer cannot be withdrawn after it has been accepted. It is a sparsely reasoned judgment and it was ignored for some 30 years. It was taken up first, and in different circumstances, in an appeal from a Scottish Court of Sessions decision[3] and then was interpreted, both in the United States[4] and in England,[5] as determining that a postal acceptance is binding once it is placed in the post.

No doubt in part because of the sparseness of the reasoning in the decision, subsequent doctrine has treated *Adams v Lindsell* both as an enigma and as an extraordinarily revolutionary decision. While most recognise that the decision is arbitrary[6] and now also archaic, and some even view it as erroneously decided,[7] it is taught across the common law world as a leading case, and the major authorities, as well as the authors of casebooks and treatises on contract, continue to imbue the decision with an exceptional importance.[8] According to Brian Simpson, the decision marks the beginning of the modern doctrine of contract as a bilateral agreement or mutual exchange of promises.[9] For Professor Ibbetson, too, it introduces Roman principles of offer and acceptance into the common law and so marks a sea change in the theory of contracts, namely the advent of the 'Will Theory' that dominated the next century of development of the law of volitional obligations.[10] Aside from its historic theoretical significance, *Adams v Lindsell* is also universally taken to be the source of the specific rule that a letter of acceptance is effective, which is to say communicated and binding, upon being placed in the post.

Technology has overtaken the antique system of postal correspondence. Electronic communications are now the norm and even though email is a species of written communication at a distance, the rule that applies treats it as an instantaneous medium and so subject to the general norm that, to be effective,

---

1 Cardozo School of Law, Yeshiva University.
2 *Adams and Others v Lindsell and another* (1818) I Barn & Ald 681, p 683.
3 *Dunlop v Higgins* (1848) 1 HLC 384.
4 *Tayloe v Merchant's Fire Insurance Co* 50 US (9 How) 390 (1850).
5 Most decisively in *Re The Imperial Land Company of Marseilles (Lewis Harris's Case)* (1872) 26 NS The Law Times 781.
6 As, eg, Collins (1997), describing the rule as anomalous; or Llewellyn (1939).
7 Thus, Nussbaum (1936). Gardner (1992) is also dubious of the rule's value. See also the decision in *Rhode Island Tool Co v United States* 128 F Supp 417 (1955).
8 The case figures in most US contracts casebooks – see Murphy, Speidel and Ayres (2003) – and in virtually all the obvious textbooks. See, eg, Poole (2001).
9 Simpson (1975).
10 Ibbetson (1999).

communication must be received.[11] The new rules, statutory and judicial, are not without significant problems and these have many of their roots in the prior law. The purpose of returning to *Adams v Lindsell*, however, is not only that of avoiding the repetition of previous errors[12] but it is also that of understanding a more complex cultural and legal history. Building upon the historical work that has shown how the decision introduced a novel and foreign or civilian conception of agreement into the common law of contracts, I will argue that it also introduced a gendered conception of bilateral consent. If *Adams v Lindsell* marked the passage from *pollicitatio* or unilateral promise to a bilateral conception of agreement or mutual consent, it did so by recognising that the parties to an *assumpsit* or debt are not one but two. The unitary concept of a promise being binding by virtue of an internal theology or faith was displaced by a concept of contracts as the 'consummation' of 'an engagement' created by 'proposal' and 'consent'. The language of engagement and consummation, as also the structuring concepts of proposal and consent, betray the historical proximity of actions for breach of promise to marry and actions for breach of other promises. It allows for the initial hypothesis that the decision in *Adams v Lindsell* also marks a gendered shift, or even break, in what was until then a unitary law. Identity made way for difference and the law of contract recognised, 'if unacknowledgedly',[13] that the subject of every contract was not one but two.[14]

The significance of *Adams v Lindsell* transpires to be greater than the mere introduction of a now defunct fiction relating to the communication of agreement at a distance. Its significance was structural and continuing. In that the decision allowed for the differentiation of offeror and offeree, or in the proper language of contracts between the master of the offer and its subject or mistress, it provides an important avenue to addressing the continuing questions that attend determination of the time when a contract is formed and in consequence whether there has been notice of relevant terms at the moment of agreement or meeting of minds. If the subject of a contract is not one but several, and if the law can recognise that dimension of difference then, whether negotiations were face to face or at a distance, the gender identity and performance of the parties, their access to information and their relative bargaining position in the exchange are all factors that can be incorporated in determining what counts as communication of agreement. While it could be argued that the postal rule covertly introduced antique norms relating to gender status into the rules governing formation of agreements, the more positive interpretation of the fiction is that it brought with it the possibility of attending to the plurality of subjects who form binding agreements and whose needs and desires gain their formal legal expression in contracting.

---

11 See Commission on European Contract Law (2000); Unidroit (1994) Art 2.6; and in the US, s 203 of the Uniform Computer Information Transactions Act adopts a time of receipt rule, and a similar provision is adopted in the revised Uniform Commercial Code currently being adopted.

12 Thus, Nussbaum (1936).

13 Ibbetson (1999).

14 On the duality of legal subjectivity, see Irigaray (1995; 1998).

Adams v Lindsell is not in any obvious sense a feminist decision. What I will argue is rather that the judgments in that case represented an unwitting shift, or even break, in the structure of contract law. This doctrinal shift both derived from the law governing the one explicitly gendered public contract mentioned in Bracton, the contract of marriage,[15] and gave birth to an implicitly gendered conception of legally enforceable promises in both the public and the intimate public spheres. At a theoretical level, communication of agreement is of the essence of bargain or of the 'drawing together' that contract represents. The requirement that there be communication depends upon an explicit recognition that there are two or more parties, and that these parties are independent, separate and different; characteristics that are ironically most evident in situations of agreement at a distance. Once difference, even if it is simply in the form of the acknowledgment of the absence of the other party, is acknowledged then the exemplary social difference, that between the genders and now also their orientations, falls within the ambit of law.

At a doctrinal level, gender had historically fallen within the jurisdiction of ecclesiastical law and not that of common law. It was the function of the Church to dictate the law that governed the private sphere of gendered relations. In drawing upon the ecclesiastical law of marriage and upon actions for breach of promise to marry, *Adams v Lindsell* can be understood as part of a long-term absorption of the spiritual jurisdiction into the common law. In more immediate terms, the borrowing brought with it, both expressly and implicitly, questions of gender difference and status differentiation that had not previously much exercised contract lawyers. It was not only that the rule was borrowed from a gendered context, but also that it was expressly forged so as to account for differences in the status of the genders. The sources and the purposes of the earlier formulation of the postal rule inevitably leave their mark upon subsequent doctrine.

Going postal

The immediate context of the decision in *Adams v Lindsell* was the advent of a new technology of communication.[16] The course of the post had historically been limited to Royal messages and messengers and the first long era of communication at a distance had been restricted to messages that announced 'state business' or otherwise delivered 'their sovereign's messages'.[17] From the *cursus publicus* of the Roman Empire to the royal currour and the *postea* of the common law, the traditional role and route of the mail had been to communicate decrees – commands, writs, judgments and laws – to a passively receptive populace of legal subjects. The communication of the post was unilateral: the messenger or mailman was the carrier of the secrets of power, the *arcana imperii heraldorum* or communicative mysteries of state, and it was the function of the subject of law to

---

15 Bracton (1968, p 97), refers to marriage as a public contract (*publice contractum*). For a lengthier discussion, see Goodrich (1999).

16 The most important source of periodisation of the mail for these purposes is Siegert (1999). See also Winthrop Young (2002). More broadly, see Derrida (1987).

17 See, eg, Legh (1562, folio 69v), discussed in Goodrich (1992, p 225).

pass on and absorb those messages.[18] The subject of law did not write: the subject of law received, observed, and obeyed.

The second era of the post came with the opening of the mail to public use. The Industrial Revolution brought with it a new requirement of subjects who could contract, who could buy and sell, who could offer and accept according to principles of reciprocity or mutuality. Unilateral stipulation of meaning gave way to bilateral conceptions of agreement and exchange. The emblematic decision from the early 19th century in this regard was not *Adams v Lindsell* but rather *Kennedy v Lee*.[19] The case dates from the year prior to *Adams v Lindsell* and it was concerned explicitly with whether a contract could properly be formed through the mail. According to Lord Chancellor Eldon: 'The question is whether this correspondence ... has formed a binding contract.' Eldon goes on to make the crucial point that where a party wishes to enforce an agreement arrived at by means of the post:

> ... the party seeking the specific performance of such an agreement, is bound to find in the correspondence, not merely a treaty – still less, a proposal – for an agreement; but a treaty, with reference to which mutual consent can be clearly demonstrated, or a proposal met by that sort of acceptance, which makes it no longer the act of one party, but of both.[20]

The requirement of mutuality gains legal expression in the concept of a meeting of minds, which is variously formulated as *consensus ad idem*, *congregatio* or *aggregatio mentum*.[21] As the meeting of minds was historically thought of in terms of consent at a given moment in time in the presence of the other party, the master of the offer, the law had to deal with contracts made through the mail by means of some species of fiction. Although the defendant in *Kennedy v Lee* clearly did not view his correspondence as legally binding, the Lord Chancellor begged to differ and determined that 'upon the whole correspondence ... I cannot but think that this letter is a virtual acceptance of the agreement made by the Defendant to close with the Plaintiff's original offer'.[22] It remains to add that the Lord Chancellor was clear, based on the facts of the case, that the contract was formed after receipt of the letter of acceptance. More precisely and interestingly, he says two things. The first is that 'if, within a reasonable time of the acceptance being communicated, no variation had been made by either party in the terms of the offer so made and accepted' there is a contract. The actual time of formation would thus seem to be after receipt of the acceptance. The Lord Chancellor, however, goes on to observe that the contract so made and accepted must be treated 'as simultaneous with the offer, and both together [taken] as constituting such an agreement as the Court will execute'.[23] Taken together, the two propositions suggest that the fiction that the Lord Chancellor had in mind was one that would treat receipt of the letter of acceptance

---

18 Bossewell (1572, folio Aia).

19 *Kennedy v Lee* (1817) 3 Mer 441.

20 *Ibid*, p 451.

21 The Latin terminology is, if nothing else, a linguistic reference to Latin sources and is taken here from *Mactier Administrators v Frith*, 6 Wend 103 (1830); and *Tayloe v Merchant's Fire Insurance Co* 50 US (9 How) 390 (1850).

22 *Kennedy v Lee* (1817) 3 Mer 441, p 454.

23 *Ibid*, p 455.

as the fictive moment of both parties being present together. The fiction, in other words, was that after the lapse of a short period of time – legally a *locus poenitentiae*[24] – post-receipt of the letter of acceptance, the court would act 'as if' both parties agreed together at the moment of receipt of the letter of acceptance.

The real significance of *Kennedy v Lee* lies more in the concept of correspondence by post being a process of mutual exchange than in its determination of when the contract was formed. The following year, and perhaps surprisingly, *Adams v Lindsell* seemingly went the other way. As already observed, the judgment was a mere paragraph in length and so is second only to the seven-word determination in *Raffles v Wichelhaus* as a fecund source of juristic speculation.[25] What distinguishes the facts of *Adams v Lindsell* from those of *Kennedy v Lee* is that in *Adams* the problem arose not after receipt of the acceptance but after a misdirected offer led to delay in the arrival of the letter of acceptance. On its facts, the determination in *Adams* follows the ruling in *Kennedy*: in the absence of any communication of withdrawal of the offer, the mere fact of selling the goods to a third party did not preclude a contract being formed. The court in *Adams*, however, famously digressed and proffered a seemingly novel reason for holding the defendants to their offer: '... if the defendants were not bound by their offer when accepted by the plaintiffs till the answer was received, then the plaintiffs ought not to be bound till after they had received notification that the defendants had received their answer and assented to it. And so it might go on *ad infinitum*.'[26]

The practical reason for holding the defendants to their offer in *Adams v Lindsell* lay in the fact of their neglect in misaddressing the letter of offer. Their offer was treated as firm and, *contra Cooke v Oxley*,[27] they were not able to withdraw the offer by what was, as far as the plaintiffs were concerned, a merely interior intention to do so: 'The defendants must be considered in law as making, during every instant of the time their letter was traveling, the same identical offer to the plaintiffs.'[28] Once the offeree had finally accepted the offer and manifested that acceptance objectively in the form of posting a letter, then equity or the fiction of the postal rule would preclude the offeror from changing his mind because such would, in effect, be allowing the offeror to actively prevent the offeree from accepting.

As observed earlier, what was determined in *Adams v Lindsell* is less significant than what the case was later taken to mean. Initially it was not much referred to or followed.[29] It was ahead of its time in that the completion of the postal system, the closing of the circuit through the institution of the pre-paid post, only occurred in 1840.[30]

---

24 The term comes from *Payne v Cave* (1789) 100 ER 502, p 503.

25 *Raffles v Wichelhaus* (1864) 2 H&C 906. See Simpson (1995, Chapter 6).

26 *Adams and Others v Lindsell and Another* (1818) 1 Barn & Ald 681, p 683.

27 *Cooke v Oxley* (1790) 3 TR 652, which held that there was no consideration for the defendant's promise to hold an offer open until 4 pm. When the plaintiff attempted to accept the offer before the appointed hour, the defendant had to agree to the bargain or else, as occurred, the deal was off. The offer did not, in this decision, continue.

28 *Adams and Others v Lindsell and Another* (1818) 1 Barn & Ald 681, p 683.

29 *Head v Diggon* (1828) 3 Man & Ryl 97; *Countess Dunmore v Elizabeth Alexander* (1830) 9 Shaw and Dunl 190; and later, see *British and American Telegraph Co v Coulson* (1871) 23 Law Times Reports 868.

30 Seigert (1999, pp 111–12); Gardener (1992, pp 178ff). For interesting digressions on the postal and the political, see Bennington (1994, pp 240–57).

It was later that case law took *Adams* to institute the fiction of the postal rule as opposed to the fiction of the firm offer, and such case law, as will be demonstrated below, relied not only upon *Adams* but also upon an earlier and lengthier tradition of *assumpsit* actions based upon promises of marriage. Before leaving *Adams*, however, the stage upon which the later cases appeared can be intimated by briefly alluding to the source of the rule in *Adams*. The *reductio ad absurdum* that the court manipulated so as to terminate the argument in the case did not come out of the blue. It was a borrowing from Roman law but it was a borrowing that had a peculiarly English twist to it.

As Simpson and Ibbetson unanimously confirm, the immediate source of the rule that the offer is to be treated as firm and continuing was Pothier's treatise on contracts of sale and, less directly, Roman law on sales at a distance.[31] What neither of these sources explain is why the shift from unilateral proposals to mutual agreements, the move from promise to bilateral exchange, should be reworked in the form of a fiction that acceptance, the letter posted by the offeree, terminates the potentially infinite regress of correspondence. Why was the offeree the party protected? Why did the courts resist the obvious authority and solution, which was to follow *Kennedy v Lee*, and indulge the fiction that the law would retrospectively treat acceptance as complete upon receipt – provided, that is, that the offeror had not objected within a reasonable time? Whatever the motive behind this specific expression of the earlier dogma, the source of this rule is ecclesiastical law.[32] Discussing the formation of agreement in spousal contracts made between parties that are absent, the issue of when the contract was formed is discussed by Swinburne, in a work published in 1686, in terms of a distinction between messengers who are agents (proctors), and messengers who 'have no Mandate being charged only with the bare dilivery of a Message or a Letter'.[33]

The marriage contract, or *spousals de futuro*, was the first type of executory contract that required mutual consent and it is precisely in terms of consent, and specifically the two parties that must consent, that the problem is posed. Swinburne immediately acknowledges the problem of mutuality and observes that where there has been an offer by letter or bare messenger the 'Approbation' – that is, the consent – of the sender would appear to be lacking because he consented at one time and the offeree consents at another time. There cannot therefore be a perfect contract because such requires 'a mutual agreement at one instant'.[34] The infinite regress that the *Adams v Lindsell* decision feared is resolved by assuming first that the offeror 'continue and persevere in the same mind, until the time of the response'. It is assumed, second, that even if the offeror has changed his mind prior to the offeree's acceptance, the fact that such 'dissent' had not been communicated to the offeree precludes it being effective.[35]

What is most striking about the fiction of instantaneous receipt of the letter of acceptance is its root in ecclesiastical law. It makes sense, however, that when faced

---

31 See *Digest of Justinian* (c 1535); and Gordley (1991, pp 45–46).
32 I have discussed the ecclesiastical sources of the rule in Goodrich (1995, pp 198–210), and so I will not belabour that specific point here.
33 Swinburne (1686), giving his source as the *Summa Angelica*.
34 Swinburne (1686, p 181).
35 *Ibid*, p 182.

with the question of how to determine whether or not there had been assent to a proposal, the common law court would turn to the jurisdiction and law that had long dealt with agreements that depended upon mutual consent, namely spousal contracts. The recourse to the spiritual law, its absorption into the domain of secular law, was neither innocent nor without unforeseen consequences. The borrowing brought with it the concern for conscience that marked the spiritual jurisdiction as distinctive. While ecclesiastical law treated women as inferior to men, it did recognise the dependence of spousal contracts (future and present) upon the assent of the woman. In doing so, it implicitly introduced into common law the vast terrain of rules that govern the differences of status and legal personality that marked the genders and formed much of the substance of the law of spousal contracts.

As the maxim goes, a fiction must always do justice – *in fictione iuris semper est aequitas*.[36] In this instance, that requirement seems fairly directly to mean that justice be done as between a man and a woman, between two exemplarily different subjects of agreement. Put in other terms, even if the parties were not male and female and the contract was one of sale rather than of 'Messages or Letters of Matrimony' as the ecclesiastical law addressed, the decision in *Adams v Lindsell* has its roots in the subjective intentions of an offeree who is differentiated from and has characteristics that are distinct from those of the offeror. There are two subjects of contract and the moment that such duality or difference is recognised then questions of gender, of orientation, performativity and, as another case put it, 'the feelings and intentions of the parties at the time of entering into such a contract' become pertinent and justiciable.[37]

Every contract is like a marriage

Adams v Lindsell would count for nothing were it not for later case law. It was *Dunlop v Higgins*,[38] and subsequent decisions running from the late 1840s to the last decade of the 19th century, that defined and legitimated the postal rule. That it was not until the 1940s, not until after closure of the circuit and the consequent erasure of distance that Seigert aligns with prepayment of postage, is no coincidence.[39] The law needed the fiction of the postal rule to deal with a series of novel situations that coincided with the universalisation of the postal system. As with most innovation in common law, the source of the new rule was a borrowing from another era of history and from a separate jurisdiction. I have alluded already to the immediate source of the rule in *Adams v Lindsell* as being a direct borrowing from ecclesiastical law, and in the same vein it is spousal contracts, and numerous common law cases of *assumpsit* for breach of promise to marry, that provide the source for the later elaboration of the fiction of the mailbox rule.

It is important not to overstate the case and so I will begin by acknowledging that the ecclesiastical rules governing spousal contracts or *spousals de futuro* are not the only source of the concept of mutuality that emerges after *Adams v Lindsell*. The

---

36 *Wilkes v The Earl of Halifax* (1769) 2 Wils KB 256; 95 Eng Rep 797.
37 *Mary Short v Stone* (1846) 8 QB 341.
38 *Dunlop v Higgins* (1848) 1 HLC 384.
39 Seigert (1999, pp 100–26); Gardner (1992, pp 178–84).

Roman law of obligations, from Gaius' *Institutes* onwards, had defined obligations arising out of contracts (*ex contractibus*) as mutual agreements, but the basis of the rule was predicated upon recognition of a debt – something had been given and had to be returned – rather than upon consent in any modern or mutual sense.[40] Pothier's much-cited opinion that an offer made by letter must be supposed to continue 'until his letter reaches the other party', is on its terms concerned with the unilateral declaration of the offeror's will, more than it is addressed to the question of consent or mutuality.[41] The most obvious source of the rules relating to mutuality was thus the contract of marriage not simply because in these cases the consent of the woman to the proposal of spousals was a condition of the contract, but also because the relational character of the obligation, its predication upon two different subjects of exchange, was much more obvious than in the secular forms of sale.

Change in the common law is usually slow and the gradual development of the postal rule is no exception. As late as 1871, the decision in *Adams v Lindsell* was deemed 'to have nothing to do with the question' of when a letter of acceptance takes effect.[42] There was understandable resistance to the new rule because it seemed to be based upon pragmatic concerns specific to the case of a misdirected offer, and because the secular law generally treated breach of contract as breach of a party's promise – the breaking of the promisor's bond – rather than as a cause of action based upon mutual undertakings. It should thus come as little surprise that, in *Dunlop v Higgins*, the issue that most taxed the House of Lords was not the time of acceptance but rather the terms of the offer. *Kennedy v Lee* had been followed in *Head v Diggon*, and so too in *Countess Dunmore v Elizabeth Alexander*, both of which directly contradict the judgment in *Adams v Lindsell*, and require actual receipt of acceptance for a contract to be formed or perfected.[43] The only other case that the court relied upon with any conviction was *Brodie v Todd*. This Scottish case, however, concerned an offer by letter that concluded 'please return in course'.[44] The court held that in law this meant the next post and failure to comply – taking two days to reply – relieved the offeror of their duty to sell. In the view of the judges in *Dunlop*, it would thus seem that the pressing legal problem facing the court was that of how to interpret the offer as inviting acceptance of the kind that actually occurred, and only secondarily was the problem that of determining the effect of a letter of acceptance.

In *Dunlop v Higgins*, the issue arose by virtue of a delay in the delivery of a letter of acceptance, occasioned by severe weather encountered en route between

---

40 Gaius (1946, p 197); Justinian (1987, 3.15); *Lectura* [1200] (1990, p 79).

41 Pothier (1806, p 161).

42 *British and American Telegraph Company v Coulson* (1871) 23 Law Times Reports 868, p 872 (*per* Baron Bramwell).

43 *Head v Diggon* (1828) 3 Man & Ryl 97. Lord Tenterden, in argument:

> the question really comes down to this single point: Must both parties be bound, or will the binding of one be sufficient? You say you were to be free for the given time, and the defendant was to be bound ... What is the form of your declaration? Why, it treats of a bargain, a complete contract; an absolute and unconditional bargain. You have proved it to be so; those counts will not do.

> *Countess of Dunmore v Elizabeth Alexander* (1830) 9 Shaw and Dunl 190 (Lord Craigie dissenting) to the same effect. The court referred to Pothier (1806) on sale, and to *Adams v Lindsell*, but did not follow it.

44 *Brodie v Todd* (1814) 17 Fac Col Dec 20.

Liverpool and Glasgow. The view of the court was that where an offer either expressly or impliedly requested an acceptance 'by return of post' or 'in the course of the post', the offer bargained for an act rather than a promise. The issues that might arise with respect to whether acceptance had occurred in a timely manner, or before withdrawal of the offer, came down to whether the offeree had complied with the offer. Citing *Stocken v Collin*, the Lord Chancellor observed that 'the real question is whether the party [that is, the offeree] has been guilty of laches'.[45] Laches, or delay on the part of the offeree, would mean failure to comply with the terms of the offer, but outside of default on the part of the offeree posting the letter of acceptance in good time was the act requested and would make the contract complete. The conclusion is thus that: 'If a party does all that he can do, that is all that is called for ... How can he be responsible for that over which he has no control'; the court goes on to add that if the offeree has posted the letter 'he has done all that he is expected to do as far as he is concerned; he has put the letter into the post, and whether that letter be delivered, or not, is a matter quite immaterial, because, for accidents happening at the Post Office he is not responsible'.[46] The posting of acceptance is 'compliance with the requisition of the offer' and perfects the contract.[47]

The question of mutuality or meeting of minds did not arise directly in *Dunlop v Higgins*. The decision in *Adams v Lindsell* was referred to only as a rule of 'common sense' relating to offers that requested a postal act rather than a promise *de futuro* (an executory promise) by way of acceptance.[48] Insofar as consent was not the issue in the case, it simply set the stage for the problems of reliance and communication that the subsequent case law would later settle comprehensively in favour of the promisee. Initially, however, with respect to the argument in *Dunlop*, the primary value of the case is that of emphasising the offeror's mastery of the offer. The reliance of the promisee upon the offeror's promise is all that is needed to bind the offeror while leaving the promise, at least in theory, with a *locus poenitentiae* or time to repent. The doctrinal root of that desire to protect the offeree can be traced most directly to cases of breach of promise to marry.

In *Hutton v Mansell*, a case of *assumpsit* on a promise to marry, the report reads: '... the promise of the man was proved, but no actual promise on the woman's side, yet [Holt CJ] held that there was sufficient evidence to prove that the woman likewise promised, because she carried herself as one consenting and approving the promise of the man.'[49] In another decision, more or less contemporary with the early postal rule cases, on an *assumpsit* on a promise of marriage where a man had proposed to a woman in the presence of her parents, Best CJ observed that '... it would be indelicate to expect that she should consent in words. No doubt the jury must be satisfied that there were mutual promises; but I think there is evidence from which they may be inferred'.[50] Finally, in *Harvey v Johnston*, a case that is cited

---

45 *Stocken v Collin* (1838) 7 Mee and Wels 515; *Dunlop v Higgins* (1848) 1 HLC 384, p 399.
46 *Dunlop v Higgins* (1848) 1 HC 384, pp 398–99.
47 *Ibid*, p 401.
48 *Ibid*, p 400.
49 *Hutton v Mansell* (1795) 3 Salkeld 17.
50 *Daniel v Bowles* (1826) 2 Car & P 553.

as authority in the postal rule decisions,[51] Creswell J states that 'The offer is, – "If you will come to this country, I will marry you". The plaintiff does come. Is that not an acceptance of the offer? ... No doubt it is. The ordinary form of declarations for breach of promise of marriage, all allege mutual promises', but this did not in his view preclude a promise implied from the behaviour or actions of the promisee.[52]

What is striking about the latter case is that it makes explicit that it is a singularity of marriage agreements that 'this contract is sustainable only where the contract to marry was mutual'.[53] The exemplary instance of an agreement that depends upon consent, which is formed by virtue of the distinction or difference between offeror and offeree, is precisely the contract of *spousals de futuro*. It is by virtue of borrowing from the rules of promises implied in fact in cases of contracts to marry that the common law developed the concept that the reliance of the promisee would determine the moment of acceptance and complete the contract. The shift from the unilateral to the bilateral conception of the postal rule is thus derived, more than anything else, from the importance of who it is that offers and who accepts.

The requirement of mutual promises has an antique root in common law. It was historically the case that promises to marry were unenforceable in *assumpsit* because the promise was of 'ecclesiastical conusance', or spiritual and enforceable only in ecclesiastical courts. Thus, in *Bunting's Case* the judges of the King's Bench '*prayeront l'opinion des Civilians*' (sought the expert opinion of the Roman lawyers) in deciding that a contract to marry was unenforceable at common law.[54] When the common law lawyers later asserted jurisdiction over marriage contracts and reversed the decision in *Bunting's Case*, they held that 'here is a mutual contract concerning a lawful act, and though the subject matter be spiritual, yet the contract is temporal'.[55] The contract was formed by the exchange of promises to marry and even if nothing else was transferred between the parties, the promises themselves were good consideration. Mutual consent was not only the form, but also the substance, of the bargain, as held in *Harrison v Cage*: 'Resolved, *per curiam*, that here were reciprocal promises; and therefore as her promise to him was good consideration to make his promise obligatory, so by the same reason his promise to her was a sufficient consideration to make her promise binding in this case.'[56]

The significance of mutual promises is borne out by its absence in a later case. Here, the plaintiff promised to marry the defendant if she would wait for the death of his master. He promised her a bond as security for his promise and Lord Eldon held that 'There is no mutuality whatsoever in this; for she is bound to nothing',

---

51 As in *British and American Telegraph Co v Coulson* (1871) 23 Times Law reports 868, p 872, col 2.

52 *Harvey v Johnston* (1848) 6 CB 295, p 304.

53 *Ibid*, pp 304–05.

54 *Bunting's Case* (1633) Moore (KB) 169.

55 *Holder v Dickeson* (1673) 1 Freeman 96, continuing to state that when bought and sold, things spiritual were made temporal (*per emptionem et venditionem res spirituals fiunt temporales*). See also *Hebden v Rutter* (1681) 1 Sid 180. On promises to marry: '*per Curiam le declar & consideration in ceo sont bone, car marriage est un preferment, et le perd de ceo est un temporal perd, et fuit adjudge bone consideration temps Roles Chiefe Jutice in Baker & Smith's case*' (the court held that the promise and consideration in this case are good, because marriage is a benefit, and the loss of this is a temporal loss, and so it was held in *Baker v Smith*).

56 *Harrison v Cage & Ux'* (1741) Carthew 467.

while adding later that 'there is no doubt, upon mutual promises actions would lie'.[57] The examples could be multiplied but the point to be made would be unaltered. The requirement of mutuality that begins its lengthy entry into the common law of secular contracts in *Adams v Lindsell* was a borrowing from the case law of *assumpsit* that dealt with highly specific and gendered promises of marriage. Far from introducing an equality of promises into the law, as is sometimes supposed, the doctrine of mutuality addressed not equality but an equity predicated upon the specific differences between promisor and promisee. Offer and acceptance were not the same thing because offeror and offeree were distinguished by differences of status, place, gender and expectation.

The later concern of the cases on the postal rule with the protection of the reliance interest of the offeree may seem arbitrary to modern eyes and something of an error, but it is in fact a rule that protects the pre-contractual interest of the female offeree.[58] Recognition of the social standing and the cultural expectations of the feminine offeree, and attention to her position and predicament, meant that equity clearly favoured protecting her reliance interest in the offer and preventing the offeror from speculating upon the time of passage of a letter of acceptance that had duly been placed in the mail. Once the offer was accepted it could not be withdrawn, a principle that also found its way into the law of contracts of sale conducted by letters. If a party in Britain offers to purchase a specified quantity of shares from a party in New York and the party in New York decides to accept and writes a letter of acceptance and then proceeds to fulfil the contract, the postal rule will operate to protect the offeree's reliance during the 10 day period that the letter takes to cross the Atlantic. The alternative would be that the offeror 'during all that time might wait and speculate whether the shares were rising or falling in price, and when he found that it was a falling market, he might revoke his offer'.[59] The reliance interest protects both the initiating position and power of the offeror and the vulnerability of the offeree in a policy and rule that emerged first in cases of promises of marriage, one of the earliest of futures contract.

Every contract that takes the modern form of mutual exchange of executory promises binds the promising parties to a future performance. Long before Lord Campbell famously declared, in *Hochester v De La Tour*, that every contract to do an act on a future day constituted an engagement, the case law on marriage contracts had recognised that where a party who had promised to marry the defendant at a future date had in the meantime married someone else, this was breach of contract and made the breaching party liable in damages.[60] This was so, interestingly, even though the woman might die before the time for performance of the original promise to marry fell due. Using the example of marriage contracts as exemplary of future commitments, Lord Campbell offered the view that: '... there is a relation constituted between the parties in the meantime by the contract, and ... they impliedly promise that in the meantime neither will do any thing to the prejudice of

---

57 *Cock v Richards* (1805) 10 Ves Jun 429, p 437.

58 The spousal contract was often termed the pre-contract of marriage, in recognition of the fact that marriage itself was a formal rite and required consummation.

59 *Re The Imperial Land Company of Marseilles (Lewis Harris's Case)* (1872) 26 NS The Law Times 781, p 783, col 1.

60 *Hochester v De La Tour* (1853) 2 El & Bl 678; *Cork v Baker* (1795) 21 Strange 34; *Mary Short v Stone* (1846) 8 QB 341.

the other inconsistent with that relation.' Just as the engaged couple 'are affianced to one another during the period between the time of the engagement and the celebration of marriage ... In this very case, of traveler and courier, from the day of the hiring till the day when the employment was to begin, they were engaged to each other'.[61] Every contract was indeed like a marriage, a fact recognised not only in the use of the word engagement but expressly acknowledged in a later case when it was remarked that 'Indeed the contract of marriage appears to afford a striking illustration of the expediency of holding that an action may be maintained on the repudiation of a contract to be performed in futuro', to which the judge, Chief Justice Cockburn, specifically added: 'To the woman, more especially, it is all-important that the relation shall not be put an end to.'[62]

Conclusion: wedded to the web

Conventional wisdom tends to the view that the postal rule was an anomaly at its inception and is now an archaism in relation to modern modes of communication and of electronic contracting. Contemporary case law and legislation overwhelmingly support the abrogation of the rule in favour of viewing email and online communication as instantaneous modes of interaction. If we study the sources of the rule today, it is, in Gardner's words, so as to avoid repeating the error in relation to newer technologies.[63] While it is certainly true that the postal rule is an archaism dating back to 17th century law on spousal contracts, it is more of an archaism than has been generally supposed, but it does not follow that it is an error or that the apparent egalitarianism of the rules now governing electronic commerce is necessarily an improvement upon the older law.

The decision in *Adams v Lindsell* was, and still could be, something of a Trojan horse. It was nothing in itself, but it opened the door to a host of much older rules that took seriously the subjectivity and the differences of actual subjects engaged in the legal formalisation of their relationship. In implicitly recognising the requirement of a meeting of minds in mutual agreement, the decision invokes an older law that was specifically built around the differences between subjects in terms of their social status,[64] their vulnerability,[65] their expectations, their specific hopes and desires. As Lord Denman puts it, in *Short v Stone*: '... we must look at this case with a view to the feelings and intentions of the parties at the time of entering into such a contract.'[66] If that seems both a sound and a surprising principle of interpretation, it may be because it states somewhat explicitly what generally is addressed more covertly in contract doctrine or left to the whim of the legislator.

The rule in *Adams v Lindsell* has the effect of drawing the process of communication of agreement to a close. It terminates the need for notification, or proof, of actual receipt of communication, upon the posting of a letter of acceptance.

---

61 *Hochester v De La Tour* (1853) 2 El & Bl 678, pp 688–89.
62 *Frost v Knight* (1872) 16 QBD 460.
63 Gardner (1992, p 192) ('there is a chance of history repeating itself').
64 *Woodhouse v Shepley* (1742) 2 Atk 535.
65 See, eg, *Atkins v Farr* (1738) 1 Atk 287; *Woodhouse v Shepley* (1742) 2 Atk 535.
66 *Mary Short v Stone* (1846) 8 QB 341, p 369.

The choice of the act of posting, or of that point in time, as the moment of consummation protects and continues to protect the offeree. Recent decisions still rely upon the postal rule to protect interests[67] and to determine both the time and the place of agreement.[68] The postal rule, in other words, can allow for attention to context and intention, to subjectivity and difference, by allowing the court to determine the time and place of communication according to a fiction that favours the offeree. The apparently arbitrary nature of the cut-off, or moment of consummation, according to the rule in *Adams v Lindsell*, is in fact far from arbitrary. It protects the offeree, for sure, by binding the offeror before, and sometimes in the absence of, any actual communication of acceptance. More than that, and more importantly than that in modern contexts of standard form contracting, the postal rule determines the content of the contract according to what the offeree knew or had notice of at the time of sending the letter of acceptance.

Contemporary infatuation with the web, and the facilitation of business over the internet, has led to the over-rapid reduction of the electronic medium to the fiction of instantaneous contracting. Treating communication at a distance, with a website, an eminent domain, or an electronic address, as if it were face-to-face interaction can have unfortunate effects when the common law has tended to treat face-to-face interaction as a metaphor of equivalence rather than of difference or of the uniqueness of actual faces. The posthumous life of the postal rule resides in the ironic possibility of translating the rules governing snail mail into the context of cyberspace contracting, so as to allow for attention to differences between the parties, failures of notice, and the strengths and vulnerabilities of the subjects, corporate and real, engaged in contracting.

English courts have held open the possibility of varying the time of receipt of acceptances by reference to the words of Lord Wilberforce in an earlier decision to the effect that where machine generated messages are concerned: 'No universal rule can cover all such cases: they must be resolved by reference to the intention of the parties, by sound business practice and in some cases by a judgment where the risks should lie ...'[69] While it would be unwise to draw too close an analogy between the shifting pattern of communication that produced the fiction of the postal rule and contemporary electronic communications on the web, there is clearly a need at least to consider the differential subject positions made possible by the internet, by use of the computer, and to develop rules that will protect those who contract by virtual means on terms dictated by the master of the website who is the modern equivalent of the master of the offer.

---

67 A strong, recent assertion of the importance of the mailbox rule for the protection of employees can be found in *Karla Schikore v Bank of America Supplemental Retirement Plan* 269 F 3d 956 (2001), p 961.

68 *Bastone and Firminger Ltd v Nasima Enterprises (Nigeria) Ltd* (1996) QBD (transcript) (applying the law of Nigeria); and, interestingly, *Schelde Delta Shipping BV v Astarte Shipping Ltd (The Pamela)* [1995] 2 Lloyd's Rep 249, where communications were by telex and the court imposed a rule of actual receipt as opposed to the view taken of internet communications where it is receipt by the relevant information system that is taken to constitute actual communication. See, eg, United Nations (2002), Arts 8(3) and 11(2).

69 *Brinkibon Ltd v Stahag und Stahlwarenhandelsgesellschaft mbH* [1983] 2 AC 34, p 42; cited in *Schelde Delta, ibid*, transcript, p 6.

Adams v Lindsell provides the possibility of certain protections for contracting subjects who are vulnerable in virtuality. It does so in principle by incorporating into common law rules that protected weaker parties in spousal contracts. It does so more specifically by attending to the risks and responsibilities of those who contract at a distance, or in its modern equivalent through a screen. Where current case law in the United States seems to favour viewing the contracting subject who visits a website as being bound by any terms contained on the website or hyperlinked to it,[70] the rule in *Adams v Lindsell* would suggest a more subtle and nuanced approach. The act of the offeree that indicates acceptance should mark the last moment of notice or conclusion of the agreement upon the terms that were in evidence prior to the act of sending the acceptance.

The details of such a continuing rule governing sending will have to be elaborated elsewhere; the purpose of this chapter is more modest. *Adams v Lindsell* drew juristic attention to gender and difference. It did so in an indirect and largely unintended way, but it can be interpreted in its afterlife as a principle of differentiation to be applied to online communications. If fictions are genuinely created to effect justice, then the work of the postal rule may hardly have begun.

References

Bennington, G, *Legislations: The Politics of Deconstruction*, 1994, London: Verso

Bossewell, J, *Workes of Armorie*, 1572, London: Totell

Bottomley, A (ed), *Feminist Perspectives on Foundational Subjects in Law*, 1996, London: Cavendish Publishing

Bracton, H de, *De legibus et consuetudinibus Angliae*, 1968 edn, Thorne, R (ed), Cambridge, MA: Harvard UP

Collins, H, *The Law of Contract*, 1997, London: Butterworths

Commission on European Contract Law, 'The principles of European contract law' (2000) Article 2.205, http://europa.eu.int/comm/consumers

Derrida, J, *The Postcard: From Socrates to Freud and Beyond*, 1987, Chicago: Chicago UP

Digest of Justinian (c 535), Watson, A (ed), 1984, Philadelphia: Pennsylvania UP, D 18 1 1 2 (*et per literas*)

Gaius, *Institutes*, Zulueta, F de (ed), 1946, Oxford: OUP, Pt 1

Gardner, S, 'Trashing with Trollope: a deconstruction of the postal rules in contract' (1992) 12 *Oxford Journal of Legal Studies* 170

---

70 The latest offerings are *De John v The TV Corp International* (2003) WL 356181 and *Ticketmaster Corp v Tickets.com* (2003) US Dist LEXIS 6483. Both decisions seem to regress from the rule in *Specht v Netscape Comms Corp* 306 F3d 17 (2002), which, at least, required a stringent degree of notice of terms that were not visible in the scroll box where the acceptance took place.

Goodrich, P, *Languages of Law*, 1992, London: Weidenfeld & Nicolson

Goodrich, P, *Oedipus Lex: Psychoanalysis, History, Law*, 1995, Berkeley, CA: California UP

Goodrich, P, 'Gender and contracts', in Bottomley, A (ed), *Feminist Perspectives on the Foundational Subjects of Law*, 1996, London: Cavendish Publishing

Gordley, J, *The Philosophical Origins of Modern Contract Doctrine*, 1991, Oxford: OUP

Ibbetson, DJ, *A Historical Introduction to the Law of Obligations*, 1999, Oxford: OUP

Irigaray, L, *Thinking the Difference*, 1995, London: Routledge

Irigaray, L, *I Love to You*, 1998, London: Routledge

Justinian, *Institutes*, 3.15, Birks, P and McLeod, G (eds), 1987, London: Duckworth

Lectura [1200] (Anon), Stein, P (ed), 1990, London: Selden Society

Legh, G, *The Accedens of Armory* (1562), discussed in Goodrich, P, *Languages of Law*, 1992, London: Weidenfeld & Nicolson

Llewellyn, K, 'Our case-law of contract: offer and acceptance', Pt 2 (1939) 48 *Yale Law Journal* 779

Murphy, E, Speidel, R and Ayres, I, *Studies in Contract Law*, 2003, Westbury, NY: Foundation Press

Nussbaum, A, 'Comparative aspects of the Anglo-American offer-and-acceptance doctrine' (1936) 33 *Columbia Law Review* 920

Poole, J, *Textbook on Contract Law*, 2001, London: Blackstone Press

Pothier, *Treatise on the Contract of Sale*, Pt I, a II III [1806], Cushing (trans), 1839 edn, Boston, MA: Little Brown

Siegert, B, *Relays, Literature as an Epoch of the Postal System*, 1999, Palo Alto CA: Stanford UP

Simpson, AWB, 'Innovation in nineteenth-century contract law' (1975) 91 *Law Quarterly Review* 247

Simpson, AWB, 'The beauty of obscurity: *Raffles v Wichelhaus and Busch* (1864)', in Simpson, AWB, *Leading Cases in the Common Law*, 1995, Oxford: Oxford UP

Swinburne, H, *A Treatise of Spousals or Marriage Contracts*, 1686, London: Society of Stationers

Unidroit, 'Principles of international commercial contracts', 1994, www.jus.uio.no/lm/unidroit.international.commercial.contracts. principles.1994

United Nations, *United Nations Commission on International Trade, Report of the Working Group IV (Electronic Commerce)*, 2002, EU Publications, www.un.org

Winthrop Young, G, 'Going postal to deliver subjects: remarks upon the German postal *a priori*' (2002) *Angelaki* 143

Chapter 5
Women Lie Back Everywhere:
The Symbolic Economy of Restitution

Adam Gearey[1]

Introduction: very little, almost nothing

To date, accounts of restitution have failed to take seriously the subject's constitutional tensions. Elaborating a problematic developed by scholars working within the area of feminist economic theory and psychoanalysis, this chapter could be read as an attempt to reveal restitution's unconscious and to enable a feminist appropriation of the subject. Can we read restitution as if it had an unconscious? How can this mode of analysis make sense? It is not supposed that this approach will shatter the possibility of a law of restitution. Rather, it could be seen as an attempt to trace the traumas underlying the discipline's sense of a coherent doctrinal self. However, as in a session with one's analyst, this chapter must impose a boundary, a limit to the material that can usefully be considered. As it would be impossible to attempt an overview of the entire subject, I will focus on a particular aspect of restitution: undue influence.

So, the notion of restitution's unconscious must be taken as more than metaphorical.[2] It relates to the tensions or the problems that constitute the subject and remain largely hidden from view. We will see that restitution's categories and divisions are based on assumptions that are not as settled as they might seem. How can this be taken in a feminist direction? The contemporary law of undue influence is predicated on the problematic of female agency. Restitution promises a return, a giving back of value that has been unjustly obtained. Property goes astray because the subject has not behaved rationally; a transaction can be impugned on the grounds that freewill was not operating. Women are associated with these interruptions, breaches in smooth running of this circuit of exchange.

We will see that feminist economic theory[3] can assist us in the development of this argument. The structures that animate restitution's unconscious can be related to a wider symbolic economy where the exchange of women as object preserves the subjectivity of men. However, in building this position we must not allow a narrowness of focus or a reductivism. We are concerned with a conjunction of psychoanalysis and economic theory so we can identify the interrelations of gender and its material contexts. Restitution intervenes at a particular moment to legitimise economic operations, to preserve faith in an epoch of capital and its distribution of

---

1   School of Law, Birkbeck College, University of London. Thanks to Sally Wheeler, Linda Mulcahy, Mary Gearey and Nathan Moore.

2   See Jameson (1981).

3   There are at least two ways of 'doing' feminist economics. One would be to work largely within the dominant paradigms, but to show how the prevailing modes of analysis fail to grasp the reality of various predominantly female experiences. The other would be to try to move outside of this paradigm, to align with the different mode of 'radical' economics that contest the assumptions and operations of capitalism. Extending this position in a Marxist or neo-Marxist direction would be to see the operation of capital as always gendered. This chapter has sympathies with the neo-Marxist position.

profits and losses, fortune and failure. Turning to the case law, we will see that the law of restitution attempts to draw and maintain a line that defines the operation of undue influence. The law can never quite identify the nature of the symbolic economy that draws these boundaries. When judges attempt to define principles, it is as if they are talking past something that remains withdrawn and disconcerting. Symbolic economy has to be forgotten to allow the principles of undue influence to emerge.

It would be a mistake to see our identification of the underlying symbolic structures of restitution as suggesting that the subject is resistant to critique. Our discovery of the tensions that produce restitution suggest that the subject is unstable. Restitution is open to manipulation, to strategic interventions, but there is no happy ending. The subject cannot ultimately be realigned or redesigned. We have to accept that doctrinal instability is an irresolvable condition. However, by this very token, there are possibilities of exploiting the tensions in the law. Restitution and undue influence may be opened to feminist argument.

The resistances of restitution

I am concerned with scholarly endeavours to organise restitution, to keep its house in order. A feminist engagement with restitution would have to go further than the merely 'technical'[4] disputes that, to date, have tended to focus on the division and ordering of the subject. Psychoanalysis is helpful as it suggests that we should read for senses that exist below or beyond the obvious. As this section of the chapter develops, it will become clear that these hidden structures relate to a particular idea of economy, politics and subjectivity.

Let us concentrate on the very definition of the subject.[5] Scholars are concerned that restitution might become something other than itself. This is a risk with all subjects, but the stakes seem higher with restitution. It may be because the subject is based on the law of unjust enrichment, and words like 'unjust' and 'exploitation' have a certain emotive content. For Burrows,[6] 'unjust' cannot be read as a 'vague appeal to individual morality; it is a reference to what the cases decide'. The foundation, then, is not to be weakened by subjective notions. Restitution is objective, rigorous and capable of principled development. Given this argument, it may be useful to examine briefly the generic structure of restitution.

We will begin with Birks' typology.[7] Although this has been criticised and revised, the following elaboration is sufficient for the limited purposes of this chapter. Restitution sees itself as policing the act of exchange. The discipline is structured by three elements that can be phrased as questions: has the defendant been enriched?; was the enrichment at the claimant's expense?; and, was the enrichment unjust? These questions can be broken down further still. 'At the expense of the claimant' contains two senses. First, that the defendant's gain

---

4 Hedley (2001).
5 Virgo (1999) provides a more detailed definition of restitution. For a sustained attack on new theories of restitution, see Hedley (2001a, pp 21–231).
6 Burrows (1993, p 21).
7 Birks (1985, p 206).

represents a 'loss' or a 'subtraction' to the claimant. This could be called autonomous unjust enrichment, as no wrong needs to have been committed. The second sense covers the situation where the defendant has gained by committing a wrong against the claimant. This is dependent unjust enrichment; the defendant's wrong has to be established and restitution is one possible form of remedy. To turn to the other two questions (has the defendant been enriched?; was the enrichment at the claimant's expense?), our concern is with the definition of enrichment. The sense is that the claimant has conferred a benefit on the defendant. What about the nature of 'unjust'? Autonomous unjust factors include the grounds of 'duress' and 'exploitation'. If we are to consider duress as a ground for restitution, then we need to clarify a central issue: how does duress constitute an unjust enrichment? This takes us towards a consideration of the factors negativing voluntariness and free acceptance. The key concept is the notion that transferor was (not) able to exercise an independent will.

The issue of independent will is related to an understanding of the competing interests that operate in exchange. A right to claim restitution is 'balanced' by a social interest in the security of receipts. Once this principle is in place it is possible to distinguish between bogus claims to restitution made by someone who had merely changed their mind after the transaction had taken place, and legitimate claims where the claimant can show that they did not intend the transfer.[8] This core meaning of the principle against unjust enrichment can now be related to one of its local manifestations: the notion of non-voluntary transfers.[9] As a category, this notion can indeed be subdivided, but the risk is that the 'unity and coherence' of the subject would become obscured. It is necessary to keep firmly in sight the generic concept: the notion that the claimant's judgment was 'not properly exercised'. If one can keep these objectives in mind, then non-voluntary transfers can be split into further subcategories without distorting the foundational theme of impaired judgment.[10] The notion of the non-voluntary transfer is thus a central distinction. How is this developed? This would take us to the notion of compulsion.

Compulsion as the use of pressure is founded on the fact that as 'social animals' we are committed to this tactic as a way of achieving desired ends. Compulsion is a rational means to an end. It would seem that there is a continuum of pressure, from outright violent coercion through to the coercion that has become so much part of our daily lives that it is invisible to us. Interestingly, Birks argues that the market works in this way.[11] An example is a power cut. If an individual has a large number of candles, they will exploit the need for them. For him this is a generic operation since the same thing happens in politics and between men and women sexually. But this is part of life, and because it is part of life, 'restitution cannot yield unthinkingly to the instinct in favour of relief for compulsion'.[12] These are all claims about the

---

8   *Ibid*, p 133.
9   *Ibid*, p 140.
10 Birks (1985) splits non-voluntary transfers into four: '(a) I did not know, (b) I was mistaken, (c) I was compelled, and (d) I was unequal.' This can be further elaborated by a division into five: (i) duress, (ii) actual compulsion, (iii) legal compulsion, (iv) moral compulsion, and (v) circumstantial compulsion.
11 *Ibid*, p 173.
12 *Ibid*, p 174.

nature of the social actor and the social world. They are essentially open to argument, but this theory of restitution refuses to engage in any argument.

The theory of the social world, as marked by compulsion, is a particular vision of how scarce resources are protected and utilised. It is as if there is a hard-wired human nature that makes compulsion necessary. Thus, any inequalities are lamentable, but, on the whole, beyond our control. However, as the argument develops, it appears that restitution is both linked to this logic and separate from it. So the task which complicates the law of restitution's reaction is the need to draw a line between pressures which are and pressures which are not normal and acceptable incidents of social life. Can this line be held? Surely, this statement demands a more elaborate theoretical notion of social life, at the very least. However, these themes are not developed as such. They become problems of demarcation, related to the tracing of the disciplinary boundaries of restitution. Boundaries have to be carefully maintained to prevent the collapsing of the discipline into ideological argument. Acceptable ways of enriching oneself are said to be difficult to draw because the drawing of the line then depends to a certain extent on society's own fluctuating moral evaluation of itself as competitive and individualistic or as collectivist and restrained.[13] What appears to underlie restitution is, thus, a political boundary, a value judgment that forces us to think about the way in which the independent will of the economic actor operates.

Restitution is thus defined by a fluctuating line, an instability that connects it with wider questions about the forms of the social world. This is perhaps the central insight into restitution's unconscious. Restitution is disturbed, as its foundations are inseparable from political ideas about 'moral evaluation'. Any division of the subject, any commentary or explanation, is thus always a discourse on political value choices. To open up this issue, we need to be able to see restitution as a field marked by conflict, struggle and irresolution. The demand for settled principles may tend towards the erasure of these tensions, but the field is still composed by the way in which they are submerged or downplayed. To develop this argument, we need to pursue a reading of the undue influence cases that employs a more explicit and critical economic perspective. This means connecting the cases with their historical and material context. The earlier cases concern colonial fortunes, or inherited wealth gained from the first manifestations of industrialisation. The later cases tend to show a different picture: matrimonial property riding as collateral for family businesses; agreements between different generations as to the care of the elderly; victims of stock market crashes.[14] What drives Birks' work on restitution may be an attempt to explain and justify the operation of the law in these difficult areas. Any proposed design of the subject may only be provisional because, as Hedley claims, restitution is organised, ultimately, by a question of 'how resources are to be allocated between individuals'.[15] These are essentially questions about 'the market and its regulation'.[16] How, though, can these tensions be exploited in a feminist direction?

At this point we need to make an imaginative and intellectual leap.

---

13 *Ibid*, p 174.
14 See *CIBC Mortgages v Pitt* [1994] 1 AC 200.
15 Hedley (2001, p 8).
16 *Ibid*, p 27.

The symbolic economy of restitution

How can feminist economics assist us in an understanding of the tensions that we have discovered in restitution? We need to ask questions about the very structure of the economy and its underpinning, the rational subject of freewill.[17]

The key issue for feminist economics is the very idea of rational exchange, a seminal idea for restitution, as we saw above. The problem for feminist economics is showing how the rational actor is not a universal, rational creature, but a construction that serves a particular political order.[18] How can this creation of the economic actor and the economic order be elaborated? We need to look into the mystery of the subject's relations to the object.

Subject-object relations are perhaps where economics and psychoanalysis touch.[19] In producing an account of economic operations that tend to be predicated on a male subject encountering objects, feminist economists have had recourse to psychoanalytical insights. Most recently, this has moved towards a questioning of the very form of property.[20]

Property serves as a way of concretely individuating its owners as subjects who own objects. Exchange of these objects allows mutual recognition. It would appear that the law is a 'central'[21] moment in this realisation of subjectivity. Law's necessity is born of this need for a mediation between subjects who recognise each other as such.

---

17 Nelson (1996, p 35) suggests that one focus for feminist economics might be to consider the 'study of markets with an eye to their social and institutional character, instead of always starting from the view that they are more or less corrupted versions of idealized (perfectly competitive, perfect information) markets'. One aspect of this would be to examine the notion of 'economic man' that underlies this model: he is an autonomous independent self-motivated by utility or personal happiness. Nelson refers to Sen's notion of 'capability' to re-orientate the study of economics towards the question of what utilisation of resources 'allows a person to be or do', and accepts that persons are rooted in different social contexts. Although Nelson's work addresses development theory, it has an obvious parallel with feminist scholars.

18 See Feiner (1995) who draws attention to the 'repressed femininity which is at the core of the neoclassical fantasy' (p 159), and reinterprets Marx's equation of the circulation of capital as mother-child-mother. The risk is that a focus on exchange draws attention away from production and from the domestic as the site of production.

19 Or, could object relations theory provide economists with a notion of interiority? Certainly Freud's own understanding of the drive and the object was to do with the interface between the world of interiority and the external world; the potentially confounding observation that people live simultaneously in an external and internal world. The theory concerns 'exploring the relationship between real, external people and internal images and residues of relations with them, and the significance of these residues for psychic functioning' (Greenberg, 1983, p 12). This approach could clearly be extended to further the Marxist notion that alienation is the product of a situation where a relationship between people has become a relationship between things. Other developments, particularly through Lacanian and Kleinian theory, could be traced in Deleuze and Guattari (1983).

20 Schroeder (1998, p xvii).

21 *Ibid*, p 50.

So, it may be that law and economy are two moments where exchange is created and then policed as a structure necessary to subjectivity.[22] In psychoanalytical theory this has tended to be associated with the notion of male subjectivity as created through the exchange of women as objects. This describes the social ritual where marriage joins kin groups together. In Western culture, this has tended to be patriarchal. The married son comes of age and enters into the community of men.[23] Historically, women were explicitly excluded from membership of this community.[24] Denying women property rights is the correlate of this exclusion. If women were to have rights they would become subjects, and hence no longer the objects exchanged between male subjects:

> ... the son sees himself and the Father as being mutually constituted as subjects through the exchange of the objects of desire. Each recognises the other as a subject objectified through objects of desire ... through this symbolic exchange ... the community of subjects is created ...[25]

This, then, is an insight into the constitution of the social through a symbolic economy or a set of exchanges that are fundamental to the perpetuation of the order of property and the social order itself. It would be easy to show that it continues to exert a hold over the law of property. Law and equity have traditionally resisted, or given begrudging concession, to the rights of a wife against her husband.[26]

If this notion of the social order is developed, it can give us a more thorough grounding of the underpinnings of the order of property and hence the order of restitution. At once, though, we have to make a distinction between different levels of analysis. Psychoanalysis is concerned with a symbolic economy and its operation. The analysis above is concerned with a sense of historical origin: a discovery of structures that can be found in the sacred and religious beginnings of the organisation of society. Psychoanalysis would be concerned with revealing the traces of these deep structures in everyday behaviour, but we do need to be careful in moving from the 'structural account' to a study of the forms of law and their operation in daily life.

In studying restitution, we are not looking at a subject that is predicated on the need to deprive women of their property. Indeed, undue influence is focused on gifts of property or commercial operations where women have been victimised and deprived of property interests. We are thus concerned with an ideological shift in

---

22 One could go on to talk of masculine and feminine positions of subjectivity. This is also an attempt to reposition the debate within feminism about female subjectivity. It moves on from any claim that there is an essential position that creates men and women as repositories of certain urges or abilities. Any sense of biology is over-encoded; we are concerned with the construction of gender through various cultural and symbolic indexes such as language, property and law. Indeed, there is a risk in associating symbolic notions of the male and female with the bodies onto which these terms are mapped. This is a sophisticated and complex theory, and the confines of space mean that we can elaborate a concern with only a single aspect.

23 Schroeder (1998, p 92).

24 For an elaboration of this position, see Aristodemou (2000, pp 29–56).

25 Schroeder (1998, p 83).

26 See, eg, the discussion in *National Provincial Bank v Ainsworth* [1965] AC 1175. Lord Wilberforce pointed out that, with the exception of certain statutory interventions, English law has 'given to the wife no interest or participation in her husband's property'.

the law. In the early modern and modern periods, the dominant forms of the ideology of the family limited female being to the domestic sphere. Despite this deprivation of full legal status, however, there was still the sense that women had a legal or economic function as the preservers of inherited wealth and the guarantors of a prosperous next generation. Control of female sexuality was bound up with this need to preserve an order of objects and lines of inheritance. The law of undue influence has its roots in sustaining this female role as the preserver of property. However, once the ideological space in which law operates has been changed so as to allow women to become full civic subjects and to hold property, the law must grapple with a profound problem. How are women to be constituted as legal beings?

The notion of the subject of free will, the economic actor, appears essential to this constitution of female legal subjectivity. We need to define those instances where one can be said not to be operating as an agent. One can thus be legitimately excused from transactions that appear formally correct in certain circumstances. The key issue is how the line between a legitimate and an illegitimate transfer can be drawn. Our concern is not so much an exclusion as the positioning of distinction that allows something to count and something to be found wanting. Tracking the development of this operation, we will see that the major problem in the contemporary law of undue influence is how to regulate the peripheral zone occupied by women. Law continues to constitute women as lying uncomfortably between full civic being and something less than rational, something to be sacrificed for a greater economic efficiency, a more global functioning.

Genealogies of undue influence

Psychoanalysis has always tried to read the most difficult of dream texts and engage with logics that are non-linear. If the truth is to be discovered, it is necessary to read against the grain. We need to borrow this method of tracking obscure or hidden meanings in reading case law. The following analysis, then, cannot be read as an exposition of the jurisprudence of actual and presumed undue influence. Moreover, it cannot pretend to analyse every important authority. We will consider a line of cases that takes us from *Huguenin v Basely*[27] to the decision in *Barclays Bank plc v O'Brien and Another*[28] and reveals the shifting contours of the law of undue influence. It will proceed as follows: after a brief review of some historically important authorities, we will begin our analysis with the most central case for the modern law, *Allcard v Skinner*.[29] We will see that the problems of this case continue into the key modern authorities, *National Westminster Bank v Morgan*[30] and *Barclays Bank plc v O'Brien and Another*. We are tracing a particular problematic. How does the law of undue influence create female agency? How is undue influence constituted? What are the boundaries that determine this concept, and how does it relate to the interests of powerful economic actors such as banks and building societies?

---

27 (1807) 14 Ves Jun 273.
28 [1992] 4 All ER 983.
29 (1887) 36 Ch D 145.
30 [1985] 1 AC 686.

Consider one of the earliest authorities that figures in the contemporary case law: *Huguenin v Basely* reveals a concern with inheritance and family property. More concretely, the case is focused on the issue of the correct transmission of property and the role that women, as wives, play in this process. If a wife is to act in such a way that the distribution of family assets goes astray, the order of succession is jeopardised. No wonder law jealously controls women's property. Law's gentle concern and ministrations protect the role of the wife as the guarantor of continuity between generations and properties. However, the wife occupies a double role. She is the angel who can guarantee the preservation of the family and its fortune but, by the token of this special nature, also the dupe and the one easily deceived: the one who must be saved from the weakness of her own nature.

The foundations of the law of undue influence go beyond a consideration of women as wives. The key problem, though, is still the constitution of female agency; an issue writ large in *Allcard v Skinner*. Note, first of all, the players in the drama. Miss Allcard, a lady of substantial means, wished to do something for the poor. She was introduced by the Reverend Nihill to the sisterhood of St Mary's at the Cross and soon became an initiate of the order. Under the rules of the sisterhood, Miss Allcard had to take a vow of poverty and renounce her worldly possessions. She also had to acknowledge complete obedience to the lady superior. Obedience meant that no one outside the order was to be consulted without express permission. Although there was no compulsion for an initiate to leave property to the sisterhood, this was the expectation. Indeed, the sisters ultimately became the recipients of certain amounts of money and the dividends of railway stocks that had been held by Miss Allcard. It might be thought, then, that the case describes an order of women with a jurisdiction over itself. Those who join the order become subject to those rules; the order exists as a world apart from the world.[31]

Miss Allcard was with the sisterhood for a little over a decade before she decided to leave the order. She tried to revoke the gifts of her property made by will, and to recover the amounts that she had already given. The sisterhood contended that it was not the lawful owner of Miss Allcard's property. The law was thus being called upon to intervene and choose between its own rules and those to which the plaintiff had effectively bound herself. The court had to mediate between this self-governing female body, the 'law' of charity that they observed and the rules of the market that operate to a secular logic.

The court resolved this dilemma not by rejecting the rules of the order, but by re-inscribing them within its own economy of undue influence. For the court, the facts of the case could only be understood as a situation where there was a presumption that the donee had an influence over the donor. From this position, the economy of giving will be recast. There is, of course, no suggestion that Miss Allcard was deceived. She was, at the time of the gift, a professed sister and, as such, bound to render absolute submission to the defendant as superior of the sisterhood (Cotton, LJ). It did not matter that she had sought advice when she joined the order; the issue was that she was unable to seek independent advice once she was a member. She

---

31 The role of the Reverend Nihill, the sisterhood's treasurer, was to occupy the Limnic space between the order and the world. Miss Allcard's money was paid into an account in the Reverend's name, and amounts were drawn out to further the construction of a hospital.

was deprived of her agency. The promise made to the Reverend Nihill was thus unenforceable. The central point is that the order's jurisdiction appeared to oust that of the court. The spiritual is raised over the secular, the law of charity over the law of the market.

Lord Justice Lindley elaborated these points. Miss Allcard was 'infatuated' with the religious life, but she was not 'an imbecile'. She was acting of her own free will. It was not a question of the law preventing people from joining religious organisations. Criticism was directed at the rule that prevented outside contact without the Lady Superior's permission. That is what disturbed his Lordship:

> I have carefully examined the evidence to see how this rule practically worked, but I can find nothing on the subject. I can find nothing to shew one way or the other what would have been the effect, for example, of a request for leave to consult a friend, or to obtain legal or other advice respecting any disposition of property, or respecting leaving the sisterhood.[32]

The rule is unclear, or perhaps what is clear is a sense that Lindley LJ glimpsed: his fear of 'spiritual tyranny'. Note, then, how the famous articulation of the notion of undue influence occurs in this context. Folly is aligned with impudence or want of foresight. The court will not impugn this kind of transaction. Such transactions are thoroughly within the world of economy where people enter into relationships and either suffer the consequences or reap the rewards. The court wishes to protect against those acts that, in some ways, conflate two orders of behaviour. Devotional acts of giving, which cannot be questioned, are extreme and irrational: a failure of good sense. Undue influence is simply another way of describing a gift made for a motive that does not appear to be one that is rational and, as such, made in accordance with rules that the court can question.

Allcard v Skinner was decided in the context of the opposition of sacred and secular spaces, the conflict between different rules and economies. Miss Allcard was the figure of a certain removal from economy. Once she was subject to the rules of the order, she was in a sacred economy and separated from the secular world. Miss Allcard could make no further claim over her property. She could no longer enjoy it or dispose of it. Her rights were extinguished. Two different logics met head on in this case. From the wider literature, it might be suggested that a decision to become a nun could be synonymous with a refusal. In the analytic language of this chapter, it is a refusal to remain in an order of exchange where one has the status of an object. A more viable sense of self can be obtained in answering a religious calling, where one is subject to different prerogatives. However, in leaving the order, in asserting title to her property, Miss Allcard attempted to enter back into the secular economy. She was asking the law to resurrect her from civic death. The court was confronted with a difficulty. It could not disturb the law of charity, nor could it cede its jurisdiction to an alternative order. By basing undue influence on a notion of victimisation, they inscribed subjecthood on the palimpsest that is Miss Allcard. The potential to become a victim is inherent with the grant of legal subjectivity to the female. From this point on, the law must understand female subjectivity, or the female as property owner, as prone to victimisation. As we will see, it is as if this

---

32 *Allcard v Skinner* (1887) 36 Ch D 145, *per* Lindley, LJ, at p 178.

notion of victimisation is both too minimal and incapable of producing a workable regime for the protection of women's property. Victimisation, then, is perhaps a term that allows the court to hide the operation of a symbolic economy at the very moment that its dynamics are recognised. To build these concerns, we need to look at the contemporary law on undue influence.

The principle in *Allcard v Skinner* becomes mapped onto a new set of facts. This transformation reveals some startling similarities underlying the surface differences. In contemporary times, the law of undue influence comes to the fore in problems associated with sureties and mortgages. The issue of the amorous relationship re-inscribes the problems of the order that creates its own jurisdiction. Historically, law had a problem with the status of the 'private' matrimonial relationship as something that should be sacrosanct and unregulated. The modern period represents a significant reversal in this ideology, but problems remain. Law struggles with the issue of how to regulate a relationship that is founded on love and intimacy. At least in some senses, marriage is not a commercial agreement. To the extent that it is founded on love, and the fact that people can behave in irrational ways under the influence of an order that exists outside rational economy, the problem reappears. Love creates its own order of compulsion, its own rules and jurisdiction, which may victimise the weaker party. How does the contemporary law of undue influence rework the issues of *Allcard v Skinner*?

In *National Westminster Bank v Morgan*, the matrimonial home was purchased with two mortgages for which both parties assumed responsibility. One might have thought that this would give the couple an equal jurisdiction, a shared responsibility for the 'family assets' and their utilisation. However, Mrs Morgan had the misfortune to be married to 'an unreliable and improvident businessman' and became increasingly entangled in his messy financial dealings. There is undoubtedly a parallel between Mr Morgan's expansion of his business without a sustaining basis and the devalued emotional currency that is exchanged between husband and wife.

Mrs Morgan's concern is with the matrimonial home. When her husband redeemed the second mortgage and replaced it with a loan secured by a charge over the property in favour of the National Westminster Bank, she took legal advice and limited the scale of the borrowing. This must have affected her husband's finances, for he later gave the bank an unlimited personal guarantee to cover borrowings by his company. A couple of months later he sought another loan. Again, his wife took legal advice, refused to sign a mortgage agreement and the loan was refused. In her own words: '... he was furious with me and there was a terrible argument between him and me on the way home which left me very shaken.'[33] Problems developed with the first mortgage and the mortgagee threatened to begin proceedings for possession. Mr Morgan arranged a loan with the bank to refinance the mortgage. On the request of Mr Morgan, the bank manager brought the documents to the Morgan's home. In an L-shaped room, with Mr Morgan lurking at one end, Mrs Morgan signed the document. The bank manager, in error, advised her that the mortgage did not cover Mr Morgan's business borrowings. Some months after this interview, Mr. Morgan died. Mrs Morgan fell into arrears with the mortgage payments and the bank began proceedings for possession.

---

33 *National Westminster Bank v Morgan* [1851] 1 AC 686, at p 689.

The House of Lords disagreed with the Court of Appeal over the foundation of undue influence. In their view, the basis of undue influence is not abuse of confidence, but victimisation. This must be coupled to a notion of manifest disadvantage. Having deployed the language of victimisation, however, the court found that Mrs Morgan failed to qualify. It is as if the law glimpsed the terms of its operation, but then denied any meaningful sense to the insight. We therefore need to read the reasoning of the court from a different perspective. Our starting point is to ask about the etymology of the word victim. The root of the victimisation is associated with the sacred. The Latin *vicitime* is cognate with the Gothic *weihan*, to consecrate, and also relates to *weihs*, holy. Dictionary definitions of sacred expand on these meanings, describing the sacred as a living creature sacrificed to some deity, a person or thing destroyed or injured in the performance of such a right; a dupe, a gull. Elaborated through psychoanalytic theory, this might suggest that the notion of the victim is central to the process through which a subject becomes an object. We could also suggest that there is a linkage between the notion of the female as victim, and as sacrifice for the sustenance of a male order. As we saw above, psychoanalysis suggests that for the regime of property to operate, women must be exchanged as objects between men. Mrs Morgan is the sacrificial victim, the object that allows the 'male' business world to continue its fantastical operation. A submerged sacred register thus seems to underlie the everyday world of undue influence.

It is precisely this submerged economy that the law cannot see, or when the law at least catches a glimpse, it must turn away. We need to return to the Court of Appeal judgment in *Morgan* to elaborate this point. A broad and a narrow understanding of undue influence circulate in this case.[34] Both understandings return to the principle that it is not the court's place to set aside foolish or improvident deals, but to intervene in those situations where a party has been victimised. At stake between the Court of Appeal and the House of Lords, however, is the range of victimisation. The House of Lords preferred the narrow understanding, effectively limiting the scope of undue influence. Most importantly, however, the House of Lords could not accept the Court of Appeal's approach because it contained a true insight into the horrors of economy: the ease with which parties can be abused. Let us outline this argument. The reasoning of the Court of Appeal is supported by a passage of Sir Erich Sachs in *Lloyd;s Bank v Bundy*,[35] in which he returns to *Allcard v Skinner*. According to this, the basis for the court's intervention depends not so much on the basis that the donee has committed a 'wrongful act', but on policy grounds. There is a need to prevent relationships being 'abused'. Once it is possible to establish that there is a special relationship, as there

---

34 *Midland Bank v Shephard* [1988] 3 All ER 17 followed in the wake of *Morgan*. It shows how dramatically the case closed down the possibilities of argument in this field. When money was borrowed from the bank, although Mrs Shephard knew of the borrowings, she was not consulted and the transaction went ahead without her consent. The court gave Mrs Shephard's arguments short shrift. She could not show 'fraudulent misrepresentation ... or ... some fraudulent concealment' (p 23). What clinches this approach is that the parties were still living together as man and wife, and that Mr Shephard swore affidavits in defence of his wife. This seemed to negate the suggestion that there was fraud, and is based on the assumption that if the marriage is ongoing then there can be no sense in which it is abusive.

35 [1974] 3 All ER 757.

is in *Morgan* between the bank manager and Mrs Morgan, then any use of information obtained is an abuse, unless the duty holder can show that the 'transaction is for the benefit of the person influenced'. This policy ground is neither dependent on showing that one party dominated the other nor on evidencing 'wrongful intention' on the part of the stronger party who gains the benefit. It rests on the notion of a 'special relationship'. If it is possible to convince the court that a special relationship exists, then the stronger party would have to show that the 'fiduciary duty of care' has been honoured.

The term 'abuse' figures in this context. If it is possible to show that there is a special relationship, then any possible use of the relevant information is, irrespective of the intentions of the persons possessing it, regarded in relation to the transaction under consideration as an abuse.[36] As Lord Justice Dunn pointed out, the mortgage itself was a 'possible abuse' of the relationship between Mrs Morgan and the bank, as it made her liable for the very thing that her actions throughout the scenario tried to avoid: liability for her husband's borrowings.

However, 'abuse' could also describe the actions of the bank in this case. *Morgan* shows that the bank gained an advantage from the remortgaging arrangement as banks are not charitable institutions, and the area office would not have approved the transaction unless it considered it to be for the benefit of the bank and its shareholders. Is the actuality of the situation glimpsed further still in the detailed acknowledgment of the peculiarity of this sort of relationship? There can be no question of a 'business relationship' – of people dealing at arm's length. The very fact that the bank manager arrived at the couple's home shows that this transaction went beyond the normal relationship of bank and customer. In this sense, there has been 'abuse' of the relationship. The word 'abuse' itself returns to the sense in which undue influence cases are bound up with property, objectification and the nature of gendered subjectivity. To abuse is not to use in a proper manner: a manner that is suitable to the 'object' – the term already, then, seems to negotiate the sense in which a person has become an object, has become victimised.[37]

We can read a continuation of these tensions in *O'Brien*.[38] The exclusion of husband and wife from the category of presumed undue influence, which raises the presumption as a matter of law, can be seen as part of a subtle argument that maintains the status quo whilst appearing to offer an even-handed approach to the issue. The relationship between husband and wife falls within a category whereby the complainant would have to establish that she had placed confidence in her husband. Of course, this means that the complaining party has the burden, first of all, of showing that the relationship was one of trust and confidence. Some might argue that the law would be set on a better foundation if it were immediately

---

36 The only way of negating this presumption would be to show that the fiduciary duty had been fulfilled or that the transaction is for the benefit of the person influenced.

37 *Goldsworthy v Brickell* [1987] 1 All ER 853, at least as far as the English case law is concerned, represents a form of qualification of *Morgan*. Although the notion of manifest disadvantage remains, a possible extension of the *Morgan* test is resisted. The foundation of undue influence is linked to a notion of abuse of trust or confidence, rather than domination.

38 In *Barclays Bank plc v O'Brien and Another* [1992] 4 All ER 983, the question of undue influence was not directly applicable, although it did underlie the questions of misrepresentation that were considered. There is insufficient space in this chapter to consider the post-*O'Brien* case law.

presumed that undue influence was exercised. What is also of importance in *O'Brien* is Lord Browne-Wilkinson's use of economic arguments. The matrimonial home is a major source of investment. To prevent the investment becoming sterile, the law must recognise that it cannot make it too difficult for this wealth to become invested in business ventures. This line of reasoning appears to recognise that the social position of women has changed to some extent but that, in practice, wives still rely on their husbands for advice in financial matters. Wives can look to the court for protection. However, the court cannot be too sympathetic to wives and impose rules that make it too difficult for institutional lenders to take the matrimonial home as security. It might be suggested that *O'Brien* ultimately affirms the sacrificial economy that runs through the other cases that we have examined.

What conclusions can we draw from this reading? The terms of the Court of Appeal judgment in *Morgan* are arguably more useful to feminist argument, as the version of undue influence is broader than the House of Lords judgment and strategically more useful in defence of women in relationships where they have been pressured into signing sureties,[39] but there is a broader point that can be made here as well. To return to a theme developed above, psychoanalytic studies, or at least those worth reading, have always drawn attention to the malleability of our controlling concepts. We cannot surrender to monolithic instances. However, any alternative development of the law must, to return to our earlier theme, also determine a boundary that will define undue influence. In turning to look at the alternative approaches to the constitution of undue influence, our concern is with how the problematic inherited from the earlier cases becomes reinterpreted. The challenge for the law is to take seriously the amorous space of the relationship, to develop concepts that might be able to make this count against other expressions of value.

The Commonwealth courts have, to some extent, been active in furthering an alternative jurisprudence of undue influence; but how do the problems of definition reappear in this law? One important, critical strand of the arguments against *Morgan* has stressed that a finding of undue influence must not be based on the need to show that the disadvantage to the weaker party was extreme. Undue influence may thus be found where a transaction was for 'reasonably equal benefits'.[40] This would relocate the entire structure of undue influence. It would cover a wider range of relationships where such an extreme economy of manifest disadvantage does not operate.[41]

We could link this argument to a related attempt to redraw the conceptual structures of the subject. A distinction is proposed between commercial relations and those whose 'sanctity' needs to be maintained. Undue influence is set to protect

---

39 A thorough review of this position would have to take into account *BCCI v Aboody* [1992] 4 All ER 955, and an engagement with the classification of actual and presumed undue influence. *Aboody* held that manifest disadvantage was a requirement for both forms of undue influence.

40 Cope (1986, p 97).

41 Cope (1986) also argued that Lord Scarman's use of confidentiality is inappropriate as it blurs the boundary of undue influence and the doctrine of abuse of confidence. Lord Scarman's construction of undue influence does not show that more must be established than merely a confidential relationship to raise the presumption. A relationship of influence does not necessarily follow from the fact that one party has some measure of influence over the other, or even that trust is reposed in that other (p 93).

the 'integrity' of the weak and momentarily weak. In *Geffen v Goodman*,[42] the law is developed so as to protect people from fraud or gifts made under coercion. In the latter instance, the court preserves the 'sanctity' of contracts, and will only intervene if there is evidence of manifest unfairness. From this position, neither confidence nor reliance can adequately describe the relationships that give rise to the presumption. The key term is 'domination', whether through 'manipulation, coercion or outright but subtle abuse of power'.[43] Domination, though, seems to be of elastic definition so that it can include the exercising of a 'persuasive influence'. Accompanying this is a qualification of the notion of manifest disadvantage. Establishing undue influence must begin with the relationship between the claimant and the defendant; the crucial question is whether there is a potential for domination inherent in the relationship.

How easy is it to determine between commercial and non-commercial contexts? It may be that the failure to hold this line between such contexts suggests that there are still unresolved tensions in this alternative vision of undue influence. Where the doctrine of manifest disadvantage has met with acceptance,[44] the distinction suggested in *Geffen v Goodman* does not seem to hold. May this be because it is impossible to say where the 'commercial' ends, and where the 'sanctified' sphere of the domestic begins? Certainly, on the facts of *Contractors Bonding v Snee*,[45] we can appreciate that familial bonds are exploited for commercial gain. In this case, the sacrificial role was played by an alcoholic and senile mother, Mrs Snee, who '… had a strong attachment to her family and was likely to agree to any proposal put to her by a member of the family whether or not it was in her own interests'.[46] She was persuaded by her son to place her house as collateral for borrowings to fund a business venture. When the business collapsed, the lender commenced proceedings for possession of Mrs Snee's property. Her argument based on undue influence failed. So, a mentally infirm lady who could only understand legal matters in the 'most superficial way'[47] and who had no real appreciation of the nature of the documents she signed or of the consequences of her action lost her only asset. What lies behind this conclusion is undoubtedly a policy consideration. Commercial lenders should not be 'fixed' with the misdeeds of third parties, unless those third parties are acting as their agents.[48] The extension of the law in this sense indicates that one of the limits of undue influence must be its operation in a market where fluidity of assets is preferred to their protection. In such a space it is unrealistic to claim that a line can be usefully maintained between the commercial and the non-commercial.

The amorous space and intimate space of the family remain a perturbation in the law of undue influence. To refer back to an earlier argument, it may be that these ambiguities reflect tensions within the court's understanding of the constitution of

---

42 *Geffen v Goodman* 81 DLR (4th) 225.

43 *Ibid*, p 227.

44 Burrows and McKendrick (1997, p 385).

45 [1992] 2 NZLR 157.

46 *Ibid*, p 161.

47 *Ibid*, p 161.

48 *Ibid*, p 171.

the half commercial, half amorous zone of modern relationships. However, this is not to suggest that greater strategic possibilities may be opened up by the Commonwealth cases.[49] Even if the dividing line between the commercial and the familial is difficult to draw, then these tensions can be deployed to ends that might further the protection of women's interests.

Perhaps this represents an alternative version of undue influence, a re-inscription of its tensions in a way so as to make for different political consequences, but one has to be careful. One cannot proceed on the basis that there is a realm of the home or the amorous sphere that is completely inured from 'contamination' from the commercial sphere. Such an inscription of the commercial and the non-commercial perhaps returns in a problematic way to a notion of separate spheres, with their different rules and economies.[50] What is required is an awareness that the amorous relationship, and the matrimonial home, are regulated spheres. This regulation must take note of the need to determine a boundary for undue influence that acknowledges the pressures placed on women by powerful commercial actors. There are hints of a possible argument in *O'Brien*. Surely the 'rich' banks have the resources necessary to make sure that the threat of unjust transactions is made as minimal as possible? Ultimately, it is perhaps too soon to say whether the law of restitution and the principles of undue influence can be re-inscribed, opened to a different economy. However, refusing to see the possibilities of progressive legal development is as great a strategic mistake as affirming a monolithic conceptual structure of undue influence.[51]

---

49 See, eg, *Garcia v National Australian Bank* (1989) 72 ALJR 1242 and the resurrection of the 'special equity theory' (sufficient action was taken to ensure that this does not invalidate the transaction). The Australian approach is the reversal of *O'Brien*: the transaction is invalid until proved otherwise. The objections to this approach return to Lord Browne-Wilkinson's arguments: such a stringent test would make institutional lenders reluctant to lend on the collateral provided by the matrimonial home. Moreover, at a doctrinal level this approach may be wrong as it bases itself on unconscionability, which is not the same as undue influence. Even though these objections could be countered and, arguably, the *Garcia* approach may in certain ways be more useful for feminist legal argument, perhaps taking sides would obscure a more disturbing issue. We remain within an economy where certain interests will be preferred to others.

50 For an elaboration of these themes, see England (1993). The economic actors are imagined as 'autonomous, impervious to social influences, and lack sufficient emotional connection to each other to make empathy possible' (p 37). It is then assumed that men act altruistically in the family, creating a dichotomy between the analysis of commercial behaviour and family behaviour.

51 In terms of a model of the family, it moves away from the conventional model that sees a patriarchal head who superintends the wealth maximisation of the family unit. This model makes conflict largely invisible. The new model would see the family in terms of 'co-operative conflict' over 'competing priorities'. These priorities are understood as 'living standards, agency and affiliation'. The first term can be understood as the welfare one gets from goods and the use of one's time, the ability of each person to recognise and promote his or her interests. Most interestingly, affiliation 'represents the need of human beings to belong and to be loved'. A legal dispute can be thought of, in economic terms, as a conflict between these conflicting priorities; thus, affiliation, to act for love, may be disadvantageous in other terms – the standard of living or one's own agency. If this is imported into the law of undue influence, it suggests that one should not be privileging commercial interests that tend to be associated with the needs of institutional lenders. Various compromises are made to preserve the integrity of the family unit by women who sacrifice their agency to this rather than to the pursuit of commercial opportunity. Even if the case law is to stick with a notion of manifest disadvantage, it could be more usefully thought through this model.

Conclusion: Reverend Nihill, it was really nothing

Perhaps undue influence leaves everything in place. Let us return to Birks' definition:

> To speak of restitution for inequality must be short hand for ... it means that there is restitution in cases of exceptional or abnormal inequality ... [this] leaves intact the proposition that there is no question of restitution for ordinary run of the mill inequalities.[52]

Undue influence is a shorthand that leaves some people short. It appears that we need to think in terms of 'exceptional inequalities'.[53] Scholarship informed by feminism attempts to delineate a general inequality that underlies specific inequalities, but can undue influence open itself to this reversal? The legacy of *Allcard v Skinner* can be glimpsed in the grappling of the contemporary case law with the question of the value of certain acts. In this way, the problem of the jurisdiction of the sisterhood, of the female space, becomes the question of the family and, most specifically, the family home. Obviously, this is not the same issue as that of charity and giving to a religious order. Our present concern is not with the divesting of property, but with the need to stake a claim over a material asset. How can an act of commitment to another be protected? How can an act of devotion, of love, or passion warrant legal protection? It is necessary to stress, at this point, that this argument is not about to raise a romantic notion of the family, or the work of the lovers, against the cold calculations of the law. Rather, it is to suggest that we must read and work within the law to see those tensions or moments that can open to different economies: impossible calculations.

References

Aristodemou, M, *Law and Literature*, 2000, Oxford: OUP

Birks, P, *An Introduction to the Law of Restitution*, 1985, Oxford: Clarendon Press

Burrows, A, *The Law of Restitution*, 1993, London: Butterworths

Burrows, A and McKendrick, E, *Cases and Materials on the Law of Restitution*, 1997, Oxford: OUP

Cope, M, 'Undue influence and alleged manifest disadvantageous transactions: *National Westminster Bank plc v Morgan*' (1986) 60 *The Australian Law Journal*, February, pp 87–97

Deleuze, G and Guattari, F, *Anti Oedipus*, 1983, London: The Athlone Press

England, P, 'The separative self: androcentric bias in neoclassical assumptions', in Ferber, MA and Nelson, JA (eds), *Beyond Economic Man, Feminist Theory and Economics*, 1993, Chicago, IL: Chicago UP

---

52 Birks (1985, p 17).

53 Birks (1985, p 204). It would be necessary to extend this analysis to the decision in *Royal Bank of Scotland v Etridge (No 2)* [2001] UKHL 44. The distinction between everyday and exceptional inequality may offer an important problematic for this case.

Feiner, S, 'Reading neoclassical economics; toward an erotic economy of sharing', in Kuiper, E and Sap, J, with Feiner, S, Ott, N and Tzannatos, Z, *Out of the Margin: Feminist Perspectives on Economics*, 1995, London and New York: Routledge

Greenberg, JR and Mitchell, SA (eds), *Object Relations in Psychoanalytic Theory*, 1983, Cambridge, MA: Harvard UP

Hedley, S, *A Critical Introduction to Restitution*, 2001, London: Butterworths

Hedley, S, *Restitution: Its Division and Ordering*, 2001a, London: Sweet & Maxwell

Jameson, F, *The Political Unconscious: Narrative as a Socially Symbolic Act*, 1981, Ithaca, NY: Cornell UP

Nelson, JA, *Feminism, Objectivity and Economics*, 1996, London: Routledge

Schroeder, J, *The Vestal and the Fasces*, 1998, Berkeley, CA: California UP

Virgo, G, *The Principles of the Law of Restitution*, 1999, Oxford: OUP

Chapter 6
Different Space, Same Place? Feminist Perspectives on Contracts in Cyberspace

Bela Bonita Chatterjee[1]

Introduction – the need for feminist perspectives?

The advent of cyberspace has given rise to new challenges and debates for the legal world, and even the most traditional areas of law are finding that they have to consider its effects. For the law, cyberspace is seen in a technical, functional sense: a kind of tool that has useful social applications. On this technical understanding, cyberspace is the virtual 'space' that is created by computer networks. The global framework of computers that creates this space is known as the internet (interconnected network). Using the metaphor of the body, the internet represents the backbone. This 'backbone' of interconnected computers supports a number of services, such as email and the World Wide Web. The World Wide Web is the system that links together electronic documents (or 'web pages'). Digital information and communication is the lifeblood of the system, and networked computers represent fixed points of entry.[2]

To cite Akdeniz, Walker and Wall, cyberspace, this once 'prosaic set of wires and switches' has now become 'a fast growing emblem of national and economic activity'.[3] Several important and sometimes unique qualities have caused it to emerge as a key commercial space. Due to its ability to transcend national borders, the instantaneous nature of communication in cyberspace and apparently easy access,[4] the importance of cyberspace as a zone of commerce has been at the forefront of contemporary political and legal policy. The advent of e-commerce has meant that cyberspace is, according to Murray, the fastest growing commercial marketplace in the world.[5] Broadly speaking, e-commerce describes all commercial activities supported through and by computers, but for the purposes of contract law, e-commerce translates as contracting using computers.[6] In response to the new marketplace of cyberspace, the perceived task of contract law is to maintain and reinforce the mechanisms of trust and security that underpin business and consumer transactions.

---

1 School of Law, Lonsdale College, Lancaster University. Acknowledgments: with thanks to Rosemary Auchmuty, Sarah Beresford, Sefton Bloxham, Dave Campbell, Megan Comfort, Fiona Cownie, Alison Diduck, Mike Doupé, Tatiana Flessas, Adam Gearey, Martina Gillen, Mathias Klang, Philip Lawton, Linda Mulcahy, Sally Wheeler and David Seymour for their support and encouragement, observations and help regarding earlier drafts of this chapter. Extra special thanks to Madeleine Jowett. (Of course, full responsibility for any errors remains with me.) I would also like to thank my Business Law group at Lancaster for journeying through contract law with me so patiently over the period of 2001–02.

2 This metaphor is borrowed from Batty and Barr (1994, pp 699–712). See, further, Terrett and Monaghan (2000, pp 1–16); Akdeniz, Walker and Wall (2000, pp 3–24); Chatterjee (2001, pp 80–83); Kohl (1999, pp 123–49).

3 Akdeniz, Walker and Wall (2000, p 3).

4 Akdeniz, Walker and Wall (2000).

5 Murray (2000); see also Abe, Sabet and Gall (2001); and Keey (2001).

6 Halson (2001); see further Nicoll (1998).

Given that there has been an emphasis on establishing cyberspace as a contractual space, the academic take, to date, has largely been to analyse e-contracts (that is, contracts made in cyberspace) and related legislation using a doctrinal approach. As Nicoll has written, 'judges and lawyers (both academic and practising) instinctively seek correlation between practice and doctrine, whether by making cases fit doctrine or doctrine fit cases' (Nicoll, 1998, p 36). Writers on contract thus tend to analyse contracts in cyberspace by using traditional methods, such as establishing offer and acceptance.[7] The general opinion appears to be that contracts in cyberspace will pose no drastically new problems or considerations for contract lawyers. As Murray argues, the law has managed to cope with every new communications medium so far, and cyberspace should be no exception: 'The law has, to date, dealt with the advent of the Royal Mail, the telephone, telex and fax machine. There is no reason to suppose the development of e-mail or the World Wide Web will affect in any way the application of the current principles of contract law' (Murray, 2000, p 18). The question for academic writers on contracts in cyberspace is not, therefore, whether these contracts are authoritative as forms of contract, but rather whether and how they meet the legal requirements of contractual form.

If cyberspace is seen as an extension of the public contractual sphere, essentially no different from the traditional marketplace, then the doctrinal approach provides a perfectly adequate analysis. The methodology of finding correlation between practice and doctrine provides a closed set of alternative answers to choose from, and no further questions have to be asked. However, in this chapter I wish to challenge and critique the current approach that contract law takes in relation to cyberspace. Using a feminist lens, I wish to re-examine this encounter in order to politicise the current doctrinal debates and to shed light on their hidden gendered dimensions. As recent feminist writers on cyberspace have suggested, it is misleading to see cyberspace simply as a neutral, technical space.[8] Cyberspace can be read not only as an economic space, but also as a political, fluid and liminal space where power relationships have the potential to be reinforced but also reconfigured. Feminist perspectives on e-contracts could therefore valuably see contracts and contract law as involving more than technical questions of form or financial interests; in other words, also be conceived of as involving relationships, power and inequality.

Feminists have already critiqued the doctrinal association of contracts with the public sphere, and this critique could be usefully extended to the doctrinal approach of seeing cyberspace as an extension of this sphere. Feminists have argued that the focus on the public sphere serves to exclude contracts associated with the private 'feminine' sphere, such as the marriage contract (Pateman, 1988; Brown, 1996; Goodrich, 1996). The marriage contract is an example frequently used by feminists to show how contracts structure gender relations – and how, indeed,

---

7 See, for example, Smith (2002); Poole (2001); Richards (2002); Murray (2000); Dickie (1998). This approach is also reflected in American and Canadian commentary, as seen in Winn and Wright (2002) and Abe, Sabet and Gall (2001).

8 See Kramarae and Kramer (1995); Kramarae (1997); Singh (2001); Wakeford (2000); Warnick (1999); Hawthorne and Klein (1999); Chatterjee (2001). See also Wall (2002) for a similar, but not overtly feminist, argument.

gender relations structure contracts. A focus on gender and sexual contracts might bring feminist legal commentators on e-contracts to note the relationship of women to such contracts, both as sexual subjects and objects: as consumers and consumed. Whereas this key point is concealed by a doctrinal analysis, a feminist perspective on e-contracts clearly reveals e-commerce and sexual commerce to be inextricably connected and worthy of emphasis. Feminist perspectives on contracts in cyberspace raise questions about the new political economies of cyberspace that are emerging, and ask who gets to access the flow of information capital and online commodities.[9]

However, in addition to highlighting the problems of the doctrinal analysis in respect of its focus on the public sphere, a feminist analysis of contracts in cyberspace might go further. Feminist perspectives might consider alternative understandings of cyberspace, and use these as the point of departure for their analyses. This involves a reconsideration of how law understands cyberspace, and what the position of women might be in relation to this space. For the purposes of a doctrinal analysis, cyberspace is an uncomplicated space, a medium that poses no novel problems. Yet if cyberspace is understood as a fluid, postmodern space, then it is a new, unpredictable space: a space literally and figuratively without precedent. This is a space where a doctrinal analysis cannot help us as we do not know what will happen next, and what has gone before is not the same. If all contracts are understood to structure our relationships, including those of gender, then might contracts made in the postmodern, unstable space of cyberspace enable these relationships to be refigured?[10]

Feminist perspectives focus particularly on power and gender, but I am aware that gender is woven into a broader matrix of identity markers. If it is accepted that identity is a social construction, then one is not only marked as gendered, but also marked by different categories. For example, one may also be marked by ethnicity, age, sexuality, class, (dis)ability, region or religion, to name but a few. Gender is not the only way we describe ourselves and for some it may not be the most important signifier. Moreover, a choice of focus on gender should not be read as suggesting that gender has an inherent homogeneity. Feminist commentators are aware that making sweeping claims about gender can serve to obscure key differences that exist between women in their own right.

However, a focus on gender can bring both powerful and positive insights, as Adam and Green comment: 'In some circles, it is assumed that we are in a post feminist era when the battles have been won and continuing to make explicit inequalities in gender is unnecessary … [however] one can still acknowledge existing inequalities, whilst performing an analysis which is upbeat and optimistic' (Adam and Green, 2001, p 4). As contract law comes under a heightened focus due to the advent of e-commerce, it seems particularly important that the understanding that the law has of e-contracts be as deep as possible. At the time of writing, the law of contract in cyberspace is very much an emergent area and by no means legally

---

9   The point that new political economies, which reconfigure power relationships, have emerged in cyberspace has previously been argued by Wall (2002, p 191). However, Wall does not investigate these economies from a gender perspective.

10 I wish to thank Sally Wheeler, Linda Mulcahy, Adam Gearey, Dave Campbell and Tatiana Flessas for discussion on this point.

certain in terms of substantive law, choice of law and jurisdictional issues.[11] For these reasons, perhaps, commentary in texts on contract law does not tend to be extensive. Even in the renowned 'heavyweight' texts such as Beale's latest edition of *Chitty on Contracts* (Beale, 2002) and *Cheshire, Fifoot and Furmston's Law of Contract* (Furmston, 2001), where one might expect substantial mention of e-contracts, discussion is minimal.[12] This is a position that surely must change, given the increasing importance of e-contracting as described above, but as it is still formative, now is arguably an ideal time for feminist arguments to influence the legal discourse. The need for legal understanding informed by feminist theory goes to the very heart of the function of the law. Ultimately, what should the function of contract law be? Perhaps given a more contextualised and grounded analysis, the law could move from being a mere framework for commerce to a facilitator of justice.

Challenging the doctrinal analysis: same place?

I The emphasis on contract as commerce

As I mentioned in my introduction, the rationale for contract law in cyberspace is to maximise the market potential. The close linkage between contract and commerce has traditionally underwritten contract law doctrine, and the association can clearly be seen in discussions of classical contractual theory. Atiyah, for example, notes that contract law has been seen as being largely concerned with the facilitation of economic exchange; 'free and voluntary exchange', he argues, 'is generally a simple but critically important method of increasing purchaser satisfaction, and even of increasing a community's wealth'.[13] Moreover, such 'free exchange' governs how this wealth is distributed through society (Atiyah, 1995, pp 4–5). Although modern contract theories have moved away from the idea of the absolute freedom of contract as witnessed by the growth in consumer protection measures,[14] the need to establish trust and certainty in order to foster business transactions still remains as a key rationale for contract law today.[15]

This emphasis on the role of contract as a framework for upholding commerce and the idea of free exchange can be seen in current legal policy on e-commerce. The main objectives of recent e-commerce directives at European Union (EU) level and related UK legislation have been to firmly establish cyberspace as a contractual space. This has been achieved by proposing the harmonisation of existing national legislation on e-commerce, as seen in the Directive on Electronic Commerce

---

11 See, further, the commentary by Murray (2000, pp 31–34); Torremans (2000, pp 225–46); and Mitrani (2001, pp 50–60) (EU and US perspectives). The chapter by Torremans was written specifically in relation to intellectual property, but is nevertheless worth considering in the context of contract law. I do not discuss choice of law or jurisdiction issues in this chapter due to restraints of space.

12 In the latter the reader is directed to fuller discussion contained in other texts in a footnote (Furmston, 2001, p 56, n 10), but discussion in the body of the text itself would be desirable.

13 Atiyah (1995, p)4

14 See, eg, Furmston (2001, pp 23–24).

15 See, generally, Atiyah (1995, pp 1–36).

(E-Commerce Directive),[16] and facilitating contract laws that are conducive to e-commerce where they are needed.[17] Examples of the latter include the recent Consumer Protection (Distance Selling) Regulations[18] and the Electronic Communications Act.[19] At EU level, establishing and supporting cyberspace as a business and contractual space will apparently bring social as well as financial rewards, thus reflecting the idea of free exchange. As the E-Commerce Directive states, promoting the single electronic market (as part of the development of a wider 'information society') will bring new opportunities for smaller European enterprises, and will be key in eliminating 'the barriers which divide the European peoples'.[20] In order to foster such an environment, cyberspace must be promoted as a safe and welcoming space, and as policy statements at EU and national level reveal, nothing must be allowed to taint the safety and security of cyberspace. Pornography, for example, is considered to be damaging to e-commerce, as it deters potential 'legitimate' consumers, and must be suppressed in order to reassure them (Edwards, 2000, p 278); further measures to support secure transactions, such as extending consumer protection to internet purchases,[21] the recognition of digital signatures, the development of cryptography,[22] as well as policing measures,[23] have all been marshalled to increase consumer confidence in cyberspace.

At first glance, the emphasis on cyberspace as a public commercial space does not appear to be problematic. However, an initial point of criticism is that the concentration on the market reinforces the connection of contracts and contract law with the public sphere, the sphere of masculine power and interest.[24] As Brown has commented (1996, p 5):

> ... contract and the market are read as coextensive. The market sphere is also male in its monopoly and masculine in its manners. Perhaps nothing could better embody – or, more precisely, disembody – men's abstracted relations with each other than the model of the discrete transaction, usually taken to supply the focal meaning of the law of contract.

If masculine interests are represented by the market, then contract law in cyberspace, as in any other space, results in being little more than a study of masculine transactions. Contracts in cyberspace thus become abstracted from the gendered social and political contexts within which they exist. The law addresses only those who have reached the (public) sphere of contracting, agents who have therefore already achieved contractual capacity and can participate in Atiyah's 'free

---

16 European Parliament and Council Directive (2000/31/EC) on certain legal aspects of information society services, in particular electronic commerce, in the Internal Market. The date of compliance was 17 January 2002. See also the related provisions on intellectual property (European Parliament and Council Directive SN/2696/00 (PI) on harmonisation of certain aspects of copyright and related rights in the Information Society).

17 See Arts 9–15 of the E-Commerce Directive, which provide for this.

18 SI 2000/2334.

19 Electronic Communications Act 2000.

20 E-Commerce Directive 2000/31/EC Recitals (1) and (2).

21 See Consumer Protection (Distance Selling) Regulations, fn 13 above.

22 See Electronic Communications Act 2000. See, further, Hogg (2000, pp 37–54).

23 Regulation of Investigatory Powers Act 2000.

24 See, eg, Pateman (1988); Brown (1996); Goodrich (1996).

and voluntary exchange'. However, the law does not look further to ask who gets to enter this sphere in the first place. Feminist commentators have emphasised how women have traditionally been excluded from the public contractual sphere for various reasons: because the law has denied them the capacity to contract by means of their exclusion from the category of rational agents, through marriage, whereby their right to contract was nullified upon the marital contract, and through gendered legislation on employment and pay.[25] As I will argue below, the criticism that women face difficulties in becoming equal contractual agents still applies to contracts made in cyberspace.

Although the law is anxious to promote a 'free' marketplace in cyberspace, as seen above, it does nothing to promote access to that space, without which contracts cannot be entered into in the first place. As noted above, the E-Commerce Directive seeks to remove commercial barriers in cyberspace though removing *contractual* barriers, but this move fails to address the layers of inequality, whether social, political or economic, which also exist in relation to cyberspace. If the directive does not address these other aspects of inequality, it will fall well short of its other objective, that of eliminating the barriers which divide EU peoples. Commercial contracts in cyberspace represent transactions that can only be made by an elite few, but the point that cyberspace is *not* a free-market place is not considered or addressed either by the directive, domestic law or mainstream legal commentators. Recent feminist commentary on cyberspace has noted how cyberspace is a space dominated by masculine interests, partly due to differences in access. As Wakeford, quoting Winner, reports, whereas some women have managed to create 'pockets of resistance', in the main, 'overall the territories of the online world reflect the unreconstructed ideologies of the population of "white male cyberboors"'.[26] To contract in cyberspace, one first has to have access to it, and access is by no means democratic; feminist writers on cyberspace have noted that there are marked differences in access to cyberspace, not just in terms of gender, but also though global economic location.[27] As Kramarae has suggested, we need to be attentive to women's different economic position in relation to computers as well as their relative lack of access (Kramarae, 1997, p 2). Although women are increasingly positioned as consumers in relation to cyberspace, Warnick comments that due to their different economic and social position, women, particularly those with families that they are expected to look after, may not have the same disposable time or income that men have in order to become consumers, and therefore contractors, in cyberspace (Warnick, 1999, pp 8, 10). Poverty is both gendered and racialised, and Warnick cites a US consumer law study to illustrate that the poorest families tend to be non-white and cannot even afford a telephone, let alone a computer (Warnick, 1999, p 10). Her conclusion, quoting Coralee Whitcomb of the National Organisation for Women, is that 'for many adult women of today, access to computer and Internet literacy is simply out of their reach' (Warnick, 1999, p 8).

---

25 See, further, Pateman (1988); Brown (1996); Goodrich (1996).
26 Wakeford (2000, p 292).
27 See, eg, Kramarae and Kramer (1995); Kramarae (1997); Warnick (1999); Singh (2001).

Although in some Western countries gender access is reported to have levelled,[28] this does not in itself guarantee that the quality or place of access is the same.[29] Kramarae, writing in respect of access, argues that as computers tend to be seen as a masculine prerogative, male access is privileged and women's access is marginalised and devalued. Women's physical access to computers in public spaces is made more difficult, she argues, by the culture of masculinity associated with computer technology. Citing the example of university computer labs, she argues that these quickly become male-dominated and hostile, sexualised environments for women (Kramarae, 1997, pp 2–3). Likewise, Pollock and Sutton, commenting on Canada's policy of extending internet access by increasing public access points, argue that 'public access points have, so far, had the tendency to follow existing hierarchies of power ... they are often in places where women would not be comfortable using the computers ... where they feel that what is being offered to them is not relevant or inappropriate, or where they find males step in to use the resources' (Pollock and Sutton, 1999, p 45). The psychology of access[30] is also a factor that has to be considered. As technical proficiency with technology is traditionally associated with masculinity, women can therefore be deterred from using computers at all. As Wajcman argues, '... the very language of technology, its symbolism, is masculine. It is not simply a question of acquiring skills, because these skills are embedded in a culture of masculinity that is largely coterminous with the culture of technology' (Wajcman, as cited in Singh, 2001, p 408).

2 The subject(s) of contracts in cyberspace – women as consumers and consumed

In addition to raising questions of access, feminist perspectives on contracts in cyberspace can critique the emphasis of doctrinal commentary on business and consumer transactions as obscuring questions of gender. In eschewing a focus on sexual contracts, and concentrating on 'legitimate' contracts, such as sale and supply of goods, the doctrinal approach works to de-legitimise any emphasis on contracts with an overt sexual or gender dimension, thereby producing a distorted legal picture of contracts in cyberspace. In respect of the women that do have access to the contractual sphere of cyberspace, feminists raise questions about their role in relation to that space, noting their interpellation as consumers, and the prevalence of sexual commerce.

I have argued above that the doctrinal approach to contracts in cyberspace stresses the importance of cyberspace as a commercial, consumerist space. However, as it claims only to look at questions of form, the doctrinal approach obscures the specific relationship of gender to consumption, thereby omitting the nature and role of women as consumers in the legal analysis of contracts.[31] Feminist perspectives, in contrast, reveal that gender and commerce are interlinked. Feminists inquire as to what types of contract are made in cyberspace, and who

---

28 See, eg, Edwards and Waelde (2000, p v).
29 See, further, Montgomery (1999, p 99).
30 I wish to thank Madeleine Jowett for supplying me with this phrase.
31 See, further, Wheeler, Chapter 2 in this volume.

makes them. In respect of those women who have access to cyberspace (a move requiring not only financial capacity, but also technological confidence and sufficient language skills),[32] their role in spending the domestic finances makes them attractive targets for online businesses (Singh, 2001, p 395). As Warnick notes, online advertisers deploy gendered rhetoric to exploit this market, appealing to traits such as femininity and domesticity in order to interpellate their female consumers (Warnick, 1999, p 4). In this way, women are positioned in a specifically gendered way in relation to consumerism and commerce in cyberspace.

In her analysis of contract casebooks, Mary Jo Frug argued that, through their descriptions of the law, casebook authors can be shown to have relied on gendered assumptions which in turn may inform or reinforce the prejudices of the reader. She argued, for example, that the general exclusion of contracts with an overt gender dimension, and use of the male personal pronoun as generic, work to imply that women are irrelevant, and effectively excludes them as being party to the discussion in their capacity as readers or as contractual agents (Frug, 1992, pp 53–60).[33] She went on to note how women do not appear as frequently as men in case examples, and that if they do, they are interpreted and positioned unfavourably in relation to men. Yet these same criticisms can be used in relation to contemporary doctrinal discussions of contracts in cyberspace. Although, as illustrated above, gender and consumption are linked, this connection is not made explicit critiqued in contract texts. At the time of writing, 'he' is still used as a generic term,[34] and writers still draw on gendered assumptions in their illustrations. For example, in Miller's work on the development of e-commerce payment mechanisms, he uses the picturesque allegory of a day in the high-tech life of an imaginary couple as an example. He writes that 'one can imagine without difficulty the scenario of a day in the life of Adam and Eve Everyman perhaps five years from now' (Miller, 2000, pp 55–56). Upon waking, Eve discovers that supplies in the kitchen are running low, and so she orders more using her 'smart' fridge, paid for from their online joint household account. Adam runs to get his train and later uses the internet to great advantage at his office. Eve also uses cyberspace to help her work, except that she is working from home as a specialist programmer. Whereas the full scenario is ripe for deconstruction on many levels, it is interesting to notice the gendered assumptions woven into these excerpts. It is Eve who takes care of the domestic running of the household (albeit aided by the smart fridge and the joint account), and despite the apparent equality of their both having professional jobs, it is Eve who is located in the home.

---

32 The point regarding linguistic skills is taken specifically from Stone, as mentioned in Warnick (1999, p 10). Stone's argument is that using cyberspace frequently requires knowledge of English. In the context of my argument, as English is the dominant language not only of cyberspace but also of commerce, access and the ability to contract is not only dependent on financial and technological skill ability, but also linguistic proficiency.

33 There is an argument that 'men' is (or rather, should be) taken to include women, an argument that is commonly cited in defence of criticism such as I have described. This position of mutual inclusiveness (expressed as notwithstanding the expression of a contrary intention) is suggested by s 6 of the Interpretation Act 1978. However, I would suggest that this does not take into account the practical (and gendered) social context in which language is used. If the male pronoun is really taken to include women, then how does this explain, for example, doctrinal criminal law texts switching to 'she' as generic in discussions of rape and sexual offences?

34 See, eg, Smith (2002).

Apart from noting the positioning of women as consumers in relation to contracts, feminist critiques of contracts in cyberspace need also to emphasise the position of women in their capacity as objects of consumption in sexual contracts. The exclusion of certain contracts from the scope of doctrinal analysis has long been revealed by feminist commentators to be a political one, and they have noted how contracts that have an overt gender dimension, the marriage contract being a prime example, are absent from mainstream contract law texts. The marriage contract is reserved for family law texts, a move which serves to obscure the way in which contracts have been used to uphold gendered power imbalances and construct gender identities, and also to reinforce the public/private divide.[35] As family law is not a 'core' subject for a qualifying law degree, the significance of the marriage contract as a sexualised, gendered contract is doubly marginalised. Regarding gendered contracts in cyberspace, it comes as little surprise that not only do texts on contracts in cyberspace continue the tradition of avoiding mention of marriage contracts, but this exclusion is entrenched in the legal provisions on contracts themselves, in that Member States of the EU can choose to except contracts governed by family law or the law of succession from the requirements of the E-Commerce Directive under Art 9(2)(d). The implication of this derogation is arguably that the importance of gender is as obscured from the vision of e-contract law as from contract law before it.

In respect of contracts associated with sexual services, the doctrinal analysis delegates these to sections on illegality. Discussion usually primly concentrates on questions of morality, thereby neatly avoiding (and obscuring) questions of gender and power. As seen above, the main emphasis of current contract law commentary is to consider cyberspace as a commercial space for 'legitimate' market transactions where harmful elements, such as pornography, are seen as deterrents to business. However, this interpretation of pornography divorces it from its highly politicised context and obscures it as a feminist issue. From the doctrinal take, the reader would be unaware that commerce in cyberspace was not only founded on the sale and purchase of goods, but also the sale and purchase of sex: through the pornography industry, through the sale of women and children as sex slaves, and through prostitution.[36] The pornography industry in particular has been deeply implicated in the development of cyberspace as a commercial and contractual space, but this connection is never mentioned in doctrinal analyses.

In an article on technology policy and cyberspace, Kramarae argues that: '... [c]urrently, many people are investigating ways to make the Internet safe for monetary transactions. Why not first make it safe for women?' (Kramarae, 1997, p 3), One aspect of this danger, which Kramarae is referring to, is the prevalence of pornography, the effects of which can be read as twofold. Not only can the free and flourishing trade in pornography help to create an oppressive atmosphere for women in cyberspace, but it can also be seen as an example of the role of women in e-commerce as (sexual) commodities in themselves. As Hughes (1995, p 156) illustrates, cyberspace is a significant market for the trade in sex:

---

35 See, further, Goodrich (1996); Pateman (1988).

36 I previously considered the relationship between e-commerce and cyberpornography in a two-part lecture series (unpublished) given at Gothenburg University in April 2000, and the ideas in this section of this chapter draw on that research. I would like to thank Mathias Klang at the Viktoria Institute, Gothenburg University, for giving me the opportunity and space on his e-commerce course to explore and develop my ideas in this area.

> Agents offer catalogues of mail-order brides, with girls as young as thirteen. Commercial prostitution tours are advertised ... technology has enabled an online merger of pornography and prostitution, with videoconferencing bringing live sex shows to the Internet.

It is difficult to estimate the scale of the pornography industry, or the value of its contribution to the economy of cyberspace, but few feminist commentators would doubt its significance. Pornography has influenced e-commerce through a subtle but effective combination of industry capability and nature of the market. Pornography is one business that guarantees a ready income; the nature of the medium of cyberspace means that consumers can find what they want relatively easily, and there is a consumer base that is willing to pay. As a quote from Thompson explains: 'All media, if they are to get a jump-start in the market and become successful, must address themselves to mass drives ... But of all these – food, shelter, sex and money – sex is the one drive that can elicit immediate consumer response' (Thompson, quoting Gerard van der Leun, 2001, p 57).

The combination of pornography as a lucrative business and the desire of pornographers to make the internet productive has led directly to the creation of methods for the product to be effectively advertised, and to be effectively charged for. It is this impetus that has given rise to many e-commerce and e-contract technologies. For example, pornography has been the driving force behind the development of content charging systems, the development of secure, fast credit card payment systems and multiple billing schemes (Bradwell, 1998, p 42). Because pornography sites can key into that immediate consumer response, those who set them up have both the motivation and the means to invest in new ways of making their sites economically productive. Only the pornography industry generates enough income to be able to do this. As Bradwell illustrates, 'e-Commerce would probably have taken much longer to get off the ground if it weren't for webmasters on adult sites demanding the technology ... we were the first company in Canada to provide e-Commerce, and it was all a result of our adult business' (Bradwell, 1998, quoting Jason King of Starnet, p 42).

In the early days of commercial contract, women were unable to contract without the consent of their husband and were, as chattels, the subject of contracts themselves (Goodrich, 1996, pp 22–23). As shown above, in the age of cyberspace, women are still in the same place as sexual commodities, although I would suggest that the position of women in relation to cyberpornography is more complicated than it seems, in that women also are now increasingly entering into the production and consumption of both lesbian and heterosexual cyberpornography (Chatterjee, 2001). The failure of legal commentators to take this form of sexual commerce represents a significant omission, and one that is clearly political.

Alternative analyses – different space?

I have argued to this point that feminist perspectives can valuably critique the doctrinal analysis of contracts in cyberspace in respect of its focus on the public sphere. However, what feminist perspectives might also do is question the assumptions about the nature of cyberspace that underlie the doctrinal approach, and question whether a doctrinal approach is even appropriate here. As argued above, doctrinal analyses of contracts in cyberspace see that space as one that presents no new problems. E-contracts are simply seen as contracts made by electronic means, as opposed to traditional paper contracts. For the law, the task therefore seems to be to determine to what extent traditional contractual doctrines and principles, which were developed to work with print medium, will be applicable to the electronic medium of cyberspace, and precisely how they will be applied. On this analysis, established principles can be extended to fit contracts in cyberspace, as e-contracts are seen as substantially the same as those 'on paper', the only difference being that they are created using a different medium. However, if cyberspace is understood to be a post-modern, disruptive medium that does not follow the rules of physical texts, then forcing it into the strictures of doctrinal (that is, paper-based) rules may produce a fixity that is undesirable. The idea here is that if contracts structure relationships, including gender relationships, they do this partly through the media that form them. Paper is a more static medium than cyberspace, hence the possibility that contracts in cyberspace might hold more flexibility. This vision of contracts in cyberspace reforming, rather than reifying, gender relationships requires a re-reading of the space of cyberspace. If the fluidity of cyberspace could be realised by the law, then perhaps the relationships that the law of contract structures could themselves be changed.

As mentioned above, feminist commentators have asserted that contracts help to create and structure gender relationships, as shown by the marriage and other sexual contracts. The law of contract is seen to be performative, repeatedly invoking prescribed meanings. Of this relationship, Douzinas, Warrington and McVeigh (1991, p 125), following Goodrich, comment that:

> [a]s physical objects, as marks, notes, or letters, contracts are inscribed within the history and rules of circulation of institutions and textual networks ... the law of contract subjects it texts to tradition. It prescribes and recognises solely certain accredited meanings. Linguistic, social and legal traditions 'fix in advance' standard meanings and proper references ... [w]e speak in tradition and repeat its contents.

The degree of fixity that the law requires is partly achieved through the nature of paper – the traditional medium of the law. As Kitsch argues, our relationship with the printed word is a close one, such that 'words on paper, whether in the form of a contract or a will or even a judicial opinion written by a judge, are the nutrients that sustain the law' (1995, p 116). The printed word has come to represent 'truth', in that it is has a permanency and stability that reassures us of its veracity and trustworthiness.[37] As it is a tangible medium, paper therefore provides contracts with a concrete identity; the contract on paper is a frozen record of the consensus, a physical, permanent trace of what was said by each party (Katsch, 1995, p 120). The status of paper in contract is therefore as much symbolic as it is practical.

---

37 Interestingly, the veracity of a written document, as opposed to that of the spoken word, has not always taken precedence for the law. Katsch provides an example from Michael Clanchy's book, *From Memory to Written Record: England 1066–1307*, where there is a dispute between St Anselm and Henry I. The dispute ends up being taken to Pope Paschal II. The reply from the Pope was written, but it was read aloud to St Anselm. The envoys of Henry I objected, claiming that the oral version of the Pope's message contradicted the written message. Some of the audience believed that the writing should not take precedence over the spoken words of three bishops, the written message being but 'the skins of wethers blackened with ink and weighted with a little lump of lead' (Katsch, after Clanchy, 1995, p 116).

However, the fixity required by the law is also provided by the system of precedent: the insistence on treating like cases as like, and looking to what has gone before in order to determine how to proceed in the future. The repeated performance of a rule lends it authority and meaning, fixed in advance. In their analysis of the postal rule, Douzinas, Warrington and McVeigh try to illustrate how the law anticipates and enforces meaning in the face of future uncertainty. Despite the requirement that acceptance be communicated to the offeror, and the emphasis on *consensus ad idem*, under the postal rule in *Adams v Lindsell*[38] written acceptances to offers can bind the offeror before the letter reaches them, or even if it never arrives (Douzinas, Warrington and McVeigh, 1991, p 125). What this also illustrates is the prime importance that the law accredits to traditional communication though paper. Its presence, symbolic as well as physical, overrides its absence. Even if the physical message does not get through, the law deems the written word on paper to be authoritative, even in its absence, and its meaning is carried on symbolically. This can be contrasted with the rule for instantaneous communications established in *Entores Ltd v Miles Far East Corp*[39] and *Brinkibon Ltd v Stahag Stahl und Stahlwarenhandelsgesellshaft mbH*,[40] where only physical receipt will suffice. Even if faxes use the trustworthy medium of paper, the fact that the words are separated from it and sent though the wires signals uncertainty for the law.

When faced with a new medium, the law needs to decide which rules should apply, and there is some uncertainty in relation to cyberspace about which choice to make. Doctrinal commentators, considering the requirements of offer and acceptance, are undecided as to whether a contract negotiated by email will require the postal rule of acceptance or the rule of receipt. Murray (2000, p 23) argues that email is popularly perceived to be an electronic equivalent of the post, and that there are several other persuasive reasons why the postal rule should apply. First, he argues that email is not like an instantaneous communication because with instantaneous communication the sender knows instantly whether the communication has been transmitted successfully. Even if the sender asks for a delivery receipt, that receipt simply confirms that the message has been delivered to a mailbox, not the offeror themselves. The receipt itself may not follow immediately from the request for it, but may be delayed by hours or even days. Accordingly, an email with a delivery receipt is more like recorded delivery post than an instantaneous communication, and should properly be subject to the postal rule. Furthermore, he points out that the way in which an email is sent is unique in that the information contained in the email is broken down into 'packets'. These packets may be sent via different routes and may not reach their destination at the same time. Indeed, some may never get there at all. This fragmentation means that emails are dissimilar to other instantaneous communications (Murray, 2000, pp 23–25).

In contrast, Poole (2001, pp 53–54) suggests that email should be treated in the same way as instantaneous communications, and that the receipt rule should therefore apply. According to Poole, email is similar to other instantaneous communications because the sender is ultimately in a position to know if the email

---

38 (1818) 1 Barn & Ald 681.
39 [1955] 2 QB 327.
40 [1983] 2 AC 34.

has or has not been sent. The contract would be binding when the email was received, but this still leaves the question of whether receipt means when the email is downloaded onto a server, when it appears on the offeree's computer, or when the email is actually read by them. Dickie (1998, pp 332–35), in his succinct analysis on the problems of offer and acceptance in e-contracts, also proposes that email acceptances should be seen as analogous to instantaneous communications (1998, p 332) and should become binding when they reach the offeror's business premises or the place of their internet service provider during normal office hours. In this way, uncertainty as to how long email can reasonably left unaccessed is minimised (1998, p 333). He points out (1998, p 334) that the email address may not indicate the physical location of the sender or the recipient. He argues that the email may merely consist of a name or number followed by the name of the service provider and uses '@compuserve.com' as an example. Where, then, will the acceptance become binding if the acceptance is sent to such an address? Dickie suggests that in this case the email would become binding either in the recipient's residence or in the country of their principal place of business (*ibid*).[41]

On one level, the debates above can be seen to illustrate the problems associated with the choice of either rule, yet we can also read these debates as illustrative of the restrictions of a doctrinal approach – the rules do not easily fit the medium of cyberspace and past precedent is not always instructive. By predicting the way to proceed, the law forecloses alternative analysis and development. As Dickie hints at, location is a problem in cyberspace, as documents as well as physical locations cannot always be pinned down. Moreover, documents in cyberspace exist in a different way than they do 'on paper'. Electronic contracts, as documents in cyberspace, have the potential to evolve over time and in space (Katsch, 1995, pp 122–23). They are dynamic and, as such, they are unstable. What this means is that documents (including contracts) in cyberspace may not be perceived to have the same qualities or levels of trustworthiness and permanency that paper documents possess.[42] The margins and edges of the paper, which act as boundaries to that document, do not exist in cyberspace (Katsch, 1995, p 120), and the relationship between the centre and the margin is subverted. Nor is the text fixed in

---

41 Article 11 of the E-Commerce Directive states (for the purposes of non business-to-business contracting where agreements to the contrary are made) that electronic orders and acknowledgments will be received when the addressees can access them; Poole concludes that the receipt rule is the appropriate one for acceptances in cyberspace (2001, p 54). Following Art 11, the downloading of the message from the server allowing access to it would constitute receipt (*ibid*). However, as Murray points out (2000, p 28), unfortunately the directive does not clearly explain the legal position of electronic offer and acceptance, or even define when a contract is concluded. There are other potential sources of guidance. Article 18(2) of the Vienna Convention on Contracts for the International Sale of Goods (1980) would also appear to support the argument that the postal rule should not apply to emailed acceptances, as does s 2.1 of the American Bar Association's Model Agreement on Electronic Data Interchange and the US Restatement (Second) of Contracts (1981) (Dickie, 1998, pp 332–33; see also Abe, Sabet and Gall, 2001, p 59). At the time of writing, the precise legal position arguably remains unclear.

42 It is still common practice, and usually desirable, to 'print out', to reproduce on paper what is on the screen in order to have a 'hard' copy. Having said this, the durability of paper is open to debate. In Stevie Davies' novel *Impassioned Clay* (1999, p 77), the heroine, Olivia, observes that:

books are ravaged by readers. Each opening brings an embrittlement; our caressive fingers deposit snails-trails of moisture along margins and text. The reader's love for the book is a wanton outpouring of acid upon its surfaces. Rot ruddies the leather binding, which dries, porous and powdered ... Alum-stiffened pages [meet] humidity in the air in a prompt rapture of acid dissolution.

such a permanent way, as it can be very easily and quickly manipulated in an electronic document, without leaving any trace of what went before. Documents can be created interactively by the parties involved, even when they are in different countries. Also, documents can be interlinked in many random and immediate ways, other than the linear modes which characterise print documents (Case, 1996). The implication of this, Katsch suggests, is that contracts in cyberspace may connect parties and documents in such ways that are hard to imagine with traditional paper contracts (1995, p 125). Katsch's position is that e-contracts have the potential to restructure the relationships we have that are created, structured and governed by contract.

Katsch's analysis sees cyberspace as an unprecedented space, where we are not restricted by the preconceptions of face-to-face dealing. Unrestricted by conventional margins, the relationships in cyberspace do not have to follow the rules laid down on paper or be prescribed by the law in anticipation. They become fluid and dynamic. If Katsch's argument that relationships in cyberspace can be rethought and restructured is accepted, then perhaps gender relations structured through and by contracts can also be refigured. The law could take a different point of departure, recognising the postmodern qualities of cyberspace, and also being attentive to the structural inequalities of gender. Rather than anticipating the past, the law of contract can develop the future in a sensitive and progressive way. This is, of course, a radical proposition, and I understand that it will take far more than shifts in contract law to produce change. Having said that, the face of contract law has arguably changed beyond anything that the founding fathers (and they invariably were fathers) of contract law could have bargained for. Whether future commentators consider wider perspectives and the potential for change remains to be seen.

References

Abe, L, Sabet, P and Gall, S, 'E-contracting – part 2' (2001) 10(4) *Canadian Corporate Counsel* 51

Adam, A and Green, E (eds), 'Equal opportunities on line: guest editorial' (2001) 31(4) *Computers and Society* 1

Akdeniz, Y, Walker, C and Wall, D, *The Internet, Law and Society*, 2000, London: Longman

Atiyah, PS, *An Introduction to the Law of Contract*, 5th edn, 1995, Oxford: OUP

Batty, M and Barr, B, 'The electronic frontier: exploring and mapping cyberspace' (1994) 26(7) *Futures* 699–712

Beale, HG (ed), *Chitty on Contracts*, 28th edn, 2002, London: Sweet & Maxwell

Beale, HG, Bishop, WD and Furmston, MP (eds), *Contract – Cases and Materials*, 4th edn, 2001, London: Butterworths

Bradwell, D, 'Sex drive' (1998) *Internet Magazine* (October) 38

Brown, B, 'Contracting out/contracting in: some feminist considerations', in Bottomley, A (ed), *Feminist Perspectives on the Foundational Subjects of Law*, 1996, London: Cavendish Publishing, pp 5–16

Case, S-E, *The Domain-Matrix: Performing Lesbian at the End of Print Culture*, 1996, Bloomington, IN: Indiana UP

Chatterjee, B, 'Last of the Rainmacs? – thinking about pornography in cyberspace', in Wall, D (ed), *Crime and the Internet*, 2001, London: Routledge, pp 74–99

Davies, S, *Impassioned Clay*, 1999, London: The Women's Press

Dickie, J, 'When and where are electronic contracts concluded?' (1998) 99(3) *Northern Ireland Legal Quarterly* 332

Douzinas, C, Warrington, R and McVeigh, S, *Postmodern Jurisprudence*, 1991, London: Routledge

Edwards, L, 'Pornography and the internet', in Edwards, L and Waelde, C (eds), *Law and the Internet: A Framework for Electronic Commerce*, 2nd edn, 2000, Oxford: Hart, pp 275–308

Edwards, L and Waelde, C (eds), *Law and the Internet: A Framework for Electronic Commerce*, 2nd edn, 2000, Oxford: Hart

Frug, MJ, *Postmodern Legal Feminism*, 1992, London: Routledge

Furmston, M (ed), *Cheshire, Fifoot and Furmston's Law of Contract*, 14th edn, 2001, London: Butterworths

Goodrich, P, 'Gender and contracts', in Bottomley, A (ed), *Feminist Perspectives on the Foundational Subjects of Law*, 1996, London: Cavendish Publishing, pp 17–46

Halson, R, *Contract Law*, 2001, London: Longman

Hawthorne, S and Klein, R (eds), *Cyberfeminism: Connectivity, Critique and Creativity*, 1999, Melbourne: Spinifex, pp 80–97

Hogg, M, 'Secrecy and signatures – turning the legal spotlight on encryption and electronic signatures', in Edwards, L and Waelde, C (eds), *Law and the Internet: A Framework for Electronic Commerce*, 2nd edn, 2000, Oxford: Hart, pp 37–54

Hughes, D, 'The internet and the global prostitution industry', in Katsch, ME, *Law in a Digital World*, 1995, New York: OUP

Katsch, ME, *Law in a Digital World*, 1995, New York: OUP

Katsch, ME, *Electronic Media and the Transformation of Law*, 1989, Oxford: OUP

Keey, J, 'Current e-commerce issues in the European Union – part 1' (2001) 10(4) *Canadian Corporate Counsel* 50

Klein, R (eds), *Cyberfeminism: Connectivity, Critique and Creativity*, 1999, Melbourne: Spinifex

Kohl, U, 'Legal reasoning and legal change in the age of the internet – why the ground rules are still valid' (1999) 7(2) *International Journal of Law and Information Technology* 123–49

Kramarae, C, 'Technology policy, gender and cyberspace' (1997) 4(1) *Duke Journal of Gender Law and Policy* 149

Kramarae, C and Kramer, J, 'Legal snarls for women in cyberspace' (1995) 5(2) *Internet Research: Electronic Networking Application and Policy* 14

Miller, S, 'Payment in an on-line world', in Edwards, L and Waelde, C (eds), *Law and the Internet: A Framework for Electronic Commerce*, 2nd edn, 2000, Oxford: Hart, pp 55–77

Mitrani, A, 'Regulating e-commerce, e-contracts and the controversy of multiple jurisdiction' (2001) 7(2) *International Trade Law and Regulation* 50

Montgomery, A, 'Everyday use: women, work and online play', in Hawthorne, S and Klein, R (eds), *Cyberfeminism: Connectivity, Critique and Creativity*, 1999, Melbourne: Spinifex, pp 80–97

Murray, A, 'Entering into contracts electronically: the real w.w.w.', in Edwards, L and Waelde, C (eds), *Law and the Internet: A Framework for Electronic Commerce*, 2nd edn, 2000, Oxford: Hart

Nicoll, CC, 'Can computers make contracts?' (1998) *Journal of Business Law* 35

Pateman, C, *The Sexual Contract*, 1988, Cambridge: Polity Press

Pollock, S and Sutton, J, 'Women click: feminism and the internet', in Hawthorne, S and Klein, R (eds), *Cyberfeminism: Connectivity, Critique and Creativity*, 1999, Melbourne: Spinifex, pp 33–49

Poole, J, *Textbook on Contract Law*, 6th edn, 2001, London: Blackstone

Richards, P, *Law of Contract*, 5th edn, 2002, London: Longman

Singh, S, 'Gender and the use of the internet at home' (2001) 3(4) *New Media and Society* 395

Smith, GJH, *Internet Law and Regulation*, 2002, London: Sweet & Maxwell

Terrett, A and Monaghan, I, 'The internet – an introduction for lawyers', in Edwards, L and Waelde, C (eds), *Law and the Internet: A Framework for Electronic Commerce*, 2nd edn, 2000, Oxford: Hart, pp 1–16

Thompson, N, 'Witness: sex on the net' (2001) *Prospect* (January) 54

Torremans, P, 'Private international law aspects of IP – internet disputes', in Edwards, L and Waelde, C (eds), *Law and the Internet: A Framework for Electronic Commerce*, 2nd edn, 2000, Oxford: Hart, pp 224–46

Wakeford, N, 'Gender and the landscapes of computing in an internet café', in Kirkup, G, Janes, L, Woodward, K and Hovenden, F (eds), *The Gendered Cyborg: A Reader*, 2000, London: Routledge, pp 291–304

Wall, DS, 'Insecurity and the policing of cyberspace', in Crawford, A (ed), *Crime and Insecurity*, 2002, Cullompton: Willan, pp 186–209

Warnick, B, 'Masculinising the feminine: inviting women on line ca. 1997' (1999) 16 *Critical Studies in Mass Communication* 1

Winn, JK and Wright, B (eds), *Law of Electronic Commerce*, 4th edn, 2002, New York: Aspen Law and Business

Chapter 7
Binding Prenuptial Agreements in Australia: The First Year[1]
Belinda Fehlberg and Bruce Smyth

Introduction[2]

Binding prenuptial agreements (or pre-marriage contracts) are a well-known aspect of family law systems in many countries, including many civil law countries, several US states[3] and Canadian provinces[4] and New Zealand.[5] Until recently, the Australian position, like the British position,[6] has differed markedly from these jurisdictions. The existence of a prenuptial agreement was viewed as relevant but not decisive to how the family court (and now also the Federal Magistrates Service)[7] would exercise its broad discretion under the Family Law Act (FLA) 1975 (Cth) to alter interests in property on separation and divorce.[8] Binding financial agreements

---

1 This article in its original form first appeared in (2002) 16 *International Journal of Law, Policy and the Family* pp 127–40, and is reproduced with the kind permission of OUP. Since this article was first published, the Federal Attorney General has introduced the Family Law Amendment Bill 2003 into Parliament, which proposes a number of amendments to the Family Law Act 1975 (Cth), including some provisions relating to 'financial agreements' (prenuptial agreements being a species of these). In particular, in response to concerns of the legal profession (as discussed in this chapter), the Bill limits the extent and nature of the advice that independent legal advisers are required to give to clients before entering a financial agreement. The Bill replaces current provisions requiring the legal adviser to advise on whether the agreement is to the financial advantage or disadvantage of the client, prudent, and fair and reasonable, with the requirement that the legal adviser must advise on 'the advantages and disadvantages, at the time the advice was provided, to the party making the agreement'. The explanatory memorandum makes clear that *legal* advice on the advantages and disadvantages is intended. The Bill also amends the legislation retrospectively so that a financial agreement will not exclude the court's power to make a maintenance order if, at the time the agreement comes into effect (rather than the time it was made – the current position), a party is unable to support themself without relying on government income support. Finally, the Bill makes it clear that financial agreements are not subject to stamp duty tax. The Bill was passed by the House of Representatives on 13 August 2003 and was introduced into the Senate on 20 August 2003. The Bill and explanatory memorandum can be accessed via the Commonwealth Parliament's home page: www.aph.gov.au/index.htm.

2 The authors would like to thank the Family Law Section of the Law Council of Australia, and the legal practitioners who participated in this study, Gerry Bean, Wendy Parker, Fiona Kelly and Martha Bailey.

3 With the exceptions of Kentucky, Michigan, Mississippi, Oklahoma, Pennsylvania, South Carolina and Vermont. Many states have adopted the Uniform Premarital Agreement Act, promulgated in 1983. See, further, Nasheri (1998).

4 Covered by provincial legislation; for example, cl D-37 of the Domestic Relations Act, RSA 1980; cl 128 of the Family Relations Act, RSBC 1996; cl F-20 of the Family Maintenance Act, SM 1987; cl F-2 of the Family Law Act, RSN 1990; cl F-3 of the Family Law Act, RSO 1990; cl F-6.1 of the Family Maintenance Act, SS 1990–91.

5 Section 21 of the Property (Relationships) Act 1976 (NZ), which gives the general power to make an agreement in contemplation of either marriage or a cohabiting relationship.

6 The current legal status of prenuptial agreements resembles the Australian position pre-27 December 2000. A proposal to introduce binding prenuptial agreements was put forward in *Supporting Families* (Home Office, 1990, p 33). See also Eekelaar (1998). For a recent discussion of the position in England and Wales, see Leech (2000).

7 If the property is worth under Aus $300,000, or with the consent of the parties.

8 See, for example, *In the Marriage of Hannema* (1981) 7 Fam LR 542; *In the Marriage of Plut* (1987) 11 Fam LR 687.

between spouses could be entered into only on separation and had to be court-registered.[9] The non-binding status of prenuptial agreements was in marked contrast to the law governing cohabiting couples, which in most Australian states allows cohabiting couples (now including, once again in most states, same-sex cohabitees) to enter into legally binding cohabitation and separation agreements.[10]

The Family Law Amendment Act 2000 (Cth) was the third – and successful – attempt to change this position.[11] The process began in February 1999 with a press statement by the federal Attorney General and ended in December 2000 with the insertion of a new Pt V111A into the FLA.[12] In between, the most significant event to occur was an inquiry by the Senate Legal and Constitutional Committee into the (then) Bill. The committee reported in December 1999, recommending that binding prenuptial agreements should be introduced, but suggesting some amendments, which were largely implemented by the government.[13]

In essence, the new FLA Pt VIIIA provides that couples may enter into a 'financial agreement' before marriage, during marriage, or after divorce, regarding their property and financial resources (both present and future), the payment of spousal maintenance, and 'incidental and ancillary matters'. For a financial agreement to be binding there are a number of requirements, including that each party to the agreement must have received independent legal advice before the agreement is entered. There is no court supervision or registration of agreements. The new Pt VIIIA thus represents two marked changes in Australian family law: the introduction of financial agreements that can be entered before and during marriage as well as after divorce, and *a movement away from court involvement in overseeing entry into private financial agreements*. The responsibility for overseeing agreements

---

9 Before the changes, separating spouses could enter binding financial agreements under s 87 of the Family Law Act 1975. Section 87 (along with s 86, which provided for the registration in court of non-binding financial agreements) was repealed by the Family Law Amendment Act 2000. Consent orders are not affected by the Family Law Amendment Act 2000, so separated spouses may still, as they could before the changes, achieve final settlement of property, spousal maintenance, and children matters (excluding child support) without a full trial, via consent orders agreed between them and made by the court, either in chambers by a registrar (Ord 14 r 2 and Form 12 of the Family Court Rules), or via minutes of consent made by the court.

10 Part IV of each of the Property (Relationships) Act 1984 (NSW), the De Facto Relationships Act 1991 (NT), the Domestic Relationships Act 1994 (ACT), and Pt II of the De Facto Relationships Act 1996 (SA) and ss 264, 265, 270, 272, 274(1), 276 of Pt 19 of the Property Law Amendment Act 1999 (Qld). These provisions allow parties to opt out of the legislative regime of property adjustment by making an agreement before or during, as well as on the termination of, their relationship. The NSW, ACT and Queensland schemes apply to same-sex as well as heterosexual de facto relationships, with the ACT scheme having the broadest application, extending to non-cohabiting 'domestic relationships'.

11 Before the most recent proposals, the introduction of legally binding prenuptial agreements had been recommended on two previous occasions: by the Australian Law Reform Commission (1987), and by the Joint Select Committee (1992). For further detail on the legal status of prenuptial agreements before the changes, and previous appearances and disappearances of proposals to make them legally binding, see Fehlberg and Smyth (2000).

12 Schedule 2 to the Family Law Amendment Act 2000 (Cth). The Act also includes provisions regarding enforcement of parenting orders (Sched 1) and private arbitration and civil aspects of the international abduction of children (the Hague Convention) (Sched 3).

13 Senate Legal and Constitutional Legislation Committee, Consideration of Legislation Referred to the Committee, Provisions of the Family Law Amendment Bill 1999, December 1999.

has, in essence, been shifted away from the court and onto family lawyers (particularly solicitors), as the providers of independent legal advice. Not surprisingly, family lawyers' concerns about their potential professional liability have featured prominently during the first year of the legislation's operation, an issue discussed later in this chapter.

The policy rationale for the recent changes was set out clearly in the federal Attorney General's Second Reading Speech[14] and the explanatory memorandum to the Family Law Amendment Act 2000. In particular, the benefits of binding financial agreements were said to be:

- greater control over property for parties to agreements (parties are able to quarantine assets acquired before, during, or after the marriage has ended. This was viewed as being '... of particular benefit to people who are entering subsequent marriages, as well as to people on the land and those who own family businesses');

- greater choice of the parties to agreements to order their own financial affairs (with the court being unable in most circumstances to change or set aside agreements);

- reduced conflict (and with it reduced emotional and financial cost) on marriage breakdown; and

- reflection of changed community attitudes and needs by the FLA.

In an article published just before Pt VIIIA came into force, we argued that there was significant reason to doubt whether the above goals would be achieved for Australia.[15] First, it appeared to us, on the basis of relevant Australian and overseas evidence, that binding prenuptial agreements were not likely to result in reduced costs and conflict on marriage breakdown but, rather, in the shifting of dispute to other areas (such as the interpretation of agreements). In the United States, for example, Sanford Katz has recently observed that '[a] special body of law has developed to test the validity of antenuptial agreements, and it can be divided into matters dealing with process and substance'.[16] A similar position has been observed in Germany.[17] Secondly, we concluded, once again drawing on relevant overseas and Australian empirical research, that binding prenuptial agreements were likely to offer men more than women in terms of increased control and choice over how property is divided on marriage breakdown, due to women's weaker economic position compared to men. For example, Barbara Atwood's 1992 United States study looked at divorce cases, reported in that year, involving challenges to the validity of prenuptial agreements, and found that in 33 of the 39 reported cases an economically subordinate wife sought to avoid the agreement.[18] Finally, drawing on data collected by the Australian Institute of Family Studies before the new legislation was enacted, we concluded that binding prenuptial agreements were not

---

14 *Hansard* (1999).
15 Fehlberg and Smyth (2000).
16 Katz (1998, p 1260).
17 Eekelaar (1998, p 471).
18 Atwood (1993). See also Brod (1994); and Nasheri (1998). See also, in the Australian context, Neave (1995, p 144).

the result of clear community support or need. These data were derived from the Australian Divorce Transitions Project, a national random survey of 650 divorced Australians. The date suggested that prenuptial agreements are rarely used – only 13 of the 650 respondents said they had a prenuptial agreement. The data also revealed a general perception, among users and non-users of prenuptial agreements alike, that such agreements are not, or would not, be useful in reaching fairer outcomes for divorcing couples. It could be argued that the introduction of legally binding agreements would result in a more positive response on these issues, but this argument would not necessarily hold on closer examination. In particular, the findings also suggested strong support for alteration of prenuptial agreements in the interests of children. Also, the respondents' general pessimism about prenuptial agreements may have been due to relationship dynamics independent of the then current legal impotence of prenuptial agreements, an issue explored later in this chapter.[19]

The central aim of this chapter is to explore how the new legislation is working one year after its introduction. After first providing a more detailed outline of the new legislative provisions, this chapter looks at the available early evidence regarding the operation of the new legislation, focusing on prenuptial agreements. This evidence indicates that currently family lawyers perceive that there are some significant impediments, which are inhibiting their and their clients' use of the new legislation.

Recent changes: law

The new Pt VIIIA of the FLA allows couples to enter into a 'financial agreement' before or during marriage, as well as after they divorce.[20] A financial agreement may cover property and financial resources (present or future), spousal maintenance[21] and other 'incidental and ancillary' matters.[22] The limits of the term 'incidental and ancillary matters' are at this stage untested.

The Act does not expressly stipulate that entering a financial agreement precludes a later court application regarding matters covered by the agreement. However, the explanatory memorandum to the new legislation indicates that this is the intention, stating that: '[i]f an agreement is binding, a court will not be able to deal with the matters with which the agreement deals.'[23] Matters not covered by a financial agreement could, however, be the subject of a later court application. For example, if an agreement were to cover property but not spousal maintenance, it would still be open to a party to later seek spousal maintenance.

A fundamental difference between court orders and the new financial agreements is that while the FLA directs the court to consider the impact of its orders on the parties, no similar requirement governs entry into financial

---

19 The findings are reported in more detail in Fehlberg and Smyth (1999).
20 Sections 90B (before marriage), 90C (during marriage), 90D (after divorce) of the FLA.
21 Sections 90B(2), 90C(2) and 90D(2) of the FLA.
22 Sections 90B(3), 90C(3) and 90D(3) of the FLA.
23 Clause 129, Explanatory Memorandum to the Family Law Amendment Bill 1999. At this stage, the ambit of 'incidental and ancillary matters' is not yet known – an issue discussed in more detail below.

agreements. In particular, s 79(2) of the FLA provides that before a court makes orders altering interests in property, the court needs to be satisfied that it is 'just and equitable' to do so. Section 74 of the FLA provides that the court may make an order for spousal maintenance that it considers 'proper'. In contrast, there is no requirement that the terms or operation of a financial agreement be 'just and equitable' or 'proper' as between the parties, and entry into financial agreements is not overseen by the court. Financial agreements once entered are not registered in the court.

I When will an agreement be binding?

Financial agreements are enforceable as long as the formal requirements for entry are satisfied and no other ground for setting aside the agreement, as discussed later, is established.

As regards formalities, a financial agreement will be binding if it is in writing, has been signed by both parties, each party has received independent legal advice and it has not been terminated by mutual agreement of the parties.[24] As no court approval is required for a financial agreement to be binding, the advice of a lawyer is the only 'outside' contact that the parties are required to have before entry into the agreement.

As regards the requirement of independent legal advice, to be validly entered into, a financial agreement must have an annexure containing 'a certificate signed by the person providing the independent legal advice stating that the advice was provided'.[25] The financial agreement must also contain a statement, in relation to each party, that independent advice has been received from a legal practitioner prior to entering the financial agreement as to:

- the effect of the agreement on the rights of that party;
- whether or not, at the time when the advice was provided, it was to the advantage, financially or otherwise, of that party to make the agreement;
- whether or not, at that time, it was prudent for that party to make the agreement; and
- whether or not, at that time and in the light of such circumstances as were, at that time, reasonably foreseeable, the provisions of the agreement were fair and reasonable.[26]

These requirements were included in the legislation at the recommendation of the Family Law Council of Australia and its Family Law Section (which is Australia's largest and most significant professional organisation representing family lawyers). The requirements are based on s 47(1) of the New South Wales Property (Relationships) Act 1984, which provides in almost identical terms for certificates of independent advice in relation to 'domestic relationship agreements' (agreements entered before and during cohabitation) and 'termination agreements' (agreements

---

24 Section 90G of the FLA.
25 *Ibid*.
26 Section 90G(l)(b) of the FLA.

entered after cohabitation has ended).[27] It has been observed, in relation to the New South Wales requirements, that for the conscientious solicitor, providing a certificate may become 'a large undertaking in time and costs', which may in turn 'provide deterrents to all but the most determined and/or wealthy [domestic] partners'.[28] Conversely, it has also been observed that the provisions have 'operated in New South Wales apparently without difficulty and without a significant history of professional indemnity insurance claims'.[29] Nevertheless, it is clear that family law lawyers – and their insurers – view the independent advice requirements in relation to Pt VIIIA of the FLA financial agreements (and particularly prenuptial agreements) as being highly onerous and difficult to satisfy – an issue discussed in more detail later.

Once an agreement has been validly entered, it is binding unless it is terminated by the parties, or one of the grounds for setting aside set out in s 90K of the FLA can be established, namely:

- fraud;
- that the agreement is void, voidable, or unenforceable (that is, common law contract grounds for refusing performance);
- circumstances arising post-agreement that make it impracticable for the agreement to be carried out;
- a material change in circumstances has arisen post-agreement relating to the care, welfare and development of a child of the marriage such that the child or applicant carer will suffer hardship if the agreement is not set aside; or
- when the agreement was made, one of the parties engaged in unconscionable conduct.[30]

The requirement that both parties receive independent legal advice is likely to limit the number of cases where some of these grounds will be successfully pleaded. Independent legal advice will not ensure that issues of power imbalance due to, for example, undue influence or unconscionable dealing are overcome, but the fact that independent advice has been given may nevertheless suffice to make the agreement enforceable.[31]

If a s 90K of the FLA ground is established, the only remedy is for the court to set aside the agreement. In contrast, under s 90KA, the court can, applying principles of law and equity, order more partial remedies – for example, setting aside part of the

---

27 Section 44(1) of the Property Relationships Act 1984 (NSW). See also s 33(1)(d) of the Domestic Relationships Act 1994 (ACT).

28 CCH Australian De Facto Relationships Reporter 32-004-32-152 (32-450-32-470).

29 Letter, dated 19 June 2001, from the Deputy Secretary General of the Law Council of Australia to the Federal Attorney General regarding 'Family law: financial agreements: certification of independent legal advice'.

30 Section 90K(1) of the FLA. For a detailed examination of the way in which these grounds may be interpreted, see Parkinson (2001).

31 For a recent case discussing the role of independent advice in the surety context, see *Royal Bank of Scotland v Etridge (No 2)* [2001] 3 WLR 1021; [2001] 4 All ER 449. See also, in the surety context, Fehlberg (1997, pp 56–58, and especially note 179).

agreement, enforcing another part of it and ordering the payment of equitable compensation. Remedies in favour of third parties may also be a possibility here.[32]

Significantly, the FLA grounds for avoiding financial agreements are narrower than the grounds that apply to cohabitation or separation agreements entered by cohabiting couples under the relevant legislation in several states. In particular, all states that have legislation providing for binding financial agreements have a more general ground for avoiding agreements. For example, s 49(1) of the Property (Relationships) Act 1984 (NSW) provides that the court can vary or set aside an agreement or any of its provisions:

> ... where, in the opinion of the court, the circumstances of the parties have so changed since the time at which the agreement was entered into that it would lead to serious injustice if the provisions of the agreement, or any one or more of them, were ... to be enforced.[33]

The FLA position is also in contrast to the equivalent New Zealand legislation, which provides that an agreement entered before marriage or cohabitation is not enforceable if the court concludes that giving effect to the agreement would 'cause serious injustice' having regard to a number of matters, including whether the agreement has become unfair in the light of any changes in circumstances since it was entered.[34] Recent New Zealand legislative changes have, however, made agreements harder to overturn. Previously, an agreement could be overturned if it was 'unjust' to give effect to it. The threshold test is now higher (although the criteria for determining whether the test is met remain the same as before). Even before these changes, there had been a gradual tightening up in judicial interpretation, making prenuptial agreements harder to avoid.[35]

It is also noteworthy that the same FLA grounds apply to the setting aside of financial agreements whenever they are entered – before or during marriage or after divorce. However, the situation of an engaged couple is likely to differ significantly from a couple negotiating after they have divorced, arguably justifying differently tailored grounds for avoidance. A more broad-based ground, similar to that operating in state cohabitation agreements, may be particularly appropriate regarding an agreement made before marriage or while spouses are happily married.

Once validly entered, a financial agreement cannot be varied. If the parties wish to change or terminate their agreement, they must make a written 'termination agreement' (requiring the same process as entry into a valid agreement, including independent legal advice).[36] A financial agreement that is binding remains binding after the death of a party to the agreement.[37] An agreement entered before or during

---

32 Foster (2001).

33 See also: s 34 of the Domestic Relationships Act 1994 (ACT); s 276(1) of the Property Law Act 1974 (Qld); s 46(2) of the De Facto Relationships Act 1991 (NT); s 39(1) of the De Facto Relationships Act 1999 (TAS); s 8(1) of the De Facto Relationships Act 1996 (SA). Binding cohabitation agreements and separation agreements cannot be entered into in Victoria under the Property Law Act 1958 (Vic).

34 Section 21J of the Property (Relationships) Act 1976 (NZ).

35 *Wood v Wood* [1998] 3 NZLR 234. See, further, Atkin and Parker (2001, Chapter 8, pp 153–69).

36 Section 90J of the FLA.

37 Section 90H of the FLA.

marriage will be binding even if its impact at the time it is enforced is to make a party dependent on the public purse.[38]

Entry into a financial agreement is, then, relatively straightforward and inexpensive for the parties, but getting out of an agreement validly entered is considerably more difficult. Mutual termination involves the additional expense of legal or financial advice,[39] while unilateral avoidance of either a financial agreement or a termination agreement requires a successful application to the court by the party seeking to unilaterally avoid the agreement. The grounds for setting aside by the court do not include a broad-based ground to the effect that enforcing the agreement would result in 'serious injustice'. In any case, at a practical level, the grounds for avoiding agreements will not assist the majority of people, who are not in a position to litigate.[40]

2 Financial agreements vs consent orders?

In practice, financial agreements are quite likely to be prenuptial agreements. Before the introduction of financial agreements, consent orders were the most popular option for separating married couples to use to make legally binding financial settlements;[41] this is likely to remain the case for such couples (with the two major exceptions being cases where spousal maintenance is an issue, and bankruptcy protection).[42] Consent orders are made by the court and thus their terms are not within the control of the parties to the same extent as financial agreements. However, if draft consent orders are acceptable to the court they do have the advantage over financial agreements of allowing parties to agree, in a legally binding way within a single document, on issues regarding the care of their children (that is, residence, contact and specific issues), as well as on financial issues (property, child support and spousal support). For family lawyers, consent orders have the added advantage that independent legal advice is not a requirement, so the risk of liability for professional negligence is substantially reduced. Consent

---

38 Section 90F of the FLA. Compare with the position regarding agreements made after dissolution, which are vulnerable in this way, and the position regarding orders for spousal maintenance under s 75(3) of the FLA which means, in effect, that the court must disregard social security entitlements in proceedings for spousal maintenance. These provisions are consistent with the policy concern expressed in *Hyman v Hyman* [1929] AC 601, that being that if spouses could contract out of the court's statutory power to order maintenance, wives would become dependent on the public purse.

39 Section 90J of the FLA.

40 Financial agreements, however, may be more readily challenged than consent orders – the grounds for setting aside consent orders under s 79A of the FLA are more restricted than under ss 90K and 90KA. In particular, consent orders can be varied if there is an 'exceptional' change in the caring responsibility for a child, leading to hardship, while challenging a financial agreement requires the lesser standard of a 'material' change.

41 Parker, Parkinson and Behrens (1999, p 580).

42 A financial agreement can be used to exclude the court's power to order spousal maintenance, a situation which cannot be achieved via consent orders. As regards bankruptcy protection, the position is that if the parties have made a 'maintenance agreement' or have obtained a 'maintenance order' before the date of bankruptcy, without the intention to defraud creditors, then the agreement or order will stand, as long as the property or cash is transferred before the bankruptcy. Orders or agreements for periodic payments can also continue. See, in particular, ss 121 and 123(6) of the Bankruptcy Act 1966 (Cth). See, further, Lindenmayer and Doolan (1994, pp 123–24).

orders, however, are only available on separation, so for those intending to marry, and who wish to enter a binding agreement regarding property and spousal maintenance, a financial agreement is the only alternative.

Impact of the changes: what do we know so far?

A significant problem in any attempt to consider how family lawyers and their clients are using the new legislation is that the new financial agreements are not approved by, or registered in, the court. The lack of a central repository for storage of agreements, combined with the short time that the legislation has been in force, limits both access to data and the amount of data available. Difficulties in researching this area may also reflect the rarity of prenuptial agreements as a form of social behaviour, as well as the often-acknowledged difficulties faced by researchers studying financial arrangements within couple relationships, especially intact relationships. All this means that family lawyers, as the only professionals with whom parties to financial agreements are required to have contact, are important sources of information about how the new legislation is operating.

Reflecting this situation, the analysis below draws on disparate evidence from three main sources within the Australian legal profession:

(a) peak organisations representing lawyers in Australia (for example, the Family Law Section of the Law Council of Australia, and the Solicitors Liability Committee of Victoria);

(b) family law practitioner writings and conferences;[43] and

(c) family lawyers.[44]

This evidence is examined as a whole to make some tentative observations regarding the early days of the operation of the legislation.

I Profiling users

One clear pattern that emerged from the available information was that use of prenuptial agreements was specific to certain groups. It seems that a prenuptial agreement is an option that appeals to some men, as well as some women, with use being more likely in relationships characterised by one or more of the following factors: a significant asset disparity between the parties (the richer party seeking a prenuptial agreement); a second marriage for one or both parties; previous Family Court involvement for one or both parties; and the presence of a family asset or business that one party wishes to quarantine.

---

43 For example, Hoban (2001) and Watts (2001). Professional workshops and seminars held since the enactment of the new Pt VIIIA include: 'Family Law Act Part VIIIA: Challenges to financial/termination agreements', Leo Cussen Institute Legal Professional Development, Melbourne, 4 September 2001 – Szabo *et al* (2000).

44 Based on a survey completed by 16 family lawyers, who are members of the Family Law Section of the Law Council of Australia (Australia's main professional organisation representing family layers, which has about 1800 members nationwide), and conversations with a further five family lawyers. The evidence reflects mainly solicitors' views (16 out of 21).

It does not appear, on the very limited evidence available to date, that men rather than women are seeking to enter prenuptial agreements. This appears to be in contrast to United States experience (for example, Atwood, 1993), referred to earlier, which suggests that prenuptial agreements are particularly likely to work to disadvantage women. Perhaps this view requires qualification in relation to older women with property and financial resources, who are entering second marriages. Certainly, the family lawyers contacted in the course of writing this chapter expressed fewer concerns regarding prenuptial agreements entered into by older clients entering subsequent marriages, compared to clients who are younger, did not yet have children and were marrying for the first time.[45]

It appears that family lawyers have experienced an increase in the level of client enquiries about prenuptial agreements since the legislation came into effect, with enquiries in most cases increasing from in the range of two or three per year to four to six per year. Thus, while enquiries have increased, it appears that interest in entering a prenuptial agreement remains a relatively rare phenomenon.

2 Problems for clients

Quite often it seems that clients who make an initial enquiry do not ultimately enter a prenuptial agreement. While there is some cultural acceptance of prenuptial agreements – at least on the part of partners who, or whose circumstances, have one or more of the characteristics listed above – other factors are often interacting to prevent agreements being entered.

According to family lawyers, one of the major factors inhibiting entry into agreements is difficulty experienced at a personal level between couples during the process of negotiating agreements. Relationship tension reportedly increased when the parties and their legal representatives began formal negotiations regarding the terms of the agreement. Family lawyers, mindful of the agreement's central purpose of offering certainty for the future, were evidently keen to sort out the fine details and to 'reality test' agreements (by asking the 'what if?' questions). However, this process was often confrontational for clients as they sat with their beloved and their respective legal representatives around the negotiating table. One practitioner, for example, said that the three clients who had contacted her regarding entry into prenuptial agreements had not gone ahead and entered an agreement due to difficulties in negotiation, leading to abandonment of the agreement, and sometimes of the relationship.[46]

---

45 It is clear that, as predicted earlier, for separating couples consent orders still tend to be used over financial agreements. The reasons given by family lawyers were that consent orders offer greater certainty, do not require independent advice, are subject to stamp duty exemption and Capital Gains Tax rollover relief and are filed in the court rather than having to be stored privately.

46 Australian Divorce Transitions Project response no 11.

At a practical level, a lack of Capital Gains Tax rollover relief,[47] a lack of stamp duty relief in relation to property transferred pursuant to financial agreements,[48] and the cost of preparing agreements were said to be further disincentives to clients considering entering prenuptial agreements.

3 Problems for family lawyers

For family lawyers, a particularly serious concern at present is the issue of their potential professional liability for providing certificates of independent legal advice, which clients require before entry into a binding financial agreement. It appears that this concern is also contributing to the low use of financial agreements, with some lawyers in Victoria currently refusing, for fear that their professional indemnity insurance will not cover them should they be subsequently sued for professional negligence, to act for clients wishing to enter financial agreements. One solicitor, for example, said that he had referred clients wishing to enter financial agreements to other solicitors, rather than acting for them himself, because '[t]he Law Institute [the peak body representing lawyers in Victoria] has advised solicitors not to enter into [financial agreements] due to the risk of being sued in the future'.[49] This example is consistent with various published materials, including a hot-pink coloured flyer sent by the Victoria Legal Practitioners Liability Committee to all practitioners in February 2001.[50] The flyer states that professional liability insurance of legal practitioners may not cover the advice that they are required to give under s 60G of the FLA, on the basis that such advice may amount to 'financial' rather than 'legal' advice.

The Law Council of Australia sought to address these concerns in a letter to the Federal Attorney General, in which certain amendments to the current s 90G, in order to clarify that lawyers are providing legal rather than financial advice, were suggested.[51] The letter also suggested other amendments to s 60G that would, in effect, release lawyers from the obligation to express a view on whether an agreement was to the client's advantage or disadvantage, prudent, and the provisions in it fair and reasonable. The letter stated that while the Family Law Council and its Family Law Section had supported the current wording in the

---

47 Capital Gains Tax applies, in Australia, to the gains made on dispositions of property. The tax rate is the individual's marginal tax rate, which in turn depends on the individual's total taxable income (including the gain). For individuals, half the gain is included in the individual's taxable income. Currently, the Income Tax Assessment Act 1997 (Cth) provides relief from Capital Gains Tax for the disposition of assets between husband and wife or involving family companies and trusts if disposition is made pursuant to court orders (which includes consent orders). No such relief exists for prenuptial disposition of assets made by financial agreement. See, further, Horan (2001, p 8).

48 Section 90L of the FLA provides an exemption from stamp duty for financial agreements, but it has been argued by Garry Watts that, traditionally, state revenue authorities have ignored such Commonwealth legislation and that a specific legislative exemption is required to be certain that this relief would be given in relation to an agreement entered before or during marriage. (There is current state legislative relief where parties are divorced: see, for example, sub-ss 68(1)(a) and (iia) of the Duties Act 1997 (NSW).) See, further, Watts (2001, p 62, note 42).

49 Australian Divorce Transitions Project response no 14.

50 Legal Practitioners Liability Committee (2001).

51 See note 29 above.

legislation in relation to independent legal advice, and similarly worded provisions in NSW have operated apparently without difficulty or significant professional indemnity insurance claims, concerns had been expressed by 'certain legal professional liability insurers' in the light of 'a number of cases in the commercial sector, which have made it plain that lawyers who are not qualified as financial advisors should not give financial advice that qualified financial advisors would give to clients'.[52] Reference is being made here to a trend evident in the law applicable to spousal and other relationship-motivated sureties – namely, an increasing number of surety claims made against solicitors for inadequate advice, leading to guidelines being provided by industry bodies (including the NSW Law Society and the Law Institute of Victoria) to lawyers, for example, to the effect that explanation (not advice) should be given.[53] In contrast, the FLA provisions require lawyers to offer much more than 'explanation' to clients – a situation with which their insurers are clearly not happy. Perhaps the greater level of concern regarding prenuptial agreements, compared to their cohabitee equivalents, reflects the greater likelihood that married couples will have assets significant enough to justify legal dispute if they later separate.[54]

Addressing the concerns regarding the provision of independent legal advice would not resolve concerns that at least some family lawyers have regarding the legislation generally. To an extent, this is a function of new legislation that has not yet been interpreted by the courts. However, among the very small sample of family lawyers accessed for this article there was a general view that the legislation is poorly drafted and contains many potential loopholes, making it hard to guarantee that a client would, in the future, have the 'certainty' that they were hoping to achieve. The complexity and resulting legal costs of preparing a prenuptial agreement often appeared to be more than clients expected.

Given family lawyers' apparent concerns about their potential professional liability and their uncertainties about the way the legislation will be interpreted, it is not surprising that some lawyers are involving other experts in the negotiation of agreements – particularly accountants and barristers. Barristers are, in some cases, being asked by solicitors to 'sign off' to the effect that the solicitor has fulfilled the independent legal advice requirements of Pt VIIIA. Other members of a client's family have also sometimes been involved to provide moral support and/or to ensure that contributions they have made to the relevant party are protected in the agreement.

As regards the impact of professional advice on any particular client, family lawyers were aware that some clients would enter agreements in circumstances where the lawyer's advice had clearly not resolved the effects of pressure on the client to enter the agreement. Thus, while independent legal advice is required by the legislation as the central means of protecting the less advantaged party to a financial agreement, there was recognition in practice of the limits of this 'safeguard'. One suggested strategy in such cases was for the lawyer to state, in

---

52 *Ibid.*

53 Solicitor's Liability Committee (1994, p 927). The NSW Law Society and the Law Council of Australia have also addressed this issue. See, further, Smith (1994).

54 Glezer (1997, p 9).

their certificate of independent advice, that in their view the client was signing under a continuing disadvantage – for example, emotional pressure. By so stating, it was thought that the lawyer may give their client a potential ground under s 90K of the FLA (discussed earlier) to seek to have the agreement set aside by the court in the future.[55] However, as noted earlier, case law in the context of suretyship suggests that the mere fact of receipt of independent legal advice may (depending on the circumstances) be enough to bind the client, regardless of its impact.

Conclusion

It appears from the available (albeit piecemeal) evidence that interest in entering a prenuptial agreement is concentrated among certain groups of the community, especially those entering second marriages with assets they wish to quarantine. There are, however, a number of practical problems that are reducing the likelihood that financial agreements will be entered before or during marriage, or after divorce. According to family lawyers, these problems relate to both their own position and that of their clients. For family lawyers, there are concerns about professional liability for independent legal advice provided, and about many loopholes and uncertainties in the legislation, which lead to problems in drafting agreements that offer clients the 'certainty' they seek. Issues for clients include practical matters (namely tax issues and the cost involved in the preparation of agreements), and also the thorny issue of undertaking detailed negotiations regarding financial outcomes on divorce when the couple is not yet married. Even if the legislation is amended to overcome practical obstacles, reluctance to undermine or disrupt the personal relationship may mean that the use of prenuptial agreements remains a rare form of behaviour in relationships.

References

Atkin, B and Parker, W, *Relationship Property in New Zealand*, 2001, Wellington: Butterworths

Atwood, BA, 'Ten years later: lingering concerns about the Uniform Premarital Agreement Act' (1993) 19 *Journal of Legislation* 127

Australian Law Reform Commission, *Matrimonial Property Report* (the Hambly Report), Report No 39, 1987, Australian Law Reform Commission

Brod, GF, 'Premarital agreements and gender justice' (1994) 6 *Yale Journal of Law and Feminism* 229

CCH Australian De Facto Relationships Reporter 32-004-32-152 (32-450-32-470)

Deputy Secretary General of the Law Council of Australia, 19th June 2001, Letter to the Federal Attorney General regarding 'Family law: financial agreements, certification of independent legal advice'.

---

55 Foster (2001); discussion in 'Family Law Act Part VIIIA: Challenges to Financial/Termination Agreements', Leo Cussen Institute Legal Professional Development, Melbourne, 4 September 2001.

Eekelaar, J 'Should s 25 be reformed?' (1998) *Family Law* 469

Fehlberg, B, 'Sexually transmitted debt: surety experience and English law' (1997) *International Journal of Law and the Family*, 11(3), pp 320–43

Fehlberg, B and Smyth, B, 'Binding pre-nuptial agreements: will they help?' (1999) 53 *Family Matters* 55

Fehlberg, B and Smyth, B, 'Pre-nuptial agreements for Australia: why not?' (2000) 14 *Australian Journal of Family Law* 80, pp 81–86

Foster, A, 'Challenges to financial agreements and termination agreements under s 90K and s 90KA of the Family Law Act 1975 (Cth)', in Foster, A and Le Moing-Ross, P, *Family Law Act Part VIIIA: Challenges to Financial/Termination Agreements*, 2001, Melbourne: Leo Cussen Institute

Glezer, H, 'Cohabitation and marriage relationships in the 1990s' (1997) 47 *Family Matters* 5

Hansard, Federal Attorney-General's Second Reading Speech – Family Law Amendment Bill, 1999, House of Representatives, 7705

Hoban, JR, 'Letter of the month: pre-nuptial agreements' (2001) 75 *Law Institute Journal* (Vic) 4

Home Office, *Supporting Families: A Consultation Document*, 1990, London: Home Office, at www.homeoffice.gov.uk/docs/sfpages.pdf

Horan, A, 'Tax rift over divorce deals' (2001) *The Age*, 23 August, Melbourne

Joint Select Committee, *Certain Aspects of the Family Law Act*, House of Representatives, 1992

Katz, S, 'Marriage as partnership' (1998) 73 *Notre Dame Law Review* 1251

Leech, S, '"With all my worldly goods I thee endow?" The status of pre-nuptial agreements in England and Wales' (2000) 34 *Family Law Quarterly* 193

Legal Practitioners Liability Committee, 'Important notice from the legal practitioners liability committee-pre-nuptial agreements', Victoria: Legal Practitioners Liability Committee

Lindenmayer, TE and Doolan, PA, 'When bankruptcy and family law collide' (1994) 8 *Australian Journal of Family Law* 111

Nasheri, H, 'Prenuptial agreements in the United States: a need for closer control?' (1998) 12 *IJLPF* 307

Neave, M, 'Private ordering in family law: will women benefit?', in Thornton, M (ed), *Public and Private: Feminist Legal Debates*, 1995, Australia: OUP

Parker, S, Parkinson, P and Behrens, J, *Australian Family Law in Context: Commentary and Materials*, 2nd edn, 1999, Sydney: Law Book Company

Parkinson, P, 'Setting aside financial agreements' (2001) 15 *Australian Journal of Family Law* 26

Smith, G, 'Third party securities and guarantees commentary', 1994, Twelfth Annual Banking Law & Practice Conference

Solicitor's Liability Committee, 'Learning from *Amodio*' (1994) 68 *Law Institute Journal* (Vic) 907

Szabo, P, Nikou, O, Milne, M and Taussig, M, *Pre- and Post-Nuptial Agreements*, 2000, Melbourne: Leo Cussen Institute

Watts, G, 'Binding financial agreements: possibilities and pitfalls' (2001) 39 *Law Society Journal* (NSW) 60–62

Chapter 8
Bargaining in the Shadow of the Flaws?
The Feminisation of Dispute Resolution

Linda Mulcahy[1]

Introduction

Few feminist writers to date have directed their attention to the similarities between the ideologies that underpin mediation and feminism, but the suggestion that mediation reflects a new feminist jurisprudence has been made and it has been argued that a transformation of dispute resolution, to better incorporate feminist values, will lead to more ethical decision-making (Rifkin, 1984). Cahn (1992), for instance, has argued that a feminised legal system would make greater use of mediation, be more appreciative of different perspectives, be aware of the relational context to disputes and the totality of the client's experience, and encourage less aggressive pre-trial tactics. This chapter explores these links in the context of disputes about contracts and considers whether mediation is capable of realising any of the political and practical goals associated with feminist projects. The particular issues I focus on here reflect ideological, methodological and pragmatic themes. These include the recognition of the importance of ethics of care in the handling of disputes, the encouragement of alternative paradigms for constructing legal relationships and the provision of a dispute resolution forum where women feel better able to voice their needs and concerns.

I take, as a starting point, the view that notions of femininity are best understood as culturally contingent. Viewed in this way, generalisations about feminine values, ways of thinking and arguing are seen as socially constructed and transient rather then genetically anchored. Indeed, it is a sign of a patriarchal society that the values associated with masculine or feminine identities can change whilst patriarchy does not. Schroeder (1990) for instance, has argued that certain values recognised as uniquely feminine by contemporary writers were experienced by European men in the Middle Ages as uniquely masculine. Similarly, it could be argued that the feminist ideals being promoted in this were guiding principles in the pre-classical period of contract law (see, further, Feinman, 1984). Whilst it is asserted that patriarchy does not depend for its existence on any one conception of masculinity or femininity, the argument that patriarchal societies, such as our own, privilege male values over female ones, whatever they happen to be, is the foundation upon which the thesis presented here builds.

There are a number of reasons why it is increasingly important for academics to reflect on the impact of shifts in state-sanctioned dispute resolution on the operation of contract law. 'Alternative' dispute resolution has been a feature of the contractual domain for some years.[2] Arbitration has proved a popular alternative to court-based adjudication in commercial and consumer contracts with the result that arbitration clauses are commonly inserted in standard form contracts; more recently,

---

1 School of Law, Birkbeck College, University of London.
2 This has led some researchers to identify a trend towards the use of non-adjudicatory techniques as long ago as 1980 (Ferguson, 1980). Others have reminded us that it is likely that mediation predates a formal and centralised court system.

however, it is mediation that has become the favoured alternative as arbitration has become increasingly formalised and complex. Unlike arbitration, which is best understood as a form of private adjudication, mediation has the potential to challenge received legal wisdom because of the emphasis placed on non-legal contexts, and changing conceptions of what dispute resolution is expected to achieve. The focus on party autonomy and empowerment and the purported respect for difference may well have the potential to endanger the foundations on which existing orders are built. Viewed in this way, the resonance with feminist scholarship is all too clear.

Those readers familiar with the extensive literature on mediation may wonder at my naivety in suggesting that the practice of mediation has the potential to challenge existing orders and ways of conceptualising disputes. Some of the most damning critiques of mediation have come from feminist and left-wing academics concerned with the ways in which the rhetoric of informalism can serve to reinforce existing inequalities rather than empower the disadvantaged. The danger, as Abel (1982) and Grillo (1991) concede, is that a complete rejection of both adjudication and mediation, because of their failure to secure protection for the disempowered, leaves us in a state of intellectual nihilism. Since one of the strengths of feminist movements has, in my view, been their commitment to an interrogation of the practical benefits of theory, it would be an act of cowardice to retreat into the comfort of deconstruction without pursuing the possibility that the fundamental assumptions of mediation movements provide a framework within which feminists can receive recognition of their call to change the paradigms on which adversarialism draws. Armed with knowledge of the ways in which mediation can abuse as well as strengthen the position of women, I argue that there are sufficient similarities between the claims of certain feminists and mediators to suggest that there is much to be gained by pursuing the connections and links. I am cynical of the claim that recent reforms to the courts have increased access to justice. I am aware of the commercial gain to be achieved by the emerging new profession of dispute resolvers. I am sensitive to the fact that substantive legal orders will not change radically because of alterations to process and setting. However, it may well be that whilst we wait for the radical change so desired by feminist writers the slow shift towards the co-operation, context and voice, heralded by the current interest in mediation, will bring unexpected harvests.

The mediation of contractual disputes

Mediation has been a familiar feature of dispute resolution in the contractual sphere for some time. This is particularly true of marriage contracts, employment contracts and landlord and tenant agreements, but it is clear that a wider range of contract disputes are increasingly being referred to mediation and that clauses permitting this form of resolution are appearing more regularly in agreements.[3] In the last

---

3 The fact that the Chartered Institute of Arbitrators claims to have opened it doors as a 'professional home' to mediators in October 1999, and is currently developing a route to Fellowship for 'Chartered Mediators', is a mark of the attention being paid to this form of dispute resolution. In a similar vein, it is worthy of note that a number of large City law firms, including some of the most traditional, have changed the names of their litigation departments, preferring broader terms which encompass arbitration and mediation. See, eg, Clifford Chance; Herbert Smith; Freshfield, Bruckhaus, Deringer; Slaughter and May; Norton Rose; and Berwin, Leighton, Paisner.

decade alone, several specialist mediation agencies have been set up, a considerable number of lawyers and others have trained as mediators and policy makers have demonstrated their support for this form of dispute resolution by funding and evaluating a number of mediation pilot schemes (see, for example, Genn, 1998; Mulcahy et al, 1999).[4] Government sponsored schemes have tended to be closely aligned to the courts and the litigation system, but mediation is also increasingly being used away from the civil justice system. Mediators have shown themselves able to deal with disputes prior to, in lieu of, during and even after litigation.[5]

Provision for the mediation of consumer disputes, which cannot be resolved at 'service level', is becoming common. The Chartered Institute of Arbitrators is involved in a number of mediation schemes,[6] and large-scale consumer mediation schemes have also been set up by companies such as Norwich Union. The increasing importance of mediation in the commercial sphere has also been signalled by the creation of the City Disputes Panel, which handles disputes in the financial services industry and claims to have dealt with cases involving a total value in dispute exceeding $4,000m.[7] More recently, a preference for mediation schemes has also been demonstrated by the British Marine Federation, the British Institute of Architectural Technologists and the Baltic and International Maritime Council.[8] The Centre for Effective Dispute Resolution (CEDR), one of the country's largest mediation providers, claims the number of mediations they have conducted rose from 100 in 1996 to over 600 in 2003. The number of commercial mediations recently rose by 24% from 387 in 2002 to 478 in 2003 (CEDR, 2002),[9] some of which involved damages of between $1.1m and $8m (CEDR, 2002).

In the wake of the Woolf reforms, government bodies have also taken a strong steering role in these developments at national and international levels. Since the implementation of the new Civil Procedure Rules,[10] there has been a reported 37% drop in the number of claims being issued in the Queen's Bench Division of the High Court and CEDR has claimed that referrals from the courts have risen proportionally year on year from 8% in 1999–2000 to 19% in 2000–01 and to 27% in

---

4   Although the take-up of some voluntary mediation pilot schemes has been disappointing, reports suggest that mediation is slowly becoming an important feature of formal dispute resolution.

5   See, eg, the Dispute Resolution Scheme for the Musicians Union which includes provisions for med-arb. Referred to on the CEDR website (see CEDR, 2002).

6   These include Brent and Waltham Council's leaseholder dispute resolution schemes and the Finance and Leasing Association mediation scheme (Chartered Institute of Arbitrators, 2002).

7   The City Disputes Panel (2002) is sponsored by the Corporation of London, Lloyds of London, Confederation of British Industry, Financial Services Authority, Institute of Directors and Bank One.

8   The Baltic and International Maritime Council has also introduced its own standard dispute resolution clause in a move to increase the shipping industry's awareness and use of mediation techniques, and other commercial players in the maritime world are considering the use of mediation clauses as a regular feature of contracts (Mackie, 2002).

9   The largest single industry sector using mediation was construction (12%), followed by banking and finance (8%), law firms (7%), manufacturers (7%), information technology and telecommunications (6%), insurers and reinsurers (5%) and shipping (3%) (CEDR, 2004).

10 During the same period, the new Civil Procedure Rules have encouraged the use of mediation and empowered judges to direct cases to this alternative forum. Introduced in 1999, the overriding objective of the Rules was to enable the courts to deal with cases through active case management by the judiciary. This included encouraging the parties to use an alternative dispute resolution procedure.

2001–02.[11] The judiciary has also supported this change by imposing cost sanctions on litigants who unreasonably refuse to engage in mediation,[12] upholding the validity of mediated settlements[13] and enforcing contractual commitments to mediate.[14] Moreover, in March 2001 the then Lord Chancellor's Department (LCD) announced that all government departments should seek to avoid litigation by using mediation and a year later the Office of Government Commerce published a dispute resolution guide for all those involved in the drafting of UK procurement contracts. At a European level, the European Commission's Green Paper on developing commercial mediation in the European Union (EU) was also published and adopted in 2002,[15] and it is anticipated by mediation providers that Member States of the United Nations Commission on International Trade Law will vote to adopt a model law of international commercial conciliation encouraging those countries with no mediation provision to use it as a basis for reform (Mackie, 2002).[16] The Insurance Mediation Directive of 2002 also supports this trend and seeks to ensure a high degree of professionalism and competence amongst intermediaries in insurance disputes.

As the momentum grows, the media through which mediation can take place are becoming more flexible in an attempt to accommodate the needs of businesses. In some instances, the traditional face-to-face format is being replaced by telephone mediations, video links and computer-assisted negotiations.[17] It is clear from recent reforms that the sort of mediation being encouraged by policy makers occurs in the course of litigation and in the shadow of the law with a view to securing prompter settlements (Roberts, 1992), but the value of mediation at all stages of the contractual relationship is increasingly being discussed outside of these circles.

---

11 They predict that, as the judiciary becomes more familiar and confident with the process, these figures will continue to rise (Mackie, 2002).

12 See *Halsey v Milton Keynes General NHS Hospital Trust; Joy and Another* [2004] EWCA Civ 575; *Reed Executive plc and Another v Reed Business Information Ltd and Others* [2004] EWCA Civ 887; *Dunnett v Railtrack* (2002) 2 All ER 850 and *Cowl v Plymouth City Council* (2002) *The Times*, 8 January. But see also *Corenso (UK) Ltd v The Burnden Group plc* [2003] EWHC 1805.

13 See *Thakrar v Thakrar* [2002] EWCA Civ 1304, in which the Vice Chancellor reversed the effect of a Court of Appeal decision declining to authorise a settlement agreed at mediation.

14 *Cable and Wireless v IBM* [2002] EWHC 2059. See also the decisions in *Dunnett v Railtrack* (2002) 2 All ER 850; *Hurst v Leeming* [2001] EWHC 1051.

15 COM (2002) 196. This asserts that the role of new online dispute resolution (ODR) services has been recognised as a form of web-based cross-border dispute resolution. It is also argued that the European Council has repeatedly stressed the importance it attaches to alternative means of settling cross-border disputes, in particular at Vienna in December 1998 and then in Tampere in October 1999 at a meeting devoted to the creation of an 'area of freedom, security and justice' within the European Union. At the Lisbon European Council in March 2000 devoted specifically to 'Employment and the Information Society', the European Council invited the 'Commission and the Council to consider how to promote consumer confidence in electronic commerce, in particular through alternative dispute resolution systems'. This objective was reaffirmed at the European Council at Santa Maria da Feira in June 2000 when the 'e-Europe 2002 Action Plan' was approved. In the employment relations field, the Brussels (Laeken) European Council in December 2001 'stresse[d] the importance of preventing and resolving social conflicts, and especially trans-national social conflicts, by means of voluntary mediation mechanisms …'.

16 See Resolution 35/52 adopted by the General Assembly on 4 December 1980, Conciliation Rules of the United Nations Commission on International Trade Law.

17 In May 2002, The ADR Group and The Claim Room launched the first European-based multilingual online disputes resolution service, which includes a virtual negotiation room and blind bidding claims settlement. Moreover, the Chartered Institute of Arbitrators is currently developing the EEJ-net scheme which focuses on e-businesses and multiple jurisdictional or cross-border disputes.

Mediation agencies have reported being called in to help design dispute resolution clauses during the drafting of contracts and during the life of a contract when negotiation becomes 'stuck'. This development stands in stark contrast to litigation, which is predominantly used when the relationship between the parties to a contract is over and good faith has been exhausted. Such flexibility will be of particular interest to those contract scholars who have highlighted the irrelevance of formal law and adversarial process to contracting parties who are in dispute or need to re-negotiate contractual provisions during the life of a contract.

The promise of mediation

Like the notion of 'feminism', the term 'mediation' has come to mean very different things to different people. Commentators have classified the different varieties of resolution that claim to come under this banner, in terms of the goals they seek to achieve, their evaluative, facilitative or transformative tendencies and the different epistemologies which underpin them.[18] Black and Baumgartner (1983) place the various forms on a continuum that classifies the different models on the basis of the level of intervention in negotiations between the parties. Others have categorised them according to their outcome orientation, with evaluative and facilitative models being seen as more settlement orientated than transformative models, which focus on changes to ways of thinking and behaviour for the future. Elsewhere, the differences between extremes have been explained in terms of the drive to save costs and time and the more idealistic tendencies of those who talk of healing and repair. This 'tinkering' with the litigation system is likely to be abhorrent to those who share the desire of many feminist commentators to change the orientation of state-sanctioned disputes settlement. I would argue that the schemes that operate away from the courts and centralised state agencies are those which offer the most stimulating intellectual challenges for the purposes of this chapter.

Despite the cultural diversity and temporality of these different forms, certain attributes could be said to underlie most stories of mediation. These include a rejection of adversarial approaches to dispute resolution; emphasis on the importance of co-operation; a focus on self-determination and voice; and an insistence that disputes must be understood within their broader contexts and away from the narrow constraints of established doctrine and *locus standi*. There are three main claims made by mediators, which are of particular relevance to feminists. First, the implicit rejection of the masculine values of the courtroom. Secondly, the privileging of values associated with feminism, which reflect an ethic of care and the importance of context and relationship. The emphasis on giving voice to different narratives offers the possibility that women's concerns and ways of conceptualising their grievances will be heard in ways which have been made impossible in the courts. Finally, mediation might be said to facilitate the broader political goals of feminists by raising awareness of prevailing masculine paradigms. In the remainder of this section, each of these three traits is considered in turn.

---

18 Eg, Bush and Folger (1994) refer to the satisfaction, transformative, conspiracy and stories of mediation, whereas Engle Merry (1992) talks of reformist, socialist, communitarian and anarchic models.

The rejection of adversarialism and the masculine

The identification of a correlation between the characteristics of masculinity and the ethos, organisation and skills associated with law and legal practice has been central to feminist engagements with the law and essential to each of the three phases of feminism. Although certain forms of mediation are closely akin to models of litigation, all emphasise the failings of court-based adjudication. It is claimed that where the courts impose decisions on the parties, mediators aspire to help the parties to reach their own agreements and party autonomy. While the courts decide cases with reference to established precedents and remedies, mediators claim to make recourse to the normative and cultural frameworks which have meaning for the parties. Where the courts and legal profession privilege adversarial techniques and objective standards, mediators argue that they focus on conciliation, communication and intersubjectivities. Given such polarisation, it should come as no surprise that a handful of commentators have argued that, whilst the courts are associated with masculine values, mediation has become associated with more feminine ideals (Rifkin, 1984; Engle Merry, 1992). It also becomes clear that the feminisation of dispute resolution remains unlikely within the courts and their precincts.

The association of masculine values with the courts will come as no surprise to feminists. It is men who have been the visible architects of the courts, civil process and doctrine and, as a result, it is masculine values that have tended to dominate the courtroom. Women were not able to vote for those who made laws until the last century, nor were they admitted to the House of Commons as representatives. They have been physically absent from the courts in any role other than victim, litigant, witness or observer for much of the history of the courts and were only able to enter the legal profession as recently as the 1920s.[19] Even today, precedent continues to be largely determined by men of English descent. As of October 2002, no Lords of Appeal in Ordinary were women, and they made up just 6% of Lord Justices of Appeal, 6% of High Court Judges, 9% of circuit judges, 12% of recorders and 19% of district judges (Lord Chancellor's Department, 2002; see also Malleson, 2003, on this point). Neither has the European Court of Justice fared much better in terms of its representativeness (Kennedy, 2002).

Feminists have also revealed the tensions between gender and professional legal identity for women. Women have been found to have been tolerated within the legal professions only when they suppress the feminine in their style of dress and working practices or practise in ghetto specialities (Drachman, 1998; Thornton, 1996; Wells, 2002). Research on images of female litigators within popular culture has also tended to question their capacity to perform effectively in the courts and the litigation system. Film and television storylines typically focus on female characters' failed love affairs and soul-searching examinations of whether to continue to practise, rather than their professional successes in the courtroom. Others have argued that it continues to be the case that it is much more common for women to be portrayed as victims or non-achievers in the legal system, whether as lawyers or clients (Corcos, 1998; Lamb, 1999).

---

19 The first woman to be called to the bar in England was Ivy Williams in 1921. The first woman solicitor was Clare Morrison, who was admitted to practise in 1923 (Barnett, 1998).

The same philosophies of rugged individualism that have guided the development of litigation as an adversarial forum have also moulded the development of classical contract paradigms based on competition. Classical contract theory is founded on the premise, born of the imagination of male philosophers, that all individuals are born free and autonomous; however, as Pateman (1988) has so authoritatively argued, feminine beings have remained subsumed under the apparently universal, sexually neutered category of the individual and the rhetoric of this vision of social relations is clearly in conflict with feminist histories of oppression. For instance, the reforms of the latter part of the 20th century, which offered women formal legal equality in employment contracts and pay, continue to sit uncomfortably with data that reveal the fiction of equal pay for equal work and the prevalence of sexual harassment against women. Viewed in this way, the rugged individualism of classical and neo-classical contract is far from being opposed to patriarchy. Rather, contract is the means through which modern patriarchy is constituted because women are not born free, but suffer from structural and institutional discrimination. Just as women were debarred from the legal profession and courts, so too were they debarred from all that the world of contracts empowers and is prepared to remedy, an argument made all too clear, for instance, in an appraisal of the doctrine of intention to create legal relations and the assumptions which underpin it.

However, it is not just the physical exclusion of women from the contractual sphere or courtroom which should be of concern to feminists. Commentators have also remarked on the exclusion of 'the feminine'. It is arguable that there is no branch of the law in which the hostile egoism of possessive individualism is more clearly reflected than in classical contract and neo-classical doctrine, which takes people away from the pre-existing web of community. Goodrich has asserted that doctrinal writers and judges alike have tended historically to legislate against the emotive and relational dimensions of contracts, a tendency he sees in psychoanalytic terms as a denial or repression of the emotive or feminine self. In its most extreme conceptualisations, he sees the legal subject of contractual exchange as a mere expression of economic relationships or callous cash nexus divorced from intimacy (Goodrich, 2001). Brown (1996) has also commented that the influential Posnerian masculinity of neo-classicalism requires 'high octane' (p 12) masculine values, such as performance, control, security of transaction and standardisation for its survival.

Just as contract law has focused on the discrete transaction between parties whose goal it is promote self-interest, so too has civil procedure served to distance litigants and it emphasises their differences in the pursuit of a winner and loser. Court-based adjudication requires disputants to put forward arguments that contradict each other, and to emphasise their own interests over those of others.[20] According to this way of thinking, exchanges are the only way in which individuals come to recognise the needs of others.

Civil procedure and the courts also remove disputes from their context by narrowing the issues for discussion into distinctive and limited legal categories that

---

20 The discourse of rights and the ethics of competitive individualism, upheld and reinforced by the courts, have been likened to other predominantly masculine arenas, such as battlegrounds (Lord Chancellor's Department, 1996) and sporting events (Frank, 1949).

stifle, rather than completely ignore, the context in which the dispute occurs. Not only do they concentrate on specific events and moments in time, but they purport to rely on linear modes of reasoning. Accounts of disputed events, which are entirely adequate by the standards of common sense morality, prove to be legally inadequate because of judicial assumptions about how a story should be told and how and when blame should be assessed (Cunningham, 1992; Davies, 1994). In Berns' (1999) terms, the monophonic judge translates the 'polyvocality' of diverse human stories into a seamless legal narrative. The emphasis placed by the judiciary on abstract principles and linear accounts also reflects the tendency of the common law to seek universal and guiding principles to frame all decisions. Emphasis on due process encourages us to ignore the suggestion that, rather than facilitating fair process, the standard of neutrality actually serves to exacerbate existing inequalities between male and female disputants by treating them as though they had access to the same power resources or are motivated by the same goals (Minow, 1991). Such generalisations assume universal truths and a neutral or objective way of seeing things, which tend to suppress alternative ways of framing accounts or grievances. It follows that court processes also serve to stifle feminist dissent by denying the possibility of competing values and epistemologies.[21]

In contemporary society, the symbiotic relationship of masculine values and court-based adjudication develops long before the trainee lawyer attends their first trial, as legal academia and practice are also masculinising agencies (Hunter, 2002). The perception that 'good' lawyers are adversarial, apolitical and competitive is perpetuated by legal educators during the academic and practical stages of training. Critics have argued that the traditional law school curriculum inappropriately privileges an adversarial approach to disputes and pays undue attention to the case-based method and masculine ideals at the expense of more holistic or contextualised understandings of grievances favoured by mediators and feminists (Bok, 1983; Carr-Gregg, 1997; Hunt, 1992). In this way, legal training imbues graduates with an inappropriate fidelity to individualism, formal legality, abstract reasoning and the judiciary (Kennedy, 1992; Abel and Lewis, 1995).

The promotion of feminist values

Gilligan's (1993) still controversial analysis of male and female modes of reasoning suggests that, whilst feminine subjects prefer to focus on context, relationships and discretion in resolving disputes, male subjects prefer to work with predetermined and logical rules that, although inflexible, produce certainty.[22] In her observations of children, she reveals how female subjects typically see moral dilemmas in terms of a narrative of relationship which extends over time. Their worlds were worlds of relationships in which an awareness of the connection between people gave rise to a recognition of responsibility for one another. Most significant for present purposes is the way in which Gilligan positions this approach as being opposed to a

---

21 For a discussion of judicial consideration of gendered assumptions of fairness, see Diduck (2001).

22 Like feminists, and relational contract theorists, mediation gurus recognise the interconnectedness of disputants rather than giving prominence to their separate and individual status.

masculinised justice model of the type discussed and specifically discusses these traits in relation to disputes. She concludes that (p 73):

> Women's construction of the moral problems as a problem of care and responsibility in relationships rather than as one of rights and rules ties the development of their moral thinking to changes in their understanding of responsibility and relationships, just as the conception of morality as justice ties the development to the logic of equality and reciprocity.[23]

In line with such arguments, some feminist legal theorists have contended that a legal system based on feminist values would privilege connection rather than competing rights and would result in dispute resolution valuing different aspects of cases. These different values have the potential to challenge current models of process in a number of ways. Bush and Folger (1994) have argued that transformative models of mediation can alter and feminise the subjects as well as the processes of dispute resolution. Mediators from a wide range of schools stress the importance of putting disputes in context rather than applying a uniform and abstract set of rules to the circumstances of each case. The relevance of privileging context is that it is said to encourage the widening of discussion so that all tensions and viewpoints that are psychologically, if not legally, relevant to the dispute are expressed. It is commonly argued that this makes a consensual and lasting settlement more likely.

Formal law with its assumption of party equality and sameness displays no such tolerance for cultural, linguistic, ethnic, value or gendered diversity. By placing emphasis on party autonomy and different ways of conceptualising the dispute, mediation also has the potential to create a space in which previously marginalised and subversive feminist arguments can be made. As a result, it could be argued that mediation provides an expressive, as well as an instrumental, function by providing opportunities for narratives to emerge that traditionally have not been heard in the courts. In their discussion of the search for the fundamental principles of mediation, Amundson and Fong (1993) draw attention to the emphasis mediators place on the appreciation of 'outsider' experience. Mediators claim that the parties should be free to construct their own stories unfettered by issues of legal relevance or rules of evidence or procedure. As a result, they adopt a conversationalist approach to the exploration of opposing viewpoints rather than one based on rules of evidence, which inhibits the free expression of grievances. Empirical studies of informal dispute resolution have demonstrated that, when free from the evidentiary constraints of the courts, litigants engage in storytelling practices which would otherwise be forbidden or frustrated.[24] Moreover, researchers have found that the extent of opportunities disputants have to tell their story is an accurate indicator of satisfaction with resolution processes and willingness to compromise (O'Barr and Conley, 1985; see also Heuer and Penrod, 1986).

---

23 Gilligan's work is not without critics who have been concerned that her emphasis on womanly virtues is undesirable as they have traditionally been used to keep women in the private sphere, or that her work encourages an overly romantic simplification of women's moral personalities. See, eg, Larrabee (1993).

24 Witnesses, for instance, have been shown to come to court with their own epistemological assumptions that conflict with the ones embodied in the law of evidence.

The emphasis which mediators place on consensus and conciliation also privileges non-material values, such as trust, respect and care, that are important to feminist writers (Riskin, 1985). Because of the focus on enhancing interpersonal communication, mediation can prompt the parties to feel and express some degree of understanding for each other. In Astor's (1995) view, mediation provides the opportunity for the underdog to communicate in a way which will build bridges that breach walls of silence. In this way, mediation provides an environment in which individuals are encouraged to express their inherent capacity for relating to the concerns of others. In contrast to the courts' emphasis on rights, mediation seeks to identify and respond to the parties' interests. As these may be shared, it is argued that the process is more likely to encourage co-operation and understanding of respective positions than adjudication does. Mediators are as likely to take account of the value systems of the disputants in the course of facilitating agreement as they are the more formal rules of legal doctrine. This opens up the possibility of challenging existing ways of seeing and doing. As Grillo argues: 'The conflict may be styled as a personal quarrel, in which there is no right and wrong, but simply two different, and equally true or untrue, views of the world' (1991, p 1560).

Conciliatory settings in which feminine values are promoted may also prompt women to voice their concerns. Mediators promise that mediation will encourage disempowered parties to become calmer, clearer, more confident and more decisive and that, in turn, this will encourage self-worth, security and autonomy (Bush and Folger, 1994). Lind et al's (1993) work with 339 university students demonstrated that women across ethnic groups had a preference for less direct, less confrontational procedures. It would seem then that the private non-judgmental nature of mediation has the effect of providing disputants with a non-threatening opportunity to explain their feelings and 'humanise' themselves to each other (p 20).[25]

Transforming paradigms?

For some more ambitious writer-practitioners, the unique promise of mediation lies in its ability to transform the character of both individual disputants and society as a whole. Proponents of transformative mediation[26] have long argued that settlement-orientated models of the kind practised by evaluative or facilitative mediators overly emphasise bargain and settlement. By doing so they serve to reinforce an individualistic world view at the cost of relational values so treasured by feminists.[27] Bush and Folger (1994) assert that the transformative model alone

---

25 Nor is the potential impact limited to female litigants. Cahn (1992) argues that research has demonstrated that female lawyers also prefer less adversarial methods of resolving disputes (see, for instance, Caplow and Scheindlin, 1990).

26 This 'transformation story' has become the underground story of the mediation movement and discussion of it can rarely be found in print. Bush and Folger (1994) suggest that mediators are often hesitant to articulate or enact transformative practice for fear of seeming too idealistic and impractical.

27 Viewed in this way, it would seem that the reforms to the civil justice system promoted by Woolf and Middleton have done little more than transplant the normative framework of competition and adversariality into a less formal sphere. This 'transformation story' has become the underground story of the mediation movement and discussion of it can rarely be found in print. Bush and Folger (1994) suggest that mediators are often hesitant to articulate or enact transformative practice for fear of seeming too idealistic and impractical.

supports and furthers a progressive shift in human consciousness and the realisation of political change which has also become the radical feminist project. They argue that transformative mediation does this by valuing behaviour that integrates strength of self and compassion for others. In their words (p 232):

> When a person marshals his or her resources and strength, standing up to obstacles and difficulties, and at the same time uses that strength in a way that not only sustains the self but attends to the needs of others, we recognise something wholly and unqualifiedly admirable and good about that kind of conduct.

The potential for disadvantaged groups to stage challenges to the status quo and overtly political accounts of the power of mediation are most likely to be discussed by proponents of transformative mediation, which tends to operate away from the courts and litigation system. Within this setting, the very popularity of mediation has been explained by a distrust of governmental agencies as tending to impose bureaucratic and outside solutions, a conviction that the courts are unresponsive to the needs and interests of disadvantaged communities and a perception that legal rules lack pragmatism. For some commentators, the resulting characterisation of mediation as a type of popular justice has encouraged the vision of this process as a form of alternative legality fuelled by the need for greater participation in, and access to, law (de Sousa Santos, 1977). Such calls to popular justice have been underpinned in some quarters by a radical political ideology, which is part of a movement to challenge racism, sexism and social inequality in society. In his defence of community mediation, Shonholtz (1984) has argued that the achievement of mediation – which has had significant social, political and psychological implications – has been the successful experiment in enabling disputants to formulate their own stories and resolve their own conflicts in ways which make sense to them. In his view, the great promise of mediation has been its potential to raise consciousness, to reawaken citizens to their dormant power to wrest this responsibility from the state and to disenfranchise the formal systems' monopoly on dispute settlement.

Mediators within the transformative school argue that conflict provides rich opportunities for growth and change. They present disputants with a challenge and a differently situated other who holds a contrary viewpoint. This offers each of the disputants an opportunity to acknowledge the perspectives of others and the chance to feel and express some form of understanding.[28] According to this model, the ideal response to a conflict is not to solve the problem but rather to transform the parties by utilising the opportunities for change. As a result, mediators focus on the statements, challenges, questions and narratives of the parties in their search for openings that afford disputants the chance to articulate their own position and acknowledge and understand the other's perspective. The emphasis is on reflection and deliberation. Empowerment of those with fewer situational powers is essential to this process, as it is argued that consideration of another's perspective can only occur when both the parties are secure about their own.

---

28 Bush and Folger (1994) suggest that this may be the reason why the Chinese have a tradition of using identical characters to depict crisis and opportunity.

Some have gone further and claimed that the transformative possibilities of mediation go beyond the individuals involved.[29] In his seminal work on the possibilities of mediation, Fuller (1971) argued that mediation is commonly directed towards the creation of new norms rather than just achieving conformity with existing ones. Bush and Folger (1994) have also drawn attention to the importance of norm creation in certain 'stories' of the mediation movement. They argue that programmes that place emphasis on community and social justice are most likely to treat formal legal rules and dominant paradigms as one of many frameworks which could be used to mould issues and evaluate possible solutions. Viewed in this way, the claim that mediation can give women more leverage to argue for their interests than they might have in formal legal processes develops a certain logic. According to Bush and Folger (pp 18–19):

> The mediation movement has used these capacities of the process, to some extent at least, to facilitate the organisation of relatively powerless individuals into communities of interest. As a result, those common interests have been pursued more successfully, helping ensure greater social justice, and the individuals involved have gained a new sense of participation in civic life.

Empirical disappointments?

Despite these ambitions, it is important to point out that feminists have also been amongst the most vociferous of critics of mediation. Despite its promise of reflecting feminist values and opportunities, many commentators have argued that far from reflecting a feminist jurisprudence, mediation serves to reinforce an objective epistemology and male ideology of law. It has been argued, for instance, that the stories told in mediation are not unfettered by the patriarchal concepts expressed by the law. Storytelling has a clear value, but it is also a process that can privilege certain speakers over others and reflects the expectations of behaviour imposed by wider communities.[30] Writing in the context of marital contracts and as a committed mediator, Grillo (1991) argues that mediation can actually be destructive to many women and some men because it imposes the same rigid orthodoxy as to how they

---

29 Bush and Folger (1994) claim, for instance, that consumer mediation can strengthen and evoke mutual recognition between merchants and consumers and that, by strengthening and evoking recognition between men and women, mediation can fundamentally change the nature of male-female interaction. In support of this, Rifkin (1984) argues more modestly, in her analysis of two case studies concerning divorce and sexual harassment, that patterns of dominance can be positively affected in the course of mediation. Certain proponents of this approach have adopted an almost religious fervour in their description of the transformative potential of mediation. So, for instance, it has been claimed that (p 83):

> ... it is striking when parties sometimes seem to reach, at least momentarily, an almost exalted state of both dignity and decency, as each gathers strength and then reaches out to the other. At such moments it seems that 'the light goes on', that an illumination of human goodness seems to eclipse in importance everything else that happens. The clear articulation of the transformative orientation conforms that these occurrences are indeed of transcendent importance, that our intuitive response to them is appropriate. But it goes further and suggests that these kinds of occurrences do not have to be, and should not be, serendipitous. They should be the very aim of the exercise, and practice should be designed and conducted to bring them about.

30 In their research on small claims courts, O'Barr and Conley (1985) note that speakers in informal dispute resolution settings employ the same narrative devices that they would in everyday conversation. It seems likely then that the same problems that occur for women in everyday communication with men will also occur in mediation.

should speak, make decisions and be as does the wider society in which it is situated. This orthodoxy is imposed through overt and covert messages about what constitutes appropriate conduct, an orthodoxy which focuses on 'the good woman' and excludes the possibility of the parties speaking with authentic voices.[31] Similarly, Erlanger *et al* (1987) contend that although mediated divorce settlements reflect flexibility, party participation and true agreement in some cases, they often also reflect unequal financial resources, procedural support or emotional stamina. Even more problematic is the epistemological concern that even when expressed, women's stories will not be understood or respected. In her work on the breakdown of violent marriage contracts, Astor (1995) has expressed concerns that the assumption that women who have been the target of violence will speak readily about their grievances in mediation is a misguided one. In her view, this is because it fails to take account of the silence that surrounds recognition of disadvantage and the substantial barriers that prevent women from relating their experiences.[32] Indeed, a key theme of feminist debate has been the ways in which lack of power and recognition have deprived women of a language with which to articulate their needs (MacKinnon, 1987). The issue of whether men could participate in feminist discourses, or know 'feminist truths', has been a contentious one. At the very least, men's dominance and control of ruling structures and the means of ideological production have afforded them considerable control over what can be defined as a credible argument.[33]

It could also be argued that the emphasis mediators place on interests, as opposed to rights, undermines the importance of rights discourse in the women's movement. Disadvantaged groups in society have always had an uneasy relationship with the courts and the notion of individualised rights because they are forced to clothe their own concerns about discrimination in the language and jurisprudence framed by their oppressors. Despite this, test-case strategies have resulted in a handful of notable successes, which have symbolic value despite their costs. Women have struggled hard for substantive rights to be embodied in legal rules and for their grievances to be heard within the public domain of the courts and some have argued that such claims have helped to enhance the position of women in society. The particular danger to which critics of mediation have drawn attention is that the secrecy and confidentiality of mediation will consign issues of interest to women back to the private sphere from which feminists have sought to emerge and that, in this way, feminist concerns will disappear from the public agenda (Abel, 1982).

---

31 In a UK context, Greatbatch and Dingwall (1989) have argued that mediators commonly act as selective facilitators who steer the process to a particular outcome. They claim that, by privileging discussion of certain topics and resolution options over others, mediators often reveal an unspoken partiality for one normative framework over another (see also Fitzpatrick, 1992; Nader, 1990; Pavlich, 1996).

32 This is fortunate as many mediation agencies will not mediate disputes involving violence, which they believe involve invasions of civil liberties that are more appropriately dealt with by the courts and police.

33 It has been argued that this outsider status fosters a double or bifurcated consciousness because oppressed groups have insight into the internal logic of the regimes which oppress, as well as experience of alternative or conflicting narratives. The same cannot be said of dominant groups who have no need to understand the perspective of the oppressed.

Conclusions and a glimmer of hope?

An overnight reversal of the norms which dominate our society is unlikely. It is both unrealistic and unhelpful to expect a process of dispute resolution to transform the litigation system's thirst for adversarialism and respect for discrete transactions in one fell swoop. However, I would argue that the current retreat from trial provides an extraordinary opportunity to change perceptions to dispute resolution in the contractual sphere. We experience huge cultural pressure to think about civil process in a particular way and this is not lightly ignored or marginalised, but the nature of what is valued in dispute resolution is changing in the wake of the Woolf reforms. Roberts (1992) argues that, despite their initial reservations, lawyers are increasingly happy to accept mediation, a finding which has led some commentators to predict that a mediatory style is becoming co-opted as an everyday part of legal practice.[34] Regardless of where the incentive for change has come from, the importance of the changes to the landscape of litigation is that alternative approaches, which I have chosen to label feminine, are being legitimated and used to challenge some aspects of the traditional order. The discourse of mediation, like that of feminism, can allow us to identify what the prevailing discourse has left out of the conventional view by questioning the inevitability of the neo-classical way of viewing disputes. Viewed in this way, the subordinated values that are prized by mediators have a key role to play in beginning to create new forms of practice.

Those who are sceptical of the relevance of these claims to the law of contract would do well to reflect on the fact that feminists and mediators are far from alone in arguing for a relational and contextualised understanding of contracts. Reformulation of traditional contract models is an imperative for a variety of modern-day scholars of a critical or socio-legal bent. Researchers in these traditions have identified a number of ways in which the judiciary have failed to understand, or respond to, the needs of contracting parties, especially those involved in long-term relationships, and the law of contract is facing something of a legitimation crisis as a result. A succession of empirical studies have demonstrated that formal law is frequently ignored or circumvented by contracting parties because of its inability to reflect the needs of the contracting parties and nuances of their relationship (see, for example, Beale and Dugdale, 1975; Bernstein, 1992; Harries, 2002; Lewis, 1982; Macaulay, 2003). For some, formal law has become more or less irrelevant to the performance of long-term contracts because of its reliance on individual self-interest and economic rationality at the cost of more widely accepted notions of common interest and flexibility, such as those espoused by many feminist

---

34 In truth, it is only fair to say that despite the claims of some socio-legal scholars that hard-nosed adversarialism is the norm in out of court negotiations in some fields, we continue to know very little about the everyday bargaining stances of lawyers since the vast majority of cases are settled without publicity.

writers (Macaulay, 1963; Campbell and Harris, 1993; Vincent-Jones, 1989).[35] This state of affairs has led academics to call for the architects of the law and the legal system to devise doctrines and processes, which give adequate expression to relationships, guided by the knowledge acquired about their empirical character (Campbell, 1999).

In common with many feminists and mediators, modern contract theorists are much more likely than their forebearers to advocate a return to models of contract that address communication between embodied subjects whose desires and needs develop and change over time. They have argued that modern contractual relationships are better understood as involving long-term bonds, concern about reputation, interdependence, co-operation, morality and even altruistic desires. The emphasis here is on belonging, rather than on the alienation encouraged by both the individualistic and discrete ideal of classical contract theory and the courts. Macneil's (1974) feminisation uses the vocabulary of relationships, trust, community and context-specific interpretation. In her discussion of his work, Brown (1996) concludes (pp 13–14):

> What a present, it seems, for feminism: an account of contract law's 'familial' understandings, that at the same time can summon the weight of legal realism and critical legal studies, to out 'the feminine' on the side of nascent counter-principles against the dominance of the discrete transaction, and the ideology of freedom and classic individualism.

If extra-legal normative frameworks remain important in contractual disputes, but are marginalised when disputes are taken to court because of the abstraction of the case from its context, how can those interested in the interface of formal law and practice ensure that contractual doctrine remains relevant when disputes arise? I suggest that if contractual performance occurs at the margins of law and outside the state justice system then we should be placing more emphasis on forms of dispute resolution, which take into account the array of normative frameworks, other than formal law, which govern the relationship of contracting parties. It is becoming clear that mediation offers a more flexible and responsive way of handling disagreements, which can take into account the everyday needs of contracting parties. If in doing so the process of mediation also has the potential to introduce

---

35 This is particularly true in contractual disputes where the slow pace of litigation is often out of step with fast moving markets. Moreover, litigation is unlikely to be appropriate to the majority of disputes, which tend to turn on the facts rather than a point of law. Disputants from the business sector may also remain sensitive to damage to their reputation caused by hasty resort to the courts. More fundamentally, the contractual doctrines utilised by the judiciary undercut the open-ended standards of the contracting parties and the finality of court-based determinations can serve to mitigate against the salvaging of relationships. Instead, emphasis is placed on the generation of rights at the time of agreement and the prosecution of disputes based on a vindication of those rights when performance gets 'stuck'. This has led to claims that the judiciary does not have the business acumen to understand business disputes, but that its ways of reasoning were geared more towards professional legal logic than an appreciation of the expectations of the parties (Friedman, 1965). Such features can make litigation unattractive when the social and business relationship between the parties, which precedes the transaction, is expected to persist after the initial deal is made. Despite the emphasis placed on trust by a succession of socio-legal studies of contracts in action, it would seem that legal process rarely makes a significant contribution to the construction of this glue that binds the parties and fills the cracks of their agreement. On the contrary, the invocation of legal process can actually serve to damage perceptions of trustworthiness when disputes arise.

feminist values into dispute resolution, then this is surely a way to strengthen calls for change. If this is the case, then it would seem that considerable headway has been made in the quest to ensure that contract law remains relevant to those who make contracts.

References

Abel, R, 'The contradictions of informal justice', in Abel, R (ed), *The Politics of Informal Justice*, 1982, London: Academic Press, pp 267–320

Abel, R and Lewis, P, 'Introduction', in Abel, R and Lewis, P (eds), *Lawyers in Society: An Overview*, 1995, Berkeley, CA: California UP

Amundson, J and Fong, L, 'She prefers her aesthetics; he prefers his pragmatics: a response to Roberts and Haynes' (1993) 11(2) *Mediation Quarterly* 199–205

Astor, H, 'The weight of silence: talking about violence in family mediation', in Thornton, M (ed), *Public and Private Feminist Legal Debates*, 1995, Oxford: OUP

Barnett, H, *Introduction to Feminist Jurisprudence*, 1998, London: Cavendish Publishing

Beale, H and Dugdale, T, 'Contracts between businessmen' (1975) *British Journal of Law and Society* 45

Berns, S, *To Speak as a Judge – Difference, Voice and Power*, 1999, Dartmouth: Ashgate

Bernstein, L, 'Opting out of the legal system: extra-contractual relations in the diamond industry' (1992) 21 *Journal of Legal Studies* 115–57

Black, D and Baumgartner, M, 'Toward a theory of the third party', in Boyum, K and Mather, L (eds), *Empirical Theories about Courts*, 1983, New York: Longman

Bok, D, 'A flawed system of law practice and training' (1983) 3 *Journal of Legal Education* 70

Bush, R and Folger, J, *The Promise of Mediation*, 1994, San Francisco, CA: Jossey Bass

Brown, B, 'Contracting out/contracting in: some feminist considerations', in Bottomley, A (ed), *Feminist Perspectives on the Foundational Subjects of Law*, 1996, London: Cavendish Publishing

Cahn, N, 'Styles of lawyering' (1992) 43 *Hastings Law Journal* 1039

Campbell, D, 'Classification and the crisis of the common law' (1999) 26 *Journal of Law and Society* 369

Campbell, D and Harris, D, 'Flexibility in long-term contractual relationships: the role of co-operation' (1993) 20(2) *Journal of Law and Society* 166–91

Caplow, S and Scheindlin, S, 'Portrait of a lady: the woman lawyers in the 1980s' (1990) 35 *NYL School Law Review* 391

Carr-Gregg, S, 'Alternative dispute resolution in practical legal training – too little too late?' (1997) 10(1) *Journal of Legal Education* 23–41

Centre for Dispute Resolution (CEDR) (2002) www.cedr.co.uk

Centre for Dispute Resolution (CEDR) (2004) www.cedr.co.uk

Chartered Institute of Arbitrators (2002) www.arbitrators.org

City Disputes Panel (2002) www.disputespanel.com

Claim Room, The, 'Stop press' (2000) www.theclaimroom.com/stop_press

Corcos, C, 'Women lawyers', in Jarvis, R and Joseph, P (eds), *Prime Time Law: Fictional Television as Legal Narrative*, 1998, Durham, NC: Carolina Academic Press

Cunningham, C, 'The lawyer as translator, representation as text: towards an ethnography of legal discourse' (1992) 77(6) *Cornell Law Review* 1298–1386

Davies, M, *Asking the Law Question*, 1994, London: Sweet & Maxwell

de Sousa Santos, B, 'The law of the oppressed: the construction and reproduction of legality in Pasargada' (1977) 12 *Law and Society Review* 5–26

Diduck, A, 'Fairness and justice for all? The House of Lords in *White v White* [2000] 2 FLR 981' (2001) *Feminist Legal Studies* 173–83

Drachman, V, *Sisters in Law: Women Lawyers in Modern American History*, 1998, Cambridge, MA: Harvard UP

Engle Merry, C, 'Mainstreaming feminist legal theory' (1992) 23 *Pac LJ* 1493

Erlanger, H, Chambliss, E and Meli, M, 'Participation and flexibility in informal processes: cautions from the divorce context' (1987) 21(4) *Law and Society Review* 584–603

Feinman, J, 'The meaning of reliance: a historical perspective' (1984) *Wisconsin Law Review* 1373

Ferguson, R, 'The adjudication of commercial disputes and the legal system in modern England' (1980) 7 *British Journal of Law and Society* 141–57

Fitzpatrick, P, 'The impossibility of popular justice' (1992) 1 *Social and Legal Studies* 199–215

Frank, J, *Courts on Trial, Myth and Reality in American Justice*, 1949, Princeton, NJ: Princeton UP

Friedman, L, *Contract Law in America: A Social and Legal Case Study*, 1965, Madison, WI: University of Wisconsin Press

Fuller, L, 'Mediation – its forms and functions' (1971) 44 *Southern Californian Law Review* 305–29

Genn, H, *The Central County Court Pilot Mediation Scheme Evaluation Report*, Research Paper No 5/98, 1998, London: LCD

Gilligan, C, *In a Different Voice: Psychological Theory and Women's Development*, 1993, Cambridge, MA: Harvard UP

Goodrich, P, 'Gender and contracts', in Bottomley, A (ed), *Feminist Perspectives on the Foundational Subjects of Law*, 1996, London: Cavendish Publishing

Greatbatch, D and Dingwall, R, 'Selective facilitation: some preliminary observations on a strategy used by divorce mediators' (1989) 23(4) *Law and Society Review* 613–41

Grillo, T, 'The mediation alternative: process dangers for women' (1991) 100 *Yale Law Journal* 1545–610

Harries, A, 'Transaction management in the NHS: the ordering of exchange relations in North Regional Health Authority', PhD thesis, 2002, University of Central Lancashire

Heuer, L and Penrod, S, 'Procedural preference as a function of conflict intensity' (1986) 51 *Journal of Personality and Social Psychology* 700–10

Hunt, A, 'Critique and law: legal education and practice', in Grigg-Spall, I and Ireland, P (eds), *The Critical Lawyers' Handbook*, 1992, London: Pluto Press

Hunter, R, 'Taking up equality: women barristers and the denial of discrimination' (2002) 10(2) *Feminist legal Studies* 113

Kennedy, D, 'Legal education as training for hierarchy', in Grigg-Spall, I and Ireland, P (eds), *The Critical Lawyers' Handbook*, 1992, London: Pluto Press

Kennedy, D, *A Critique of Adjudication*, 2002, Cambridge, MA: Harvard UP

Lamb, S, *The Trouble with Blame: Victims, Perpetrators and Responsibility*, 1999, Cambridge, MA: Harvard UP

Larrabee, J (ed), *An Ethic of Care: Feminist and Interdisciplinary Perspectives*, 1993, New York: Routledge

Lewis, R, 'Contracts between businessmen: an empirical study of tendering in the building industry' (1982) 9 *Journal of Law and Society* 153

Lind, E, Huo, Y, Tyler, T, … *And Justice for All: Ethnicity, Gender and Preference for Dispute Resolution Procedures*, 1993, Working Papers Series, Chicago: American Bar Foundation

Lord Chancellor's Department (LCD), *Access to Justice*, 1996, London: HMSO

Lord Chancellor's Department (LCD), 'Statistics – women in the judiciary' (2002) www.lcd.gov.uk/judicial/womjudfr.htm

Macaulay, S, 'Non-contractual relations in business: a preliminary study' (1963) 28 *American Society Review* 55

Macaulay, S, 'The real and the paper deal: empirical pictures of relationships, complexity and the urge for transparent simple rules' (2003) 66(1) *MLR* 44

Mackie, K, 'Mediation – how is it relevant to the maritime community?' (2002) www.cedr.co.uk/index.php?location=/library/articles/bimco.htm

MacKinnon, C, *Feminism Unmodified: Discourses on Life and Law*, 1987, Cambridge, MA: Harvard UP

Macneil, I, 'Restatement (second) of contracts and presentation' (1974) 60 *Virginia Law Review* 589

Malleson, K, 'Justifying gender equality on the bench: why difference won't do' (2003) 11(1) *Feminist Legal Studies* 1

Minow, M, 'Feminist rescission: getting it and losing it', in Bartlett, K and Kennedy, R (eds), *Feminist Legal Theory: Readings in Law and Gender*, 1991, San Francisco, CA: Westview Press

Mulcahy, L, with Selwood, M, Summerfield, L and Netten, A, *Mediating Medical Negligence Claims: An Option for the Future?*, 1999, London: HMSO

Nader, L, *Harmony Ideology*, 1990, Palo Alto, CA: Stanford UP

O'Barr, W and Conley, J, 'Litigant satisfaction versus legal adequacy in small claims court narratives' (1985) 18(4) *Law and Society Review* 661–701

Pateman, C, *The Sexual Contract*, 1988, Cambridge: Polity Press

Pavlich, G, *Justice Fragmented: Mediating Community Disputes under Postmodern Conditions*, 1996, London: Routledge

Rifkin, J, 'Mediation from a feminist perspective: promise and problems' (1984) 2 *Law and Inequality* 21

Riskin, L, 'The special place of mediation in alternative dispute processing' (1985) *University of Florida Law Review* 7, pp 19–27

Roberts, S, 'Mediation in the lawyers' embrace' (1992) 55(2) *Modern Law Review* 258–64

Schroeder, J, 'Feminism historicized: mediaeval misogynist stereotypes in contemporary feminist jurisprudence' (1990) *Iowa Law Review* 1136

Shonholtz, R, 'Neighbourhood justice systems: work, structure and guiding principles' (1984) *Mediation Quarterly* 5, pp 3–30

Thornton, M, *Dissonance and Distrust*, 1996, Oxford: OUP

Vincent-Jones, P, 'Contract and business transactions: a socio-legal analysis' (1989) 16(2) *Journal of Law and Society* 166–87

Wells, C, 'Women law professors – negotiating and transcending gender identities at work' (2002) 10(1) *Feminist Legal Studies* 1

Afterword: Feminism, Liberalism and Utopianism in the Analysis of Contracting

David Campbell[1]

The basic finding of 'critical' or 'contextual', or, as I shall say here, 'socio-legal' contract scholarship has been that there often is a great distance between the formal provisions of a contract and the actual contracting behaviour of the parties; between the 'paper' and the 'real' deals.[2] The formal provisions can get lost somewhere in this distance, and disputes are resolved in ways which evidence the 'non-use' of those provisions.[3] The basic, implicit claim of the 'classical' law of contract articulated in 'traditional' or 'formal' contract scholarship is that contracting is tightly governed by the formal provisions of the contract. Non-use therefore has been very strong counter-evidence to the classical law, and, after long struggle, has proven to be the 'death' of it, with Stewart Macaulay, whose terms we use whenever we talk about these issues, as I have done here, being the 'Lord High Executioner'.[4]

One cannot overestimate the importance of the finding of non-use, but its limits are becoming clear. It is, as it were, a negative finding. In order to refute the classical law, it is not enough to show that its claim that contracting is governed by the formal law is uncompelling. We have to offer an alternative, superior explanation of contracting. If we cannot explain the actual behaviour of the parties by reference to the formal provisions of the contract, how do we explain it? Assuming that we are allowing the formal provisions some role in this explanation, but not the overweening role the classical law accords it, how do we describe this reduced role? In my opinion, which I have expressed many times previously so shall state but briefly here, a very thorough job of criticism has been carried out, to the point where further criticism of the classical law is superfluous, but this negative work has not yet been matched by similarly successful positive work of constructing an alternative theory to the classical law.

So far, the two most well-developed alternative theories that have emerged from socio-legal contract scholarship are relational contract and welfarism, and I would now rank with these the reflexive theory, which has been the outcome of a recent shift in thinking by Hugh Collins,[5] formerly one of the leading proponents of welfarism, though doing so may be a little premature. The excellent chapters brought together in this volume confirm that feminist contract theory must be

---

1   Professor, Department of Law, University of Durham.
2   Macaulay, S, 'The real deal and the paper deal: empirical pictures of relationships, complexity and the urge for transparent simple rules', in Campbell, D *et al* (eds), *The Implicit Dimensions of Contract*, 2003, Oxford: Hart Publishing, p 51.
3   Macaulay, S, 'The use and non-use of contracts in manufacturing industry' (1963) 9 *The Practical Lawyer* 13.
4   Gilmore, G, *The Death of Contract*, 2nd edn, 1995, Columbus, OH: Ohio State UP, p 1 n 1.
5   Collins, H, *Regulating Contracts*, 2000, Oxford: OUP, pp 128–32.

considered as a fourth alternative theory.[6] Feminism's contribution to the negative work of criticism is well known: I do not suppose the classical law has ever been subject to more vigorous criticisms than those mounted in Dalton's and Frug's striking papers.[7] There are contributions aplenty to this effect in this volume, and I will largely leave them to speak for themselves. I would, however, be derelict in my duty were I not to praise the richness of the accounts of contracting that support these criticisms. I will, invidiously, give but two examples.

That Sally Wheeler's chapter is so learned, unorthodox and interesting as to entirely sustain comparison with Brian Simpson's later historical papers on contract[8] is a product not only of the quality of her scholarship, but also of the fertility of the feminist approach, which allows the employment of the impressive range of interdisciplinary material Wheeler uses to describe, for example, the agency relationship that was the corollary of the denial of legal personality to wives in cases such as *Debenham v Mellon*.[9] I personally find less persuasive Peter Goodrich's latest reflections on *Adams v Lindsell*,[10] but it goes without saying that it is difficult not to be swept along by the lavish erudition of one of current legal scholarship's most distinct, entertaining and thought-provoking voices.[11]

Leaving aside this quality of actually being interesting, so rare in that current writing which merely interminably persists in the method of the traditional scholarship,[12] what I find particularly pleasing about these chapters is the way that positive theories of obligation and dispute resolution emerge from them. Perhaps the most accomplished chapter in the sense of reflecting an obviously thoroughly grounded and relatively well settled position is Linda Mulcahy's, whose work is becoming a reference point in the study of alternative dispute resolution (ADR). ADR turns on showing the superiority of the 'settlement' to the 'vindication of rights' mentality,[13] but, my goodness, how feeble most efforts to do this have been. One is driven to distraction by one's inability to get students to desist from their use of the not merely inaccurate, but hackneyed and unhelpful, contrast between the 'Rolls Royce' of litigation and the 'Morris Minor' of ADR but, of course, the poor

---

6   In this country, the most substantial piece of evidence for this had been H Biggs (ed), 'Gendered readings of obligations: strict lore or strict legal forms' (2000) 8(1) *Feminist Legal Studies (Special Issue)*. Alice Belcher's paper in this *Special Issue* is of particular relevance to the point I wish to make in this chapter: Belcher, A, 'A feminist perspective on contract theories from law and economics' (2000) 8 *Feminist Legal Studies* 29.

7   Dalton, C, 'An essay in the deconstruction of contract doctrine' (1985) 94 *Yale Law Journal* 997 and Frug, MJ, 'Re-reading contracts: a feminist analysis of a contracts casebook' (1985) 34 *American University Law Review* 1065.

8   Simpson, AWB, 'Innovation in nineteenth century contract law' (1975) 91 *Law Quarterly Review* 247; Simpson, AWB, 'Quackery and contract law' (1985) 14 *Journal of Legal Studies* 375; and Simpson, AWB, 'Contracts for cotton to arrive: the case of the two ships *Peerless*' (1989) 11 *Cardozo Law Review* 287.

9   (1880) 6 App Cas 24.

10 (1818) 1 Barn and Ald 681; 106 ER 250.

11 The point of this chapter, which I shall make in criticism particularly of Auchmuty, has implications for Goodrich, P, 'Gender and contracts', in Bottomley, A (ed), *Feminist Perspectives on the Foundational Subjects of Law*, 1996, London: Cavendish Publishing, p 17.

12 Weinrib, EJ, *The Idea of Private Law*, 1995, Cambridge, MA: Harvard UP.

13 Collins, H, *op cit* fn 5, Chapter 14.

dears are only reproducing what they read in the leading works.[14] How very different is Mulcahy's sophisticated account of the co-operative attitude which is needed to make ADR (and almost all litigation, if truth be told) work, and her argument that this attitude will more likely be the result of adopting a feminist normative stance is very compelling indeed.

An at first glimpse paradoxical illustration of Mulcahy's argument is provided by Belinda Fehlberg and Bruce Smyth's account of the difficulties Australian legislation, intending to a facilitate a specific form of planning for dispute resolution, binding prenuptial agreements, has encountered. We are told that the use of these agreements has remained low, and one of the reasons for this is the parties' reluctance to provide for dispute resolution in this situation, for resort to the paper legal deal conflicts with the normative expectations of the real marriage deal.[15] Though they do not discuss it at length, Fehlberg and Smyth raise the issue of how far it is the nature of the paper agreement that exacerbates the difficulty of the situation, for certainly the advice which is offered seems to turn on narrow, non-co-operative ideas of 'quarantining' (as they put it) each parties' assets.

I must admit that I become less convinced by feminist contract scholarship not merely in this book, but in general, the more I move, as it were, back from dispute resolution to agreement, though it is here that feminism has made its most striking impact on my thinking on recent developments in contract. In a line of cases culminating in *Royal Bank of Scotland v Etridge (No 2)*,[16] the foreclosure of mortgages on domestic homes, which have been pledged as security for unpaid loans to a husband's[17] businesses, has been challenged on the ground that the (joint) owner wife acted under the undue influence of (leaving aside the lender) her husband when agreeing to the security. Though I have but little respect for the classical doctrine of agreement, I read the duress, undue influence and inequality of bargaining power cases in which that doctrine is criticised with dread, for they lack any coherent principle and, in the face of their incompetence, merely add a bewildering pleonasm in which to express that incompetence. The contrast could not be greater with the forthright statement of what is wrong and what should be done that Rosemary Auchmuty provides in her chapter, the most recent in what I think will prove to be an important set of pieces on this issue.[18] Her belief that the marital relationship (indeed, heterosexuality as she defines it) is essentially exploitative allows her to make a clear policy statement, something that has been

---

14 For a recent authoritative statement of the litigation solicitor's view (rather more cogent than most) see Davis, S, 'ADR: what is it and what are the pros and cons?' in Caller, R (ed), *ADR and Commercial Disputes*, 2002, London: Sweet & Maxwell, p 1.

15 Cf Campbell, D and Collins, H, 'Discovering the implicit dimensions of contract', in Campbell, D *et al* (eds), *op cit* fn 2, pp 30–31.

16 [2002] 2 AC 773.

17 By no means all these problematic mortgages have involved marital or cohabitation relationships, but they have involved, eg, mothers and children, and Auchmuty (and Hadfield, in a paper I am about to discuss: see text accompanying below) might have given the implications of this more thought: see Richardson, M, 'Protecting women who provide security for a husband's, partner's or child's debts: the value and limits of a child's perspective' (1996) 16 *Legal Studies* 368, which is cited but not really taken on-board by both Auchmuty and Hadfield.

18 See also Auchmuty, R, 'Men behaving badly: an analysis of English undue influence cases' (2002) 11 *Social and Legal Studies* 257.

beyond any of the cases on which she comments: 'a ban or limitation … on the availability of the family home as security for business debts … would represent a prioritisation of what is important to most women – their home and family – over the masculine concern for business profits.'

Subject to solving some tricky issues about devising an adequate rule, I myself think it right to ban the use of domestic homes in this way when dependent children are involved, and perhaps in almost all other cases. I suspect my policy would be more restrictive than Auchmuty's. However, I depart from her in that I believe that the wives in almost all of the cases she discusses were responsible for their agreements, for I do not believe that her account of the marital relationship, though I acknowledge its strength, annihilates that responsibility. I cannot deny that I think that account is a little overdone,[19] but this relatively minor point is not the one I wish to make here. I would prevent agreements of this sort, but when so doing I believe I am placing a restriction on the choice of parties, even the wives in these cases, which *prima facie* I am loath to do. I am anxious not to be misleading when I say that this type of restriction used to be described as 'paternalist' in a positive way in the socio-legal scholarship.[20] This usage has gone out of fashion, not so much because of its misleading connotations in relationship to feminism, but because confidence in overriding the voluntary choices of the parties to contracts has diminished and what Collins calls respect for 'autonomy' has grown in relative importance to paternalism.[21]

This use of autonomy, so central to Kant's ethical philosophy, tells us that liberal values are working their way back into contract, something I welcome, for my own socio-legal approach expresses a 'liberal socialist'[22] commitment to a liberal notion of justice, coupled with a belief that socialism is necessary to 'preserve and even

---

19 Bigwood, R, 'Undue influence: "impaired consent" or "wicked exploitation?"' (1996) 16 *Oxford Journal of Legal Studies* 503. Since writing this chapter, I have read Bigwood, R, *Exploitative Contracts*, 2003, Oxford: OUP, in which this point is now made in the course of the most substantial review now available of the Commonwealth law of duress, unconscionability, etc.

20 Collins, H, *The Law of Contract*, 1st edn, 1986, London: Weidenfeld & Nicholson, Chapter 8.

21 I have charted this in respect of the shifts in Collins' textbook between the 1st and 3rd edns, in Campbell, D, 'Reflexivity and welfarism in the modern law of contract (review of H Collins, *Regulating Contracts*)' (2000) 20 *Oxford Journal of Legal Studies* 477. Since writing this chapter, I have read the 4th edn, 2003, where the shift to autonomy is even more emphatic.

22 I grasp the opportunity to draw to readers' attention to what, with Bernstein's well-known *The Presuppositions of Socialism*, 1993, Cambridge: CUP, is, in my opinion, the best work of political theory that has emerged from the Marxist tradition: Rosselli, C, *Liberal Socialism*, 1994, Princeton, NJ: Princeton UP. This book is so little known that I will quote at length from p 86 in the hope of persuading readers to have a look at the book:

> Socialism is nothing more than the logical development … of the principle of liberty. Socialism … is liberalism in action. It means that liberty comes into the life of poor people. Socialism says, the abstract recognition of liberty of conscience and political freedoms for all, though it may represent an essential moment in the development of political theory, is a thing of very limited value when the majority of men, forced to live as a result of circumstances of birth and environment in moral and material poverty, are left without the possibility of appreciating its significance and taking any actual advantage of it. Liberty, without the accompaniment and support of a minimum of economic autonomy, without emancipation from the grip of pressing material necessity, does not exist for the individual; it is a mere phantasm.

enlarge the atmosphere of liberalism'.[23] This definitely is not what Auchmuty wants: she gives a much higher value to feminist equality than is consistent with liberalism;[24] and no doubt none of the other contributors want it either. I fully acknowledge the power and attraction of feminist equality set out by Auchmuty, but it seems to me that Auchmuty does not much care about the value of autonomy, and so can put forward restrictions on capacity to contract without much regard for the costs inevitably bound up in there being restrictions. This seems to me to threaten to make feminist contract theory something of an oxymoron, for highly regulated contract will not be contract, because contract has unregulated choice at its heart. Though Wheeler is good enough to mention that she is in agreement with my attempt to give competition a central place in the relational theory,[25] the overwhelming feel of those chapters in this volume that, expressly or implicitly, take a stance on the issue is that freedom of contract need not be accorded too much respect, and we should be ready to sacrifice it to other political goals. I feel obliged to try to enter a note of caution about this.

In his sometimes scathing comments on the way the currently highly fashionable restitutionary scholarship has attempted to address undue influence, Adam Gearey helpfully draws attention to one of the ways in which feminism is deepening the discussion of inequality generally: feminist economics' critique of the assumption in neo-classical economics that 'economic man' is motivated by self-interest in the sense of rational individual utility-maximisation.[26] (To drive home the point I wish to make, I will call these economics liberal economics.) I am certain that the further development of the feminist critique of undue influence must be linked to these economic issues, but, as I understand it, to do so in the terms of economic theory involves assessing the possibilities of rational price formation in the absence of competition, and this is not an issue which can be discussed here. What can be discussed, however, is the ethical nub of the issue, and I propose to link Auchmuty's chapter (via Gearey's) to the feminist critique of the core liberal claim of contract, the idea of desert, put forward by Gillian K Hadfield in her 'An expressive theory of contract: from feminist dilemmas to a reconceptualisation of rational choice in contract law'.[27] In this paper Hadfield takes, if the anachronism be allowed, Auchmuty and Gearey further by developing criticisms of certain contracts,

---

23 Orwell, G, 'Inside the whale', in Orwell, G, *Collected Works*, vol 12, 1986, London: Secker and Warburg, p 110. Orwell earlier had written: 'Socialists ... have never made it sufficiently clear that the essential aims of socialism are justice and liberty': *The Road to Wigan Pier*, in Orwell, G, *Collected Works*, vol 5, 1986, London: Secker and Warburg, p 199. See also Cole, GDH, 'Western civilisation and individual rights', in Cole, GDH, *Essays in Social Theory*, 1962, London: Oldbourne, p 156: 'I for one am not the less individualistic in my outlook for being a socialist: indeed I regard socialism, not as an end, but as a means to the enlargement of individual capacities and liberties.'

24 See, further, Auchmuty, R, 'When equality is not equity: homosexual inclusion in undue influence law' (2003) 11 *Feminist Legal Studies* 163.

25 Campbell, D, 'Ian Macneil and the relational theory of contract', in Macneil, IR, *The Relational Theory of Contract: Selected Works of Ian Macneil*, 2001, London: Sweet & Maxwell, pp 20–28.

26 Gearey cites Nelson, JA, *Feminism, Objectivity and Equality*, 1996, London: Routledge, which I believe is the most authoritative single statement of the argument.

27 (1998) 146 *University of Pennsylvania Law Review* 1235. See also Hadfield, GK, 'The dilemma of choice: a feminist perspective on [MJ Trebilcock's] *The Limits of Freedom of Contract*' (1995) 33 *Osgoode Hall Law Review* 337.

including what she calls 'spousal guarantees', into a general criticism of the liberal economics of 'rational choice', and from this the liberal ethics of choice which have been given their best statement in modern contract scholarship in Charles Fried's *Contract as Promise*.

Hadfield, like Auchmuty, entirely understandably concentrates on the downside of freedom of contract, which emerges when we compel parties to live with the consequences of agreements they wish they hadn't made by enforcing a remedy for breach of those contracts: the doctrine of sanctity.[28] It can plausibly be argued that the welfarist strain of contract scholarship has been entirely motivated by abhorrence of these consequences to argue for departure after departure from sanctity.[29] Fried's achievement was to show that the freedom to make such contracts as one wanted was not the only upside of freedom of contract. Sanctity itself had an upside, for it was only by enforcing choices that parties regretted that the law of contract showed respect for the parties' choices and therefore their autonomy:

> If we decline to take seriously the assumption of an obligation because we do not take seriously the promisor's prior conception of the good that led him to assume it, to that extent we do not take him seriously as a person. We infantilise him [as we do quite properly when we release the very young from the consequences of their choices].[30]

I believe this is true. I think the law of contract must make parties live with the consequences of choices they regret, otherwise the distribution of goods by desert, and the contribution this makes to the formation of character, is rendered senseless:

> It is a first principle of liberal political morality that we be secure in what is ours, so that our persons and property not be open to exploitation by others, and that from a sure foundation we may express our will and expend our powers in the world. By these powers we may create good things or low, useful articles or luxuries, things extraordinary or banal, and we will be judged accordingly – as saintly or mean, skilful or ordinary, industrious and fortunate or debased, friendly and kind or cold and inhuman. But whatever we accomplish and however that accomplishment is judged, morality requires that we respect the person and property of others, leaving them free to make their lives as we are left free to make ours. This is the liberal ideal ... This ideal makes what we achieve our own and our failures our responsibility too – however much or how little we may choose to share our good fortune and however we may hope for help when we fail.[31]

As Fried's caveat about hope for help tells us, it is not a necessary implication of the liberal position that all goods should be distributed by desert. Though some liberals, or more properly libertarians, do so, most do not. Even Hayek found a secure place for social security in his thinking,[32] and the delimitation of the

---

28 Hughes Parry, D, *The Sanctity of Contracts in English Law*, 1959, London: Stevens and Sons, Chapter 1.

29 Baker, JH, 'From sanctity of contract to reasonable expectation' (1979) 32 *Current Legal Problems* 17, and Collins, H, 'The sanctimony of contract', in Rawlings, R (ed), *Law, Society and Economy*, 1997, Oxford: Clarendon Press, p 63.

30 Fried, C, *Contract as Promise*, 1981, Cambridge, MA: Harvard UP, pp 20–21; quoted, with the omission of the clause in square brackets, in Hadfield, GK, 'An expressive theory of contract: from feminist dilemmas to a reconceptualisation of rational choice in contract law' (1998) 146 *University of Pennsylvania Law Review* 1235, p 1256.

31 Fried, *ibid*, pp 7–8.

32 Hayek, FA, *The Constitution of Liberty*, 1960, London: Routledge and Kegan Paul, Chapter 19.

contractual 'sphere' from other social spheres, which has almost always been *de facto* a part of liberal thought,[33] seems to have been successfully formalised.[34] A market socialism, which is more or less my own political goal, has been stated on the basis of a primary market sphere, in which distribution is by desert, which is limited by social security.[35]

I am not certain it will help,[36] but let me give a personal illustration, which I think will hit home with readers as it will be personal to most or all of them as well. I am continually confronted by students and junior colleagues who make what I am certain are poor choices. However, until they go beyond a certain point, which is much more easily reached in their case than it would be with regard to my other fellow citizens to whom I do not believe I owe a fiduciary duty, I would not do what little I can to make my students and colleagues alter their actions (as distinct from trying to persuade them to change their minds) because I respect their autonomy, and I believe this requires me to allow them to go to hell in a hand basket if they so choose, or, hopefully far more often, learn from their mistakes. They can form their character only by going through this process, and I reluctantly acknowledge that this means that some will spoil their character more than temporarily, and with this perhaps their careers and their lives. Acknowledging this, the attractions of behaving otherwise, in a paternalistic fashion more in line with my fiduciary duty, are clear, and I suppose I owe the successive governments which have so degraded university education whilst I have been an academic a vote of thanks, for they have alleviated the burden of responsibility I feel by making it impossible for me to take the interest in my students that I used to do as the sheer weight of their numbers now prevents this.

Hadfield's paper is, at first glance, more sympathetic to contract than Auchmuty. She sees what I think is the basic issue very clearly: 'Is it possible to protect women from the oppressive consequences of harmful, constrained choices ... without divesting women of agency?'[37] However, she does not believe that a choice between mutually exclusive alternatives, a dilemma as she says, is necessarily involved and she believes that a thoroughly feminist reworking of contract, utilising Elizabeth Anderson's *Value in Ethics and Economics*:[38]

---

33 Siedentop, L, 'Two liberal traditions', in Ryan, A (ed), *The Idea of Freedom*, 1979, Oxford: OUP, p 153.

34 Walzer, M, *Spheres of Justice*, 1983, Oxford: Martin Robertson.

35 Miller, D, *Market, State and Community*, 1989, Oxford: Clarendon Press; and Miller, D, *Principles of Social Justice*, 1999, Cambridge, MA: Harvard UP.

36 I am encouraged to write in this way by Auchmuty, R, 'Agenda for a feminist legal curriculum' (2003) 23 *Legal Studies* 377, p 395.

37 Hadfield, GK, *op cit* fn 30, pp 1236–237.

38 Cambridge, MA: Harvard UP, pp 1–90.

offers ... a way out of this dilemma by providing a foothold to a contract logic that does not see the decision to refrain from implementing a person's earlier choice as a failure to represent her autonomy.[39]

Anderson, Hadfield tells us, maintains an 'expressive' concept of choice rather than the 'instrumental' concept found in liberal economics, which reduces all values to one commensurable scale expressed in money. The expressive concept is, in contrast, value-pluralist and recognises that when parties makes consumer choices they are expressing their commitments to a wide-ranging set of values, such as an art lover disclosing a commitment to art when spending a considerable sum on a painting. Whereas instrumental choice, involving private expenditures of money, invites no public justification, expressive choice requires such justification, for its purpose is to express an underlying value and such values have meaning only as they are shared with others. When the expression fails, as when a purchase intended to express a creditable intention to improve oneself turns out to be bad because one's choice turns out to be mistaken, then, Hadfield tells us, this can be reversed without loss of autonomy:

> A contract logic based on Anderson's theory of expressive choice might require enforcement of contracts for mortgage guarantees ... But enforcement will not be due to indifference to the reality of evolving rational choice, or because a woman's choice has nullified the background claims that she has to relief from loss of her home ... Rather, enforcement will be required because the full picture of those background claims, including the reliance interests generated by her choice and the policy interests others have in the protection of a convention of contractual choice, justifies enforcement. If enforcement is not justified, it will not be a failure of respect for the autonomy of the woman who made the promise. It will not be because she is not capable of rational choice or in need of exceptional protection from the courts. It will, indeed, be because she chooses rationally, both at the time of her contract and at the time she changes her mind, and because contract law understands what this means.[40]

I fear I have failed to convey Hadfield's argument properly because I do not understand it, or, rather, I understand it only as an attempt to avoid rather than resolve the dilemma she identifies. I simply do not see how her argument about expressive choice allows her to say one can reverse parties' choices without infantilising those parties. They may indeed change their mind over time, and will do so in the cases which cause legal trouble, but letting them off does relieve them of their contractual choices, and I cannot see how we can do this and hold them responsible for those choices simultaneously. The whole point of letting them off when we do so is to excuse them their responsibility.

---

39 Hadfield, GK, *op cit* fn 30, p 1258. Hadfield has another argument, which distinguishes between the consequences of a choice and such consequences imposed by law, about which I will omit discussion because of reasons of space as I believe it only a little better than the argument I will discuss. A synopsis of this argument is given in the introduction to the symposium in which Hadfield's paper appeared: Adler, M, 'Law and incommensurability: introduction' (1998) 146 *University of Pennsylvania Law Review* 1169, pp 1178–179. This synopsis is accurate, but is able to be so only because it completely ignores Hadfield's claim to have resolved the dilemma at the heart of her paper.

40 Hadfield, GK, *op cit* fn 30, pp 1281–282.

Furthermore, I fear Hadfield has failed properly to understand the nature of liberal economics,[41] which *are* value-pluralist in that they recognise the infinite multiplicity of economic actors' values, but are committed to being, so far as this is possible, neutral between those values. When one first gives the matter thought, one tends to think that economic co-ordination will require a wide-ranging consensus over goals; in sum, a plan. The extraordinary claim for the market as a 'system of natural liberty' is that, accepting a basic political consensus over distribution being conducted by means of exchange, then co-ordination, and indeed the best co-ordination, will be produced by myriad, independent, voluntary choices. To put it this way, planning is not required for order, and indeed the best order has to be unplanned. Liberal democratic society's best claim to legitimacy rests not on the moral value of particular social goals set by that society but on the extent of the freedom of its citizens to set their own goals. One may say that the goal of liberal democratic society should be to eschew the pursuit of social goals. In particular, the claim that the market economy is efficient is not a claim that that economy efficiently produces a particular set of morally valued goods, but that goods are allocated through the choices of economic actors.

Though liberal economics as such does, as Hadfield claims, work with reductions to money and refuses to second-guess the preferences expressed in purchasing decisions when these are the product of voluntary choices, this hardly means that economists are prevented, in their capacities as private citizens or moral philosophers or whatever, from believing that those choices are important because they express moral values, and from holding views about the moral calibre of those choices. What liberal economists qua economists refuse to do is paternalistically trump choice because they have a higher respect for autonomy than paternalism (and when they trump, they allow that they themselves, as liberal economists, have been trumped).

I do not see how Hadfield avoids the choice between paternalism and autonomy, and, I'm afraid, I think she goes off on all sorts of tangents in an increasingly desperate attempt to waffle around it, ending with exactly the same dilemma with which she started, resolved nowhere but in her own rhetoric. One can, of course, reject (liberal) autonomy as an ethical value, as some feminists, for all too readily understandable reasons, do,[42] and I believe Auchmuty moves towards doing this; Hadfield, however, wants to accept both autonomy and its paternalistic opposite; and this one cannot do. I urge readers to turn to Hadfield's paper, for it carries the strand of argument in this volume exemplified by Auchmuty's (and Gearey's) chapter(s) a little further, and, I think it will be seen, in doing so simply vanishes into thin air.

---

41 Still the best expression, in respect of our concerns here, is Robbins, L, *An Essay on the Nature and Significance of Economic Science*, 2nd edn, 1935, London: Macmillan.

42 Held, V, 'Non-contractual society: a feminist view', in Hanen, M and Nielsen, K (eds), *Science, Morality and Feminist Theory*, 1987, Calgary, Alberta: University of Calgary Press, p 111; and Nedelsky, J, 'Reconceiving autonomy: sources, thoughts and possibilities' (1989) 1 *Yale Journal of Law and Feminism* 1; see, further, Grimshaw, J, 'Autonomy and identity in feminist thinking', in Griffiths, M and Whitford, M (eds), *Feminist Perspectives in Philosophy*, 1988, Bloomington, IN: Indiana UP, p 90; and Sedgwick, S, 'Can Kant's ethics survive the feminist critique?' (1990) 7 *Pacific Philosophic Quarterly* 60.

It is inevitable that Hadfield makes no concrete suggestions for law reform that would fully realise her aims, for those aims cannot be stated sufficiently concretely to allow this. It is essentially this lack of concreteness about how to turn aspiration into law that raises, I think, a question mark against Bela Bonita Chatterjee's exciting proposals for a contractual regime for cyberspace. Chatterjee sees well enough the shortcomings of the contractual regime for earthbound contracts, and hopes to avoid these in the 'unprecedented', 'new medium' of cyberspace. I do not want to comment on Chatterjee's specific comments on, for example, the rules for determining when and where contracts are formed in cyberspace, but to point to a lack of concreteness in those comments which, to my mind at least, robs the aspirations they articulate of some of their force. It is not, I believe, merely limitations of space but limitations of a clear idea of what precisely we are to do, which can be expressed in terms of concrete suggestions, that causes Chatterjee to raise one's expectations higher than I think they can ever be satisfied.

I recognise that my argument against Hadfield depends on acceptance of formal logical notions of non-contradiction that certain feminist epistemologists have challenged.[43] Though, strangely enough, I feel I would be competent to pursue the argument down this line, I do not want to do so, for if I did I would merely restate what I want to say about the characteristic of feminist theory which Hadfield exemplifies,[44] which is that it is unacceptably often unable to resist the impulse to claim to have one's cake after having eaten it. One can see the attraction of Hadfield's reasoning. It would be better if we could both make parties live with the consequences of their actions and spare them those consequences at the same time. My own liberal socialism which mixes desert and social security gives in to exactly the same impulse, but does so in a spirit of acceptance of a compromise between these distributive principles which involves the partial sacrifice of both.[45] In my opinion, Hadfield's claim to avoid this compromise represents a utopian strand in her thought, and in feminist thought, with both of which, writing as a disillusioned old Marxist, I can entirely sympathise, but beg feminists to think about carefully.

The problem Engels and Marx addressed was, of course, the alienation (and consequent exploitation) of labour, and their first solution, in the initial works of their collaboration, was to make labour a pleasure, in a most important sense to make labour as such disappear:[46]

> [A]s soon as the division of labour comes into being, each man has a particular, exclusive sphere of activity which is forced upon him and from which he cannot escape.

---

43 Ramazanogly, C, 'On feminist reason: male reason versus female empowerment' (1992) 26 *Sociology* 207; see, further, Antony, L and Witt, C (eds), *A Mind of One's Own: Feminist Essays on Reason and Objectivity*, 1993, Boulder, CO: Westview Press.

44 In any case, what I would aspire to say has been said by Holmwood, J, 'Feminist epistemology: what kind of successor science?' (1995) 29 *Sociology* 411. See also Holmwood, J, 'Gender and critical realism: a critique of Sayer' (2001) 35 *Sociology* 947.

45 Though I do not agree with the way he does so, I am anxious to point out that Ian Macneil has done more to give a theoretically sophisticated statement of the implications of this compromise for the law of contract than can be found in all the rest of modern contract scholarship (Fried and Fuller excepted) put together: Macneil, IR, 'The many futures of contract' (1974) 47 *Southern California Law Review* 691, pp 696–712, Chapter 4.

46 Marx, K and Engels, F, 'The German ideology', in Marx, K and Engels, F, *Collected Works*, 1975, London: Lawrence and Wishart, vol 5, p 77.

He is a hunter, a fisherman, a shepherd or a critical critic, and must remain so if he does not want to lose his means of livelihood; whereas in communist society, where nobody has one exclusive sphere of activity but each can become accomplished in any branch he wishes, society regulates the general production and thus makes it possible for me to do one thing today and another tomorrow, to hunt in the morning, fish in the afternoon, rear cattle in the evening, criticise after dinner, just as I have a mind, without ever becoming a hunter, fisherman, shepherd or critic.[47]

I must say that I used to believe in the possibility of this implicitly, but now all I can say is, er, yes, and move on shamefacedly; Engels and Marx did more or less the same. Though they retained the aim of turning labour from a burden into 'life's prime want',[48] they did not think all of labour could be like this, and in their later works they sought to distinguish between 'necessary labour', which would satisfy 'necessary needs', and 'free labour', which partook of the realm of freedom they had earlier envisaged:

[The] realm of freedom actually begins only where labour which is determined by necessity and mundane considerations ceases; thus, in the very nature of things, its lies beyond the sphere of actual material production. Just as the savage must wrestle with Nature to satisfy his wants, to maintain and reproduce life, so must civilised man, and he must do so in all social formations and under all possible modes of production. With his development this realm of physical necessity expands as a result of his wants; but at the same time, the forces of production which satisfy these wants also increase. Freedom in this field can only consist in socialised man, the associated producers, rationally regulating their interchange with Nature, bringing it under their common control, instead of being ruled by it as by the blind forces of Nature; and achieving this with the least expenditure of energy and under conditions most favourable to, and worthy of, their human nature. But it nonetheless remains a realm of necessity. Beyond it begins the development of human energy which is an end in itself, the true realm of freedom, which, however, can blossom forth only with this realm of necessity as its basis. The shortening of the working day is its basic prerequisite.[49]

Engels and Marx did not give any clear guidance about how to distinguish necessary from 'luxury' needs,[50] and with them necessary from free labour; nor did they say anything about the organisation of necessary labour which gave one any hope that it could be different than labour under capitalism, quite the contrary in fact.[51] There is a dreadful vagueness at this point in their work – just the point where it was essential that lots should have been said – but nothing could be said, because on any plausible philosophic anthropology, labour cannot be made completely pleasurable, though it might well be made far more pleasurable than it now is. Engels and Marx tragically overstated their case, turning what could (and to a great extent is despite its shortcomings) an immensely powerful critique of bourgeois justice into a complete rejection of the categories of thought in which it made any sense to talk about 'justice' or 'injustice' because, despite their

---

47 *Ibid*, p 47.
48 Marx, K, 'Critique of the Gotha programme', in Marx, K and Engels, F, *op cit* fn 46, vol 24, p 87.
49 Marx, K, 'Capital, vol 1', in Marx, K and Engels, F, *op cit* fn 46, vol 35, p 807.
50 *Ibid*, p 530.
51 Eg, Engels, F, 'On authority', in Marx, K and Engels, F, *op cit* fn 46, vol 23, p 422, which would be a shocking piece were it at all well known.

interminable protestations to the contrary,[52] they sought a utopia in which the problems of finite resources and conflict in relationships which give the terms 'justice' and 'injustice' any meaning were all resolved.[53] We know that under communism society would be able to 'wholly cross the narrow horizon of bourgeois right and inscribe on its banner: "From each according to his abilities, to each according to his needs!"'[54] However, it is impossible to devise the concrete institutions that would allow this, and the militant attempt to impose these utopian outcomes against a 'way of the world' that just will not change as it should consequently has involved some of the most deplorable wounds humankind has managed to inflict on itself.

I am by no means arguing that feminism has the same totalitarian potential as Marxism did, but I am arguing that it is subject to the same utopian shortcomings. As Alfred Schmidt observes, we can now easily see that Fourier's belief that when humankind has managed to achieve a rational, combined order in its eighth social period, it would itself be able to cultivate more or less all the Earth, eliminate extremes of temperature, turn the seas into an inexhaustible source of refreshment ('the kind of lemonade known as *aigresel*'), domesticate useful fish, etc, is utopian in a bad sense;[55] but Marxism and feminism are both prone to the same utopian error when they argue that ineluctable existential choices will be resolved when we change our social organisation,[56] and lambaste anything that falls short of this as mere reformism. When feminist contract theory puts a low value on autonomy, it invites a repugnant paternalism. When it denies that acceptance of autonomy has costs, it becomes utopian. A feminist law of contract must avoid both.

I hope these comments of, as I say, a disillusioned old Marxist serve a useful purpose, though I fear that it may be beyond the pale to ask feminists, many of whom are very conscious of shortcomings in the way feminist issues have been addressed by Marxism,[57] to pay any heed to what is often tedious, the ramblings of a recusant about sins he is conscious of having committed himself. The chapters in this volume show that feminism certainly can make a considerable contribution to the critique of the classical law of contract, and they link to an economic and philosophical literature in which feminism is putting forward a powerful general critique of bourgeois individualism. However, if they do not place a pre-eminent value on autonomy, feminists cannot really respect the law of contract, for a law of contract that does not turn on autonomy and choice becomes something like a law of planned, paternalistic exchanges, that is, not contract at all; this is where I think Auchmuty in particular is heading.

---

52 Engels, F, 'Socialism: utopian and scientific', in Marx, K, and Engels, F, *op cit* fn 46, vol 24, p 281.

53 Campbell, D, 'The critique of bourgeois justice after the failure of Marxism', in Kerner, A *et al* (eds), *Current Legal Issues in the Czech Republic and the United Kingdom*, 2003, Prague: Charles UP, p 9.54, Marx, K, *op cit* fn 49, p 87.

55 Fourier, C, *The Theory of the Four Movements*, 1996, Cambridge: CUP, pp 47–56.

56 Schmidt, A, *The Concept of Nature in Marx*, 1971, London: New Left Books, p 163: 'The peculiar error that a fundamental change in the whole universe will go hand in hand with the proper organisation of human relations.'

57 Sargent, L (ed), *Women and Revolution: The Unhappy Marriage of Marxism and Feminism*, 1981, Boston, MA: South End Press.

If my comments are of any value, they should show the necessity of avoiding utopianism in the way the very powerful feminist critiques of inequality, in general, and of its reproduction through the law of contract, in particular, are formulated. Feminism, which is, of course, a collective noun embracing a wide range of ethical standpoints, including the relatively liberal,[58] is perfectly well able to do this. It was from 'an economic-feminist perspective' that does respect autonomy that Megan Richardson analysed the use of domestic homes as security and identified the problems with, and took a cautious attitude towards, banning the use of this security.[59] Further, when it comes to taking a non-utopian line, lawyers, who must pay attention to practical detail if their work is to be any good at all, might even give a lead to those whose disciplines allow a freer rein to speculation. Mulcahy's Chapter 1 to this volume, which seeks to develop a feminist 'ethics of care' whilst seeking to avoid 'a mush of altruism', illustrates what I broadly think is the most productive line to take.[60] I must, however, conclude by fully acknowledging that I do not think the strand of feminist thinking eloquently expressed by Auchmuty, who is 'not content to look to either courts or parliament to act in defence of women', and whose recent proposals for reform of the legal curriculum make no mention of the value of legality whatsoever,[61] would be unduly excited by my modest proposal.

---

58 Eisentstein, ZR, *The Radical Future of Liberal Feminism*, 1981, London: Longman.

59 Auchmuty approves of one of Richardson's specific proposals: Auchmuty, *op cit* fn 18, p 279.

60 I saw this chapter in draft only long after I had written this Afterword, and have decided against entering into the long comment on it, which it deserves, because it would involve some revision of what I had already written.

61 Auchmuty, *op cit* fn 18.

Index